Kay Pope was born in London in the western suburb of Ealing in 1935, but when her parents bought a small hotel in partnership with friends after World War II, she lived the latter half of her childhood on the sea front in Bexhill. She attended Battle Abbey, a boarding school a few miles inland from the nearby seaside town of Hastings, before moving on to secretarial college in London. It was this that led to a life changing event as shortly after taking up her first job on The Evening News she met Dudley Pope. They married a year later when Kay was just eighteen.

She had always wanted to travel and had dreamed of faraway places when, as a child, she could see the Royal Sovereign lightship flashing on the horizon out of her tiny attic window. When Dudley told of his dreams of writing whilst cruising the world on his own sailing boat, she was ready to sign on as first mate. For nearly thirty years the couple lived on board, along with their daughter, Jane.

Besides typing all Dudley's books, acting as teacher to her daughter and painting the boat Ramage, Kay began collecting seashells after they first sailed to the West Indies. This became a family hobby, as the family snorkelled among coral reefs together, and one new species found was named after her. She also wrote articles describing their seashells in two magazines devoted to malacology, both for amateur collectors like herself, and marine biologists.

The best part of this life, however, was being with Dudley and together meeting new people as he sailed and researched his books, and of course the sailing itself, particularly in the Mediterranean and her much loved West Indies. Widowed now, Kay lives on the island of St. Martin.

CABO TRAFALGAR
IN THE
MOONLIGHT

PEN & SAIL: MY LIFE WITH DUDLEY POPE

KAY POPE

HOUSE OF STRATUS

This edition published in 2012 by House of Stratus, an imprint of Stratus Books Ltd., Lisandra House, Fore Street, Looe, Cornwall, PL13 1AD, U.K.

www.houseofstratus.com

Typeset by House of Stratus.

A catalogue record for this book is available from the British Library and the Library of Congress.

ISBN 978-0-7551-2278-3

For
Jane Clare Victoria
with Love

AUTHOR'S NOTE

This is the story of my life after meeting Dudley Pope: our both working on a London evening newspaper, then moving to Italy, and later sailing in our cutter Golden Dragon to the West Indies, with our baby daughter Jane, and living among the islands of the Antilles.

Of course, a large part of our lives was Dudley's work as an author. I shared in this, however, typing all of his manuscripts and we worked both hard and well alongside each other, whilst visiting many places and bringing up our daughter, including arranging her schooling on board.

I have always felt I was specially blessed in my marriage: I shared Dudley's working life which many women do not experience, although the wives of farmers, parsons and country doctors are often the exception. We married in 1954 when many women still stayed at home, had children and did not continue with their careers. Their objective was to encourage and support their man, but otherwise stay in the 'wings'.

My husband was a fine seaman; and sailing and writing sea stories were his life. We lived on board boats longer than we ever lived on shore. In Italy we discovered the fun of snorkelling and once in the West Indies, this led to collecting seashells and a passionate hobby began.

Dudley wrote eleven naval histories and twenty-four novels, eighteen of which feature Nicholas Ramage who progresses from a lowly lieutenant to captain of a 74-gun ship of the line in the Navy of Nelson's time. Sometimes the Ramage novels are set in places where we lived, or visited, and my husband also used the research we had gathered for the background of his naval histories.

After writing a renowned biography of Sir Henry Morgan, Dudley also wrote another series featuring generations of 'Ned Yorkes', beginning in the late seventeenth century and ending in the Second World War.

This book is therefore about life with an eminent naval historian and novelist, the sharing of his triumphs and frustrations, travel and living in Italy and the Caribbean, and the sea and sailing. It is the story of uninterrupted love between two people who shared in everything, including as its sub-title suggests, 'Pen and Sail'.

I would like to extend heartfelt thanks to many friends who have encouraged me to set this unique story down, but must mention and give special thanks to John Gold, one of my husband's oldest friends. After reading an early draft, John posed a series of questions which demonstrated where improvements could be made, and also offered more general advice.

Kay Pope,

Le Pirate,
Marigot,
St. Martin,
F.W.I.

CHAPTER ONE

The Beginning 1952–54

One of the girls who worked in the clippings library stuck her head round the office door and said: "Dudley Pope has shaved his beard: he looks so handsome!" I now knew the name that went with the beard, and it was obvious this man was considered one of the more desirable bachelors on the paper.

Dudley told me later he could not understand what was going on that morning, because so many of the girls from the library kept popping in to ask him if he had this or that folder of cuttings.

I was seventeen at the time, shy and had just found my first job. Little did I realise how my life would eventually change from the path I had embarked upon, or guess at the adventures to come!

Having decided to work on a newspaper after finishing secretarial college, I needed to join a trade union, which was the only way in. One foggy afternoon in November I had walked across Blackfriars Bridge, down the road towards the Elephant and Castle until I found the NATSOPA[1] office. Feeling distinctly nervous, I said I wanted to join. This caused no comment, and I was asked to pay my dues. I then said I wanted a job on a newspaper. A ledger was produced from under the counter and it transpired there were two available: one in the Editorial Department of *The Evening News* and the other in the Circulation Department of the *Sunday Dispatch*. Before I could open my mouth, a man standing next to me turned and said: "You take

National Society of Operative Printers and Assistants

the *News* job, miss, it's an 'appy paper'."

A telephone call was made and I was given an appointment immediately to see a Miss Joanna Gabbedey. So I found my way to *The Evening News* building, which was in Carmelite House in the street of the same name, one block up from the Thames Embankment. I was interviewed, seemingly approved of, and told to start work the following Monday at 9 a.m. on a month's trial. I was to be assistant to Miss Gabbedey, who was in turn the editor's secretary.

After the first four weeks it appeared I had settled in well and was kept on. John Marshall, the editor, was a large amiable man and when there was not enough work for me to do I was given all his press cuttings to stick in several large scrapbooks. Later on, I typed the manuscript of one of his amusing cricket tales. After arriving each morning, he first held an editorial meeting with the heads of each of the departments, before going through the day's post. He would go through the readers' letters marking those he considered worthy of publication with the word "Give". These I took to the Features Department and put them on the desk where an intimidating man with a beard sat facing the wall, in a small side room which he shared with Gus, the cartoonist. During the following weeks, Gus began to waylay me for a chat.

Several weeks later, after lunch in the canteen with the printers and linotype operators, I went out for a walk along the Thames Embankment only to run into Gus and Dudley. Gus, of course, stopped to talk to me and then, to my horror, excused himself by saying he had work to do and left me with his companion. I was completely tongue-tied, but Dudley was never at a loss for words. As we walked along the Embankment past Captain Scott's ship, the *Discovery*, every now and then he would stop to ask if he was boring me. But my heart was singing and soon afterwards our courtship began, commencing with a theatre invitation.

Gradually, I came to learn about Dudley's early life. His father had died when he was an infant and he was brought up by his mother and grandparents at Mersham in Kent. An early memory was the bicycle that became too small for him and having to cycle back and forth to school in Ashford whilst waiting a long time for a larger one.

When Dudley was in his early teens his mother became housekeeper to a widower with two children. He went with his mother to the farm, but could not adapt to the discipline of this new family life. After only six months and perhaps not for the first time, certainly not the last, he showed characteristic independence, packed his bag, mounted his bicycle and moved back to his grandparents. Another memory, in these years before the Second World War, was the smell and black smoke of burning cattle which were killed during outbreaks of foot and mouth disease. He did not see such black smoke billowing again until war had begun. The War brought about the evacuation of his school to the West Country, where it became a boarding school. Dudley and a few other boys, whose parents could not afford the boarding fees, stayed behind in Ashford. He was now aged fifteen.

In the summer of 1940 the Battle of Britain began over Kent's skies and heavy bombing raids continued until May 1941. Ashford, with its large railway junction, was a target along with London and other cities, and so school became sporadic for the remaining children. Significantly, however, Dudley did well in History and English. When aged twelve his grandfather had enrolled him at the public library and they went together to borrow books. He became a voracious reader; his grandfather had the 'Captain Marryat' books on his bookshelf and Dudley read and reread *Peter Simple, Mr. Midshipman Easy*, and *The Pirate and the Three Cutters*. Thus the early seeds were planted for his later interest in the Napoleonic period, the Navy and sea power.

At weekends and holidays he would take off with his bicycle and head for the coast, passing through Romney Marsh to Hythe and Dymchurch. There the Martello towers stand at intervals along the coast, built to defend Kent from the invasion of England planned by Napoleon – but who eventually invaded Russia instead. So it was, at this early point in World War II, there were fears Hitler also planned to invade Britain, but like Napoleon, he also turned eastwards to attack Russia. When talking of these days, Dudley recalled the German Messerschmitt Me 109s, returning to Germany after dropping their bombs, which often flew low and raked anything with gunfire they saw moving on the roads. Whilst cycling down to the marsh, this forced him to shelter in roadside ditches. He well remembered the smell of the stinging nettles around him from those times. Also, when the RAF and German fighters had their aerial dogfights, he saw parachutes, some burning and twisting as they came down in the fields.

Because Dudley had been in the school OTC[2], he joined the Smeeth branch of the Home Guard. They managed to salvage a small anti-aircraft gun from a crashed German bomber, but found no ammunition. The gun was loaded on to a cart, which they borrowed from a farmer, for manoeuvres in the summer evenings. Dudley also took his turn as an air-raid warden, sitting up in the church tower on watch and then doing his school homework below in a pew with a torch when all was quiet. One day his grandfather, who was a little deaf, was cutting a rose in his garden when Dudley heard a lone German Messerschmitt approaching low over the house. He rushed out and threw himself on top of his grandfather, while bullets studded the ground around them. After it was over his grandfather asked, rather crossly, "What did you do that for boy?", and then with some considerable shock saw the shredded rose tree, its trunk split down the middle and only a headless rose stalk in his hand. Many of Dudley's friends, older than himself, had left to join the RAF, and it was aeroplanes, rather than ships, which interested him at this time. By the end of 1941 he was sixteen, but would have to wait two more years before being called up. However, as soon as he passed his Matriculation Examination at school he decided not to wait, but to join the Merchant Navy as a cadet. From this moment onwards the sea would be the major interest in his life.

At an interview with the Silver Line in the City of London, he claimed he was seventeen years old and was accepted. With his new kit he was sent off to Liverpool where he shipped aboard the *Silver Willow* to join three other cadets, who shared a cabin.

One boy, Dickie Perkins, was from Ashford. At this time, the *Silver Willow* was bringing palm oil from West Africa calling in at Lagos in Nigeria and Freetown, Sierra Leone. Whilst in Liverpool, getting ready for a subsequent voyage, Arctic clothing

2   Officer Training Corps

was brought on board, and the boys felt they were doomed for an Arctic convoy. As it happened, it was another run in convoy to Lagos, and once they were there, they bartered the clothing with Nigerians for fruit. The cadets had a wind-up record player in their cabin, but their only record was of the arias from *La Bohème*. To the day Dudley died it upset him to hear these popular arias, as the memories of lost shipmates remained painful for him.

An average convoy sailed with between thirty and forty ships, in six or seven columns with five or six ships in each column. They were escorted by a few Royal Navy destroyers, corvettes and trawlers. The *Silver Willow* was armed with four Bofors guns to defend against air attack. Each gun was in the charge of a cadet and manned by DEMS[3] gunners, who were volunteers from the Royal Artillery. As the convoys neared the African coast, they often sighted a German reconnaissance 'plane, which would circle the convoy just out of range of the guns. It would have taken off from an airfield in north-west Africa, then occupied by Germany.

The cook and deckhands on board the *Silver Willow* were Chinese. When there were no potatoes left, rice was served. In Lagos, the purser bought sacks of yams, but when they were eaten, there was only rice.

The Third Mate made life difficult for all the cadets and particularly for Dudley, who stood watch with him on the bridge. As a result, when sent down to the galley for cocoa Dudley sometimes caught a cockroach and put it in the Third Mate's mug. Later, though, in the way strange things happen, this man was to save Dudley's life.

As well as attending classes to learn navigation, using the sextant, and seamanship, which involved learning to splice heavy wire hawsers used to hoist cargo, the cadets were set to painting the deckhouse and inside the bulwarks, working under the bosun. With the heat and humidity in the Tropics, the paint continually developed huge blisters and bubbles. The Customs officers in Liverpool knew the Chinese had opium on board, but they could never find it. On one occasion, they came on board with hammers and broke every paint bubble on deck, much to

---

3   Defensively Equipped Merchant Ships

the fury and disgust of the bosun.

In November 1942, the convoy in which Dudley was sailing was attacked during a North Atlantic winter gale, a few hundred miles south-west of Madeira. A pack of German U-boats mistook the convoy for forces sailing to North Africa for the *Operation Torch* landings. The leading ships of the convoy were attacked on successive nights and the losses mounted. The *Silver Willow* was the third ship in her column, and during the previous two nights they had seen the ships ahead of them torpedoed and sunk. With the *Silver Willow* now the leading ship of her column, it was her turn to be attacked. When torpedo tracks were sighted from the bridge, her helmsmen was ordered to turn to avoid them, so that they passed either side of the *Silver Willow* and hit the next ship astern. The bad weather continued with the wind blowing a strong gale.

Everyone was wearing life jackets; the captain, officers and Dudley, as the cadet on watch, were on the bridge, when the *Silver Willow* was finally torpedoed at the bow. Dudley was blown off the bridge, down several decks, and was unconscious for some minutes. He came to, thinking he was blind, but in fact blood from a small cut on the lobe of one of his ears had run across his face and into his eyes.

Two lifeboats on the windward side of the ship were lowered, but the sea swamped them immediately, and they were lost when the ropes holding them were lifted out of their hooks by the large seas. On the leeward side, at the third lifeboat station, Dudley saw the Chinese throwing their suitcases into the lifeboat as it was lowered, where an officer already on board, promptly threw them into the sea. At the fourth and last lifeboat he found the Third Mate, who was getting into it, who ordered Dudley in and the boat was lowered. As it neared the sea, a large wave lifted one of the rope falls out of its hook, so the boat hung by one and then suddenly turned upside down as it fell into the water. Dudley was trapped in a tangle of ropes wrapped round the boat.

The Third Mate remembered Dudley carried a large knife tucked inside his lifejacket. He reached for it and cut all the ropes, freeing him. At the same time, the lifeboat drifted along the ship's hull. The sea was covered with a thick layer of oil, as the torpedo had entered one of the palm oil tanks in the forward hold. As the two of them clung on to the upturned boat it was suddenly washed into the hole made by the torpedo. The waves made an eerie booming noise as they rebounded inside the tank. Then the backwash sucked them out, and the lifeboat was blown free from the ship. However, drifting in and out of consciousness, Dudley realised later he was no longer with the boat and was alone in the sea. He remembered to switch on the little red light on his lifejacket before becoming unconscious again. The Atlantic Ocean in November is bitterly cold and the Third Mate wasn't seen again. Nor was the boat.

Sometime later, Dudley woke and felt a terrible pain on his face; before realising it was caused by the little Merchant Navy buttons near the cuff of a sleeve someone was using to wipe his face so as to see who it was. "Why, it's that bugger Pope," said his shipmate, Cadet Dickie Perkins. Only one lifeboat had got away safely and it was all the men could do to row, keeping the boat head to wind for fear of capsizing in the huge seas. By mere chance, Dudley had drifted down directly onto them and they just managed to reach out and grab him as he went by. A little later, the Captain drifted alongside in the same way, and as they tried to roll him over the gunwale, he kept saying: "Be careful! Be careful!" They concluded the old boy had stove in some ribs, but later seated on a thwart the Captain dove his hand into his lifejacket and brought out a bottle of whisky, which was handed round for all to share.

There were a few other officers in the lifeboat as well as the Captain, Dickie Perkins, and Dudley. At times an oar was swept away by the heavy seas as they struggled to keep the boat upright and headed into the wind. They had only a small ration of water each day because they could not open the emergency food lockers in the lifeboat. After two weeks, someone spotted what looked like a huge ship coming up astern of them, but as it drew nearer the smaller it became. They were seen by the lookouts and the ship manoeuvred in a circle so that the wash from the propellers could smooth the sea a little. Boarding nets were thrown over the side and when the lifeboat was alongside, the survivors were able to grab the nets and climb on board. However, Dudley had an injured finger from the time the Third Mate freed him from the entangling ropes alongside the sinking *Silver Willow,* and so found he was unable to climb up the net. Finally, a crew member came looking over the side with a torch to make sure no one was left behind, and went down to help him. Like everyone else, because they had so little to eat and drink, he was almost too weak to stand, but on getting below, Dudley found he was in the company of shipmates and friends from other ships of the convoy which had also been lost.

After barely registering this, he realised the ship had begun to gather way, but there was then the most terrible crash which sounded like another submarine torpedo attack. As the survivors rushed to the door to get out on deck, they heard laughter behind them. The ship, the *Kalimantan,* from Malaya and named after the province there, was a shallow, flat bottomed river steamer. She was manned by a Royal Navy volunteer crew who were taking her to Scotland, to be prepared for service in the Normandy landings of 1944. But for now, as she rose to the crest of every Atlantic swell, she crashed down on the other side, and did so all the way to Glasgow.

The food supplies on board were exhausted, and all that was left were tins of tomatoes, which they ate out of the small cans they came in. Upon arrival in Glasgow, they were taken to a hotel for a meal, which none of them could eat, the first mouthful sticking in their throats.

By this time, Dudley's finger was becoming very painful, but he said nothing because he wanted to get home as soon as possible and not be detained in a hospital in Scotland. He travelled south to London, arriving at Paddington with his captain and other survivors, all of whom had clothing stained with salt and palm oil. Just as Dudley headed off alone for Charing Cross to catch a train to Ashford, he was arrested by a policeman who thought he was a deserter. Fortunately, he was able to find his captain and all was explained.

Dudley found his grandfather, now a widower, at home in his familiar place at the fireplace, knocking the ashes from his pipe. Being deaf, he did not hear Dudley come in, but on turning, calmly said: "Hello, boy, I knew you were all right. You must go over to Littlestock to see your mother." There, Dudley's arrival was more dramatic: his mother fainted when he walked in the door. She had received a telegram many weeks before saying he was "missing, presumed lost at sea." After a visit to the doctor, Dudley was taken into hospital because the fourth finger on his left hand had a cut tendon. A surgeon attempted to rejoin it, but too much time had elapsed for this to be successful and so it was decided to amputate. Shortly afterwards, gangrene set in and Dudley went through an excruciating period of having his hand plunged in scalding water to try to combat the infection.

Ashford Hospital was in a cul-de-sac and living close by in a house near the end was the family of Dickie Perkins. Dickie visited Dudley every day whilst on leave and when he returned to sea his father went instead. Then a terrible moment came when Dudley overheard the surgeon talking to the ward sister. He said that they may have to have the arm off that "young man". But before that could happen, the sister bore down on him one morning with a huge syringe filled with a yellow liquid which was an early form of penicillin, still in its developmental stage at that time. It saved his arm and hand. As he was recovering, Mr. Perkins received another telegram from the shipping company. Dickie had joined an oil tanker which also carried aviation fuel in drums on deck. Dudley was asked by Mr. Perkins if there was any hope for his son this time. He knew there was not, because he had seen a tanker blow up in his last convoy. As he had been senior to his friend, he always felt badly afterwards that had it not been for his hand, he would have been on board the new ship and not Dickie. But Dudley never forgot the friends with whom he shared a cabin on board the *Silver Willow*.

By the time he was fully recovered, Dudley had turned eighteen and then received his call-up papers. He decided he wanted to join the Royal Navy and duly applied. But at the subsequent interview he was dismissed after a few questions and told: "You've done your bit for the country lad, go out and get busy in civilian life!"

At this point he had no idea what he wanted to do, but a family friend to whom he had written whilst at sea, was impressed enough by his letters to suggest he take up journalism, which led him to the *Kentish Express* as a trainee reporter. There, he earned one shilling and sixpence per week plus sixpence bicycle allowance. He also learned the basics of journalism: covering all the local news from agriculture to the court sessions in Ashford. At only twenty, he moved to Fleet Street, first joining an advertising agency and then *The Evening News.* His first task was as a reporter covering stories of wartime Britain. Later, he specialised in Royal Naval affairs and general sea stories, including shipping disasters around the coast of Britain, as all things maritime interested him. On a visit to Greenock, near Glasgow, he saw the *Kalimantan,* the ship that had rescued him and his shipmates in their lifeboat. She had been restored and repainted white for the Tropics and was ready to return to Malaya.

By 1949 Dudley was a sub-editor, sitting at the large table in the Sub's Room with a dozen or so other men, editing news stories as they came in, and later going upstairs to the stone to see the pages set up by the printers. Two men at the table became good friends, John Gold and Steve Camp, and it was Steve who introduced Dudley to sailing. Following a holiday together, sailing a chartered boat in the Solent, Dudley went sailing whenever he could. He joined the Junior Offshore Group, otherwise known as the JOG. They were an enthusiastic group of young men who, in the summer, spent their weekends racing yachts of under twenty feet from the south coast ports of Britain across to French ports such as Dunquerque, Calais, Étaples and Fécamp. Crewing these yachts was a hard and fast way to learn to sail. When he had enough experience Dudley bought one of these little boats and called her *Red Gryphon.*

One summer, he sailed across the North Sea, through the Kiel Canal to Denmark and as he cruised the Danish islands, received a great deal of attention and hospitality. There was much comment about the size of *Red Gryphon* and also the fact that she was the first British yacht to sail across the North Sea to visit Denmark since before the War. Later, he wrote a book about this trip which eventually led to a career as a full-time author. When the manuscript was completed, he sent it to several publishers, one of whom was interested enough to publish it subject to some changes. But Dudley had become discouraged and learned, as with many would-be authors, that it is very difficult to get a first book published.

However, another publisher, William Kimber, later contacted

Dudley to commission a non-fiction book on a naval action during World War II. Kimber suggested several titles, but Dudley preferred ideas of his own and it was finally agreed that he should write a history about the small coastal forces in the Mediterranean. By this time, he had moved from the Subs table to the Features Department at *The Evening News*, becoming a feature writer and naval correspondent. So it was, at the end of 1952, when I joined the paper and came to know him.

Occasionally office tickets allowed us to go to the theatre or, in the summer, to the Promenade Concerts at the Royal Albert Hall. The first time we went out together was to see *Paint Your Wagon*. We also exchanged notes in the office and Dudley wrote many letters to me. We were so in love and very early in our relationship it was just assumed we would marry. One evening, we had an argument about the office dinner and dance. Being young, I naturally wanted to go, but Dudley did not. The next day I received a long letter from him stating his reasons: he could not dance and had no wish to spend an evening with people he worked with all day. The letter continued:

"While I am writing I ought to repeat something else I said this evening: for us, for the next few months, it will be – as long as you feel you can help – more work than pleasure. It may seem tedious, and at times I get a bit irritable. But the thing is this: we must look ahead. For me to be a successful author, with the freedom that that implies, then I must work. If I have, say, four books published then we are free: no more offices. Just work damned hard for a few weeks (months) and then – weeks of rest. But one can do nothing without hard work. So, where [your friends] *for instance are going (we'll say) to the theatre a couple of times a week, and dancing on the other nights, we are dictating and typing. The difference is this: one day we may be rich enough to say – 'now we cruise the world for 3 years'; or 'we'll buy that lovely Queen Anne house in Lymington.' These are, to some extent, dreams at the moment; but it is the evenings at the Admiralty and the typing afterwards, and later the sheer grind of typing the MSS, that will make those dreams reality. And with the reality, the independence which only money can*

give; and that is the happiness which money can give you. You see that my profession is – counting in authorship – not a profession like the usual one where one waits for the man above you to die: one has to force oneself on. Otherwise one stays still. Look at the Subs table at 'The Evening News' – loaded with men who have accepted their fate. But Graham Greene and Evelyn Waugh were journalists like me. So was Hemingway. Somerset Maugham, A.J. Cronin and C.S. Forester were all failed medical students. But all worked damned hard in the early days, which is what I have to do. Whereas before I was doing it for myself – and that's not much of a spur – I am now working for you as well, and that makes me want to make a success, so that I can share my life with you and give you some of the things in life which you ought to have – travel, comfortable home, good clothes and so on. But it will only come through plain hard work, and lots of luck. Especially luck. This may sound an awful long sermon and maybe you won't be able to read my writing anyway . . . Darling Kat – I love you far more than I thought I could love anyone: each day there is something about you that I discover anew and each day I fall in love with you again and again. Anything I want in this world I want for you, and you alone. The only thing I don't want for you – is yourself. I want that for myself. I had, in the course of a short but rather cynical life, thought that my "phantom love" – the woman of my dreams, if you like – did not exist. I am still completely amazed that I have now met her, and that not only do I love this "dream" woman, but she also loves me. At times we will, perhaps, have slight misunderstandings. These will be made worse, rather than better, by the fact we work in the same office, because whereas if we only "disagreed" in the evenings, then I could hold you and kiss you and we wouldn't disagree any more. But in the office – well, we have to "behave" Kat – I love you. Never doubt that and try to be patient. I love you, D. "

By the spring of 1953, the research was well advanced for his book *Flag 4*, with Dudley visiting the Historical Section at the Admiralty most evenings. The Navy's small high speed craft played an important role during the War with their actions among the islands of the Adriatic, the east and west coasts of Italy, and along the shores of North Africa. They were the fast motor torpedo and gun boats (M.T.B.s and M.G.B.s), working in flotillas, which raided enemy-held ports and important installations, such as petrol and ammunition dumps. They also sank hundreds of lighters and schooners which were increasingly needed to carry important cargoes of stores and ammunition as the roads were cut by Allied bombing. From the outset, Dudley was determined to write a serious historical study of these little ships. Flag 4 in the naval code book meant 'Attack with torpedoes' and when the book was published the full title was *FLAG 4, the Battle of Coastal Forces in the Mediterranean.*

Upon leaving *The Evening News* around 4 p.m. Dudley would use a pass he had to research and take notes from action reports in the Admiralty, both Allied and also German Naval records that had been seized at the end of the War. He was also able to sometimes trace survivors through reports submitted by the captains of the boats involved and then visit them to hear their personal stories. For the first time, Dudley experienced the excitement and fascination of research. The finding of the odd clue that makes the picture complete; going into the minute detail of what men said just before going into action; and the enjoyment of meeting naval officers and then comparing their recollections with what they had written in their reports at the time.

This same year, Dudley sold his little *Red Gryphon* and soon bought a William Fife 8-metre, which was 48 feet long. He changed her name to *Concerto* and later painted her red. She was lying on the river Clyde and two friends volunteered to bring her south to Newcastle where Dudley joined them. Arriving on a very wet morning and going on board, he was horrified to find most of the decks leaked. The driest part of the boat was under the side deck by the cockpit, where he found one friend sleeping under a yellow rubber dinghy and the other under a sail. *Concerto* was then taken to Newhaven where I could visit Dudley on Sundays throughout that summer and he taught me to sail. Naturally my parents were very concerned that their daughter of seventeen was dating a man ten years older. My father later warned me against marrying a writer, who is most likely to have an artistic temperament as many creative people have. I remember him telling me that it would not be an easy life, but there was no gainsaying me.

I lived with my family in the Geneva Hotel on the sea front at Bexhill-on-Sea. My parents were partners with friends who had been neighbours when we lived in Middlesex. They sold their homes, gave us four children a good education at boarding schools, bought the hotel and we became one large family. Up to the age of eleven I had a happy and uneventful childhood. I was four years old when Germany invaded Poland and World War II began. My brother and I were relatively untouched by the War: we had an Anderson shelter in the sitting room which was rarely used, although I remember one night when bombs fell fairly close by. My mother brought home whale meat and dried bananas, which none of us liked and we also kept a few chickens, whilst my father supplied many vegetables which he grew in the garden. When home for the school holidays in Bexhill, I often had a little room on the top floor overlooking the sea and I went to sleep each night seeing the Royal Sovereign lightship flashing on the horizon – keeping guard and warning ships of the rocks and shoals out there. I always loved the sea and used to dream about sailing one day and visiting places all over the world.

Dudley had similar dreams. One summer evening we viewed some paintings hanging on the fence by the Thames Embankment and Inner Temple Gardens. Afterwards, we sat on a bench there and Dudley revealed that one day he wanted to sail round the world and make his living entirely by writing books. If this did not appeal to me and if I regarded our evenings out together as just an affair, then we should stop seeing each other. But this was my dream too and perhaps I should confess now that I am a gypsy at heart: my wish came true when I married a sailor and although I did not see the whole world, I happily lived with Dudley on board boats for many more years than we ever lived on shore.

In the middle of July, Dudley went into Charing Cross Hospital to have his appendix removed. Joanna allowed me to have my lunch hour during one of the hospital's visiting hours, so I could see him each day. Immediately after leaving hospital, he asked my father for my hand in marriage, we became officially engaged and would marry in a year's time. I then received this letter in the office:

"*Tuesday, August 30, 1953.*

Dear Miss Hall,

I read about your engagement to Dudley Pope in The Times *yesterday, and while offering you my best wishes, I feel I ought to warn you about this fellow whom I have known for some years. He is rather temperamental, obsessed by boats, and alternatively depressed (99% of the time) or crazily cheerful (one % of the time). His financial situation is terribly involved at the moment, verging in bankruptcy, and his prospects of ever having any money are, I feel I should warn you, absolutely nil. He has few other interests outside boats. You appear to be one. The others are music (bigotedly classical, and loathing most modern music except French cabaret music), and books and just sitting on the beach watching boats. He is extraordinarily bad-tempered before lunch, and usually not much better after lunch. So you see you must be crazy really. I trust you will not be offended by this short intimation of what you have taken on. I am, madam, Yours sincerely, Dudley Pope.*

With the announcement of our engagement I also received a charming letter from John Connell, who each day wrote the leading article in *The Evening News*. He described himself 'an old Grouser' and bade me tell Dudley not to make me happy, but to keep me happy.

Dudley began writing *Flag 4* in October and I began typing it for him a few hours each evening on the hotel typewriter, as well as at the weekends. We decided not to see each other on Sundays, but concentrate on the book instead. This was to be my future life: helping Dudley with his books and boats. A letter he wrote to me at this time, enclosing more of the manuscript for me to type, said:

*My darling – It sounded all right the night before when we
agreed you stay at Bexhill and type; but it is a dreary business
when Sunday comes and you are not here . . . it's so very lonely.
I did not feel so very lonely before I met you, when I was alone –
well, I was just alone. Now when I am not with you I am more
than alone – half of me isn't here at all: I seem lost. That is, I
suppose, the essence of love – that when two people fall in love
with each other they cease to be two separate persons – somehow
they fuse into one, like two pieces of molten glass poured in the
same mould. Perhaps it is a good thing that once in a while you
do not come over – it makes me stop taking things for granted. I
get so used to the idea of you coming over on a Sunday . . . then
you suddenly don't come and I sit and think about it and realise
how much I need you. It's like not knowing how dark it is until
you switch the light out. John Donne, a poet I shall introduce you
to one of these days, wrote in the 16th century (my memory's
bad – it was something like this): "I wonder, by my troth, what
did I do before I loved, Was I not weaned 'till then, but suckled
on childish pleasures, foolishly?"*

*I know what he means. I can't see how I ever went on living
with the emptiness that there was in my life before I met you.
I suppose there was the fact that not having been really in love
before, I did not know what was missing. Anyway, all that
emptiness has gone: we have met, we are in love, and we are
going to be married soon. We have a home, we have faith in each
other and a respect for each other. We have a good start with the
book coming out. We have all the future here in front of us. If
we can only work hard for a year or two to take advantage of the
chances offered, then I think we can have the life we want – a
free life, without the soul-destroying monotony of office life . . .
I love you, my darling Kat, to an extent which perhaps you don't
realise. I wish you were here now, then I could kiss you instead of
having to kiss you in my imagination.*

*I must dash to catch the post – I don't see you until Tuesday .
. . I love you,
Yours D.*

P.S. Don't number these pages, but the Chapter number is all right and so are the footnotes, so you can follow them. I'll put the page numbers in later with a pen. "

Dudley stayed with us at Christmas and we discussed wedding plans. We hoped *Flag 4* would be finished by the end of February and we planned to marry on 17 March. My paternal grandmother was Irish, so we chose St. Patrick's Day. Dudley liked that date because it was an easy one for him to remember. On 8 January 1954 he wrote to me:

"Exactly one year and one month before I was due to be married I wrote in my diary (Feb 10/53): . . . Asked Kay (I don't even know her surname!!) if she'd like to come to the play. She agreed and was delightfully shy. Feeling on top of the world, though I can't think why . . .' (I can now though!!) The same day I wrote: 'Find I'm thinking of a wife!! Which shows what a crazy romantic I am . . .'

Then, on Feb 12, I wrote: 'Pleasurably excited at thought of going to see 'Paint Your Wagon' with Kathleen Hall. Snowing all day. Met her and she was sweet: completely self-possessed, shy but controlled, gay in a young way, bright and with so much of that light-heartedness that I have not got, never had, never will have . . . I thoroughly enjoyed the evening – far more than I have any other visit to the theatre I have ever made . . . She was 6 when I was at sea: I am ten years older. It's a long time, I think – yes, I am thinking that.'

Then Feb 13, the next day: 'The stalwart Gus was very pleased – 'I'd like to see you two fixed up.' I must say, since I've had perhaps a total of 20 minutes conversation with her – my mind is wandering that way; but it's silly, because I have so much to do before that . . . oh all these are dreams and I must face up to that . . .'

So you can see you had caught me right from the start!!! I love you.

I worked on at the office until 10.15 pm last night and got to page 105. I shall, I hope, have the worst of the book – i.e. past the Sicily invasion – done this weekend. From then on it should be much easier . . . I gather from other people that men usually, at this stage, get very nervous about marriage – 'cold feet' in fact.

All I can say is that far from getting cold feet I only wish we were getting married today. You know it seems that most natural thing in the world that we should fall in love. Maria last night asked me when and where I proposed to you, and I realised then that I don't think I ever did propose to you in that sense: it seems to have been accepted from quite early on – which is what I mean when I say it has all happened so naturally. The only fear I have is that I might prove a disappointment to you . . . I hope not and shall try very hard to avoid it . . . Kat, my sweetheart, much as I love you, I must do some work . . . Yours D."

Thus it came about at lunch time on Friday, 12 March, Dudley clambered into a taxi to deliver his manuscript to his publisher. At midday the following Wednesday, at St. Peter's Church in Bexhill, I entered the west door on my father's arm and saw the man I loved so much and who would be my companion for the next forty-three years, waiting for me at the altar.

CHAPTER TWO

The Decision

Before *Flag 4* was completed, Dudley had made notes for the next two books he hoped to write. They were two World War II actions which interested him; both had a significance of their own and neither had been written before. As Dudley rapidly gained confidence in his writing, the idea slowly came to him that perhaps he could eventually establish himself as an authoritative writer on naval history – yet written in a readable style for all sections of the public. Further back in his mind was the wish to write about Nelson and the naval battles during the Napoleonic War. Dudley never wrote about a subject which did not interest him, so that when beginning research for a new book, he derived enormous enjoyment learning about his subject. He wrote chiefly for himself but, for him I was his average reader and anything I did not understand, he rewrote more clearly.

I continued working at *The Evening News* after we were married but, because sometimes sensitive staff matters arose in the editor's office, I was transferred to work for the News editor, who in those days was Frank Starr, a small man, barely taller than myself. He and his wife, Doris, were at the performance of *Paint Your Wagon* to which Dudley took me on our first date and I think he kept a fatherly eye on us both.

Living on board *Concerto*, we travelled together back and forth to London daily. During the train journey Dudley often reviewed his ideas for his research and writing, while I very often went to sleep with my head falling on his shoulder, since we were up before six o'clock each morning. For our summer holiday we sailed *Concerto* across the Channel to Le Havre one weekend in June. This was my first sailing trip of any distance offshore, because the year before we had sailed from and returned to Newhaven on fine summer days with light breezes and calm seas. Colin Mudie, Dudley's best man at our wedding and who also had been a member of the Junior Offshore Group, came with us and since he had to return on the ferry from Le Havre on Sunday evening to be back at work next day, we sailed despite a poor weather forecast. During the night the wind became strong blowing Force 7 from the south and because our course was to the south, it was a rough and wet crossing. I was sent below to sleep and they left me in my bunk until the morning. My sleep was only disturbed at times by the thunderous flogging of the canvas sails as the boat changed course, going about on to the other tack, with the noise of the sheets passing through the blocks along the deck above my head. Being young, I could sleep at an angle of 45 degrees, wedged against the bunk board or the side of the boat, depending which tack we were on. When I awoke the following morning, Saturday, it was just beginning to get light. But as soon as I got up and tried to put some warm clothes on, holding on for dear life as the deck heaved up and down beneath my feet, I became dizzy and queasy. There was no alternative but to lie down again on the bunk and shut my eyes. In that position everything was all right. So this is seasickness, I thought. In the afternoon the rain squalls cleared and the wind did not seem to howl so much in the rigging. But the sea was still rough and the cabin danced as crazily as it did before. Dudley shouted down the hatch that they could see France and suggested I came on deck for some fresh air. But it was still hard to stand upright. I got dressed by degrees, with so many warm clothes to put on. Dudley came below and helped me with the oilskins and I went on deck feeling not at all well. The sea looked grey and very rough indeed. I was a lump of misery that sat in the cockpit by the tiller, wishing that one of the waves would pick me up and carry me away. I felt my marriage was over before it had hardly begun. I knew there was no way Dudley would ever give up sailing, and how could I cope if I was so terribly seasick?

Then he told me to steer the boat and sing! Having no choice, I did and gradually began to feel better. We reached Le Havre just after dark and anchored in the harbour.

We stayed two weeks in Le Havre and made friends with the members of the yacht club who then had their headquarters in a wooden hut. There was another palatial yacht club there which fulfilled a more social function than sailing. During that time we also visited Paris and then two friends joined us from England. We sailed to Trouville where we stayed another week and then, well fortified with seasickness tablets, we sailed to Newhaven Harbour with a brisk south-west wind on our quarter, taking exactly thirteen hours.

By September the proofs of *Flag 4* arrived to be read through to correct any printing errors and at the same time, complete the index. Dudley had already made a list of all the names of people, ships and places in alphabetical order in an address book, and all that was needed to be done was to go through the proofs very carefully, filling in the appropriate page numbers. Dudley found this a very tedious task this first time, although it soon became part of the routine when writing his non-fiction books. For him at this point it is too late to make any radical changes and feelings of dissatisfaction with the book would turn to worry and depression until after publication when, perhaps some good reviews appear in the newspapers to make all the hard work worthwhile. This happened often when the page proofs arrived and, being the optimist in the family, I did my best to encourage and reassure him. In fact, this first time it was exciting to see the title and Dudley's name on the dust jacket when we received the first copy of *Flag 4*. But we both found we could not read the book. We knew the story so well by then, that it was hard to take in what we read. When it was published in November, we were happy to see a copy displayed at Smith's bookstall in Victoria Station. We watched the papers and magazines impatiently for reviews and there were a few in the London newspapers, including *The Evening News*.

By the following summer we had almost completed the research for the next book which was *The Battle of the River Plate*. It was later published in America with a different title: *GRAF SPEE, The Life and Death of a Raider*. This story interested Dudley because it was the last battle fought without the use of radar and air power. It was also the first British naval action of World War II.

In December 1939 the hunting group under the command of Commodore Harwood, consisting of three lightly armed cruisers, the *Ajax, Achilles and Exeter,* caught the German pocket battleship *Graf Spee* in the South Atlantic Ocean and inflicted enough damage on her that Captain Langsdorff took her into the River Plate. Langsdorff obtained permission to enter the territorial waters of Uruguay, where he scuttled the *Graf Spee* with a double explosion a few days later and she settled on a sandbank off Montevideo. Dudley applied for a pass for me to accompany him to the Historical Section at the Admiralty and while we were doing the research there he dictated a great deal of the material on to a small tape recorder, which I transcribed later at the weekends. He also volunteered to work Saturdays at the paper, when the Historical Branch was closed, allowing his colleagues to have the weekends off with their families. In this way, he was able to spend one whole week day at the Admiralty taking notes from the documents.

But the research did not only involve going to the Admiralty. We were also in touch with the officers who had served in the three ships during the battle. We met Sir Edward Parry who was the captain of the *Achilles* and he and his wife welcomed us into their home in Kent and shared our times of elation and dejection. They followed the progress of the book very closely, and gave Dudley much encouragement. Dudley also visited Lady Harwood, the widow of Admiral Sir Henry Harwood, who was in command of the squadron and was the victor of the battle. He had been finding it hard to recreate in words the character of Sir Henry solely from the officers' descriptions who served with him. Quite clearly he had a great personality: as Commodore of the South America squadron at the beginning of the War, he had done an enormous amount of good work in establishing friendly relations between the Navy and various South American governments. His hearty, typically English approach, mixed with his inaccurate but far from halting Spanish, made him a great favourite. Yet Dudley felt something was missing from the picture that he had formed in his mind of this brave sailor.

One of the most moving experiences Dudley ever had was

listening that afternoon to Lady Harwood reading some of the letters that the Admiral had written to her just after the battle, while the two damaged cruisers, *Ajax* and *Achilles* waited outside Montevideo, expecting the *Graf Spee* to come out any minute and finish them off. With the *Exeter* lying crippled and out of the fighting, they would have had little chance of stopping her:

"Things are tricky at the moment as we don't know if he is coming out again, I have the most difficult problem to catch him again. If he escapes me all the good we have done will be upset – not all, but a lot of it. The mouth of the Plate is so wide and there are so many ways out that it is very difficult. Probably another battle – and who knows? I hope for the best. If yes, or no, you will know before you get this . . ."

In fact, he had told his captains afterwards that he put their chances of surviving at about thirty per cent. Lady Harwood told Dudley that the first thing she knew about the battle was when she came out of a cinema and saw the headlines in an evening newspaper. By the end of the day Dudley realised that he had at last found the final pieces of the jigsaw puzzle which he had been piecing together over the past months to create the first complete and accurate account of The Battle of the River Plate. The words written by men about to go into battle, when they think they will not live to see their wives again, are always very moving.

Until Dudley went to Goring, Admiral Harwood had seemed to be an extremely competent and brave naval officer; but lunching at the table that Sir Henry had lunched at, sitting in the drawing room, looking into the garden which no doubt Sir Henry had thought about longingly as he waited off Montevideo, Dudley saw that other side of him – the husband and the father. Lady Harwood showed Dudley a photograph, which she allowed him to reproduce in the book, of the *Graf Spee* at anchor. In his characteristic handwriting, Admiral Harwood had marked the shell holes and sent the photograph to his eldest son, who was then thirteen years old. The book was published in 1956 by Weidenfeld & Nicolson. It received greater attention in the press than *Flag 4* and it was satisfying to read good reviews after all our labours.

The book was condensed in *Lilliput* magazine, and serialised in a Liverpool paper. The reviewer in *The Sunday Times* wrote: Dudley *"had drawn copiously both on German and on English documents, and he presents both sides fairly and with judgement. His account of the actual battle is equally clear. He has brought to life not only the action, but the last macabre hours off Montevideo."*

A director of the American publisher in Philadelphia, J.B. Lippincott, was in London on a business trip. He found a copy of Dudley's *Battle of the River Plate* in a bookshop and took it back to the United States where it was decided to publish it.

The same year Captain Scott's ship the *Discovery*, moored on the Thames Embankment, was threatened with closure because the Scouts could no longer take care of her and the museum on board. Dudley wrote an article which began a campaign to save her with the help of Peter Scott. Readers responded with letters to *The Evening News* and several said what a shame it was that these old sailing ships could not still be working.

Dudley wrote more articles in *The Evening News*, not only about the *Discovery*, but also the Sail Training Association which was formed soon afterwards by Bernard Morgan and Peter Godwin and supported enthusiastically by Lord Louis Mountbatten. The first Tall Ships' race was held in July 1956 with sea cadets on board the ships of many nations and sailed from the Solent, off the Isle of Wight, to Lisbon. Dudley found a berth on board the three-masted schooner *Creole* owned by the Greek ship-owner Stavros Niarchos and he watched with amusement the intense rivalry between the permanent Greek crew on board and the crew of the *Ruyam*, a beautiful Turkish yacht in the race. It was a matter of honour for *Creole* to reach Lisbon first, but the winds were light for most of the race and the smaller *Ruyam* arrived first. The *Moyana*, a ketch built in Argentina, won the race, arriving in Lisbon ahead of the large Norwegian Sail Training Ship, the *Christian Radich*. Tragically the *Moyana* was lost at sea in a storm on her return voyage to England, but all those on board were saved.

Dudley found Stavros Niarchos a fascinating man: at this time Aristotle Onassis was his brother-in-law, as they both had married daughters of the shipping magnate, Stavros Livanos. Before World War II Niarchos had a fleet of trading ships with his uncle and lost part of it during the hostilities. But when the War was over he had about two million dollars of insurance money and began to build a fleet of oil tankers. Later came the supertankers which could carry large cargoes of oil. By 1956 with the Suez Crisis and the canal closed, he was in a perfect position to keep oil supplies flowing with his supertankers as they carried oil from the Persian Gulf to Europe round the Cape of Good Hope.

Some time after Dudley had covered the Tall Ships Race and returned to the office it became apparent he was unwell and he came close to a nervous breakdown. Travelling to London each day and at the same time writing The Battle of the River Plate in the evenings and days off, left him both physically and mentally exhausted. For a highly strung, imaginative person like my husband, his work on *The Evening News* frustrated him enormously. He was tactless and sometimes his colleagues found him difficult to work with. When he disagreed with something Dudley always said exactly what he thought and, having got it off his chest, would happily resume work unaware of the crushed feelings left around him. Dudley was writing on defence and naval topics and he held very strong views, disagreeing with the policies of the Government and the Ministry of Defence at that time. But when his articles were edited his opinions were often cut so they did not appear in the paper. For Dudley this was not only frustrating but also infuriating.

In the evenings he would rage about the office to me and his frustration certainly contributed to his near nervous breakdown. His doctor recommended a period of rest and we stayed with my family at the hotel in Bexhill, where Dudley could relax while I went to the office each day. There are always plenty of maintenance jobs to do on a boat, and had we remained on the boat he would have found himself doing this and that all day long.

I took my three weeks holiday later in August while Dudley was still on sick leave. We decided to visit Cornwall, meandering slowly by car staying in little bed and breakfast guesthouses. A distant cousin had contacted Dudley at *The Evening News* the year before and suggested they meet. Hugh's father had drawn up a large Pope family tree, working on it for many years during summer holidays in Cornwall. He visited churches, beginning in the Padstow area, searching for the names of the Pope family in the registers for births, marriages and deaths and going back to the early fifteenth century. The family had lived in a manor house at St. Kew for three hundred years and moved to Plymouth in the early nineteenth century. They became ship-owners and had their yard at Turnchapel, across from the Cattewater near Batten Castle. Having gained so much family history, Dudley later used family and place names when he created his hero, Lord Ramage, for the series of novels he wrote set in the time of Nelson's Navy. Ramage's father, John Uglow, tenth Earl of Blazey, would have his family home at St. Kew, while Uglow was the maiden name of Dudley's great-grandmother. We visited St. Kew on our holiday and found the manor house that once belonged to Dudley's forebears.

By September that year Dudley had more or less recovered his health. We decided to sell our boat and live in London. It would mean we should no longer waste time and energy in travelling and have longer evenings at home to work on the next book. We were just beginning the research for *73 North* which Weidenfeld's had commissioned him to write as well as *The Battle of the River Plate*.

Every book Dudley had published was contracted by his publisher. It specified among many things, the approximate number of words, usually between 70,000 to 80,000, the date when the manuscript would be completed and delivered to the publisher, and the royalty payments.

The first is often paid on signing the contract, a second payment when the manuscript is delivered and a third when the book is published. Once a hardback book has earned the advance, further royalties are paid every six months with a statement giving the number of books sold. The royalties are based on the percentage of the book's sale price and an author might expect ten per cent on the first 1,500 copies sold, while this percentage will increase slowly to perhaps seventeen per cent when there are more than 15,000 copies sold. Paperback royalties are based on lower percentages, perhaps beginning at four per cent and rising to six or seven.

Shortly after, we were offered an apartment on the fourth floor of an old building at the Holborn end of Chancery Lane. There was no lift, but we loved it, and we could hardly have been closer to the office. We used to cut through the Inner Temple and across King's Bench Walk, then turning eastwards find our way to Carmelite House.

During most of 1957 we were busy with 73 North, completing the research at the Admiralty and meeting the officers and men involved in the story. Later, in the year Dudley wrote the book, which was about the attack on convoy JW 51B and like all the Arctic convoys, carried equipment for the Russian Front, which included tanks, fighters, bombers, lorries, munitions and aviation fuel. It was one of many convoys that sailed to Russia and the battle that raged around it within the Arctic Circle, at 73 degrees north, had a far greater consequence which was not realised until after the War when the Minutes of the Führer's Naval Conferences were published. Dudley had been intrigued to read that Hitler had decided to decommission all his warships larger than a destroyer simply because he was infuriated by the failure of the attack on convoy JW 51B. The German Navy was ordered to concentrate on attacking the allies' convoys of merchant ships with the U-boat fleet instead. This convoy had an escort of five destroyers under the command of Captain (later Admiral) R. St. V. Sherbrooke. The German attack force had one pocket battleship, one heavy cruiser and six destroyers. The British destroyers, using bravery and bluff, succeeded in driving the German ships off until they were reinforced by two cruisers. Captain Sherbrooke was severely wounded during the battle, losing an eye; for his gallantry and skill in winning this action, and thus saving the convoy, he was awarded the Victoria Cross. But he was also supported by a fine and brave band of officers, most of whom we met.

Dudley also contacted Admiral of the Fleet Lord Tovey who

from 1940 to 1943 was Commander-in-Chief of the Home Fleet based in Scapa Flow, a beautiful natural harbour in the Orkney Islands. He organised the escorts for the Arctic convoys and sent them on their way, sending signals to warn of impending German attacks from packs of U-boats.

Later, Lord Tovey very kindly agreed to write the foreword for *73 North*, and he and his wife visited us one evening at our home in Chancery Lane. During the evening he regaled us with a story about an amusing incident when he was on a M.T.B. in the Mediterranean at the beginning of the War. A shell exploded nearby and blew his cap off, leaving the cap band with badge still in place round his head. Lord Tovey was a short man and we could visualise him as a younger man standing on the bridge of his M.T.B. with the cap band across his forehead. How Dudley wished he had met Lord Tovey earlier when doing his research for *Flag 4* as he could have included this anecdote in his book. Just before *73 North* was published, we invited everyone who had helped us, with their wives, to the Cock Tavern in Fleet Street to meet their former captain and each other again. It was a very convivial evening and fun to have contrived this reunion.

Moreover, they continued to have a reunion every year for many years to come. The publication of *73 North* was most exciting with the publishers renting a window at a bookstall at Waterloo Station, which created a great deal of comment among our friends. It was also very well reviewed in the national and provincial papers and was serialised in the same Liverpool paper that ran the serialisation of *The Battle of the River Plate*.

73 North was also well received in America and Dudley was greatly encouraged. John Connell in *The Evening News* began his review by saying:

> *Dudley Pope's new book, the third work of naval history, which this distinguished young writer has published in the past few years, is by far his best. In '73 North' Mr. Pope has a magnificent theme which he tackles magnificently . . . This is history written like Alan Morehead's 'Gallipoli' and Chester Wilmot's 'The Struggle for Europe' by someone who has learned his craft as a journalist . . . He has a strong but well-disciplined sense of*

drama, and a sober respect for the limits of historical truth . . . It
is a major achievement."

Alan Ross in *The Observer* wrote that Dudley. *"Creates exactly the*
atmosphere, builds up the tension; and the climax, when it comes, has
an explosive and dramatic force . . . Altogether, '73 North' must be
about the most exhaustive study of a naval action ever to be written."

It made all the hard work so worthwhile, as also the sacrifice
of not seeing our friends as often as we wished or going out in
the evenings to the theatre. While we were still both working for
The Evening News we worked every evening and weekend when a
book was in progress. As soon as we came home, Dudley took a
short nap in his chair while I made some tea. After half an hour
he would wake refreshed and ready to begin work on the book.
He wrote all his non-fiction books by hand, as it was too difficult
to manage a typewriter with his notebooks and papers around
him on the desk. He was painstakingly careful to write accurately,
and checked the facts in his notes against their sources. When the
first draft was finished, he went through it, editing, cutting and
rewriting while I typed the manuscript again, chapter by chapter.

The first civil war in Lebanon broke out in May of 1958 and
Dudley learned that the U.S. 6th Fleet in the Mediterranean was
about to land a force of Marines in Lebanon at Beirut. The office
sent him to cover the story and he was away for several weeks. By
this time Dudley was deputy to Harold Walton, the foreign editor
and the day he left, Harold came to the News Room to reassure
me not to worry as he had Dudley well insured against injury or
death! Instead of leaving me happily reassured as he hoped, he
left me worrying about his safety. But in the postcards and letters
Dudley sent me, he said he was never in any real danger as all the
taxi drivers were rebels and knew where the combat lines were
drawn up. Dudley also described some of the difficulties he and
other journalists experienced before they could begin to send
stories back to the office:

"There were incredible delays in getting going on the story. We

arrived at the airport at 2 pm and it took until 9 pm to get a visa. Curfew is 8 p.m. Next day we had to get Press permits, cable permits, curfew permits and a new visa (they gave us only 48 hours at first) . . . This is a wonderful red-tape country, it took me 36 hours to get enough permits even to file a cable. Hope Harold realises this. There are hordes of pressmen here – all nationalities . . . The Press competition is tough, the Express, Mail and Chronicle for instance, all have three men each. They want me to go to Jordan today, but I can't get a visa (Embassy shut) and anyway, I think this is the more important news centre. All the U.S. headquarters are here.

"I can't get through to the office by 'phone, nor them to me. Cable takes hours. I'm writing to Harold care of you because censors will open my letter if addressed to the office . . ."

Later on a postcard Dudley wrote:

"Excelsior Hotel, Beirut. Darling heart – another week begins – and I wish I was with you. This city is one of the most delightful I have ever seen – and I am living in splendour, but it is of no interest without you. I forgot to tell you I love you. They seem to be using my stories – I'm told I had the splash [the story on page 1] *on Saturday. But it's drying up here and I hope it won't be long before I'm home again with you. Look after yourself beloved Kat and don't worry about your own – D."*

As Dudley remained frustrated with the office, life on the paper became more intolerable for him. He hated discipline, but yet had the most incredible self-discipline while writing his books at home. When a book was in progress, all his thoughts were concentrated on that book, and he worked on it every day.

At every opportunity I would tell him the office was not worth worrying about to the detriment of his health. To leave the office where it was when he walked out of the building each evening and not bring it home with him. To become a full-time author was still his goal, without the need of the supplementary income from journalism. But it takes courage to throw up a good joint income for the uncertainty of authorship, where your pay cheque only arrives twice a year. There would be good years and bad years.

Dudley's creativity always amazed me: ideas came to him while travelling on a train or when out driving the car, or even in the midst of some maintenance job on the boat.

The ideas flowed best when he was relaxed. He always had a notebook handy to jot down phrases or as ideas came to him. He suffered with nervous tension all his life, caused by his creativity and it was something he had to learn to live with and control. Although Dudley understood people, their motives or their failings, he was often intolerant and would not suffer fools gladly. We learned from relatives that his Pope grandfather, George, who was a Church of England missionary to the Tamils in southern India for forty years, had been the same and his temperamental outbursts were legendary.

Dudley said things which would have been better left unsaid. It was this last characteristic which made it hard for him to work with other people and he was the first to admit this. He had a very quick mind, and I always found it impossible to argue with him. He could muster all his arguments before I could even rationalise mine. In any dispute between us everything was said and then forgotten. He never held a grudge and he apologised later when he thought he had been unkind.

One of his oldest friends, John Gold, who had sat next to him at the large table in the Sub's Room some years before, made this fair assessment to me of Dudley's character when I told him I was writing this book: "I think very few outside the family knew Dudley as well as I did. He was a very, very complex character, difficult at times, very demanding, occasionally cruel in the remarks he made, but always utterly loyal. He will forever remain one of my greatest friends."

Dudley made his plans carefully, with a great deal of thought and preparation. He said it was because he was lazy and it is easier to get it right the first time. But he also admitted when he was young he was hasty and slapdash and learned through mistakes to be cautious.

I am a patient and easy going person, an optimist, who believes things happen for the best. In an argument I have the misfortune of being able to see both sides and it would annoy Dudley when he was criticising someone, if I came to their defence. When Dudley lost his temper with me, I would let his anger flow over me. Later, if I still felt justified in my point of view, I would judge when it was safe to discuss it again. Small things angered him, the larger problems he could face calmly.

He was never very communicative early in the morning and hated getting up. But one dull Saturday morning when I was lazily thinking of going to the kitchen to make some coffee, he really startled me when he suddenly sat up in bed and said: "Well, that's it. I have finished with the paper. I am going to resign!"

With this statement made, Dudley sank down into the bed again and began to consider the implications of what he had just said. Up to that point he had worked fourteen years on *The Evening News*. No one will be surprised to know that between the decision made that April morning two and a half years elapsed before it was put into execution. But afterwards, whenever Dudley grumbled about the office, I always seized the opportunity to say: "Why let it bother you? You are wasting your breath, you cannot change anything. Anyway, we have decided to leave! So how much longer must we live and work in London?"

"Yes well, we'll wait bit longer and see how well this next book sells," he would reply. We had a great deal to think about that dull Saturday morning. We still had our dream, perhaps not sail around the world, but cruise with our boat in warm waters, and dropping our anchor in some foreign port for a while to allow Dudley to write his sea stories and perhaps even novels. But we had to consider first if we were we going to earn enough money from writing books? Where were we going to live? In England or abroad? In a house or a boat? How wonderful it would be, if only we had enough money saved, to buy a boat, fill it up with stores and sail off to the Caribbean! Or a cruise to the Aegean!

Was Dudley going to continue writing naval history? Besides a house or boat in which to live, we would also need a reserve of capital with which to launch ourselves: for having left our salaried jobs on *The Evening News*, there would be no income for the first six months or until Dudley delivered his next manuscript and received an advance royalty payment. Or better still, we had to choose a moment when there was a book in print that was earning money for us to live on. However, it is always difficult for an author to assess his future income.

But it did not matter that morning: from then on we both felt happy that the decision had been made.

After writing three contemporary naval histories, Dudley turned back one hundred and fifty years to the Battle of Trafalgar in 1805. By the time 73 North was published he was already visiting second-hand bookshops to buy books about that period. The first thing he had to do was to learn how to sail a square-rigged ship of the line like the Victory, now lying in her dry dock at Portsmouth. He would stagger into the flat with his parcels of books, filthy from the dusty bookshelves, hot and sticky from climbing up all the stairs to our flat on the fourth floor and shamefaced at the amount of money he had spent. There were books on sails, rigging, gunnery and seamanship; biographies of Nelson and books on the life and times of the early nineteenth century, all of which would be useful for reference in the future.

His own sailing experience helped him considerably and he also visited the Victory to walk round her decks, imagining himself in the year 1805 and taking in the atmosphere. He studied the mast, rigging and sail plans with photocopies obtained from the National Maritime Museum, covering his desk and the sitting room floor night after night. There were also plans of the hull and the interior, showing the layout of the different decks below; drawings of the 84, 74, and 64-gun ships; of frigates, sloops and bomb ketches. For Dudley felt, without this knowledge, his book on the battle would be as dry and dull as those accounts in our history books at school. His task was immense: he wanted to write history that everyone could enjoy; he was going to write all the little everyday events that happened to Nelson, his officers and his seamen. Many times Dudley was afraid he would fail and yet, if he could succeed, he knew he could write an enjoyable but nevertheless perfectly accurate naval history for everyone to read. He hoped he could write countless other books on his favourite period of history that he discovered as a schoolboy when he visited the Public Library in Ashford with his grandfather.

Again, Dudley enjoyed the research immensely, learning everything he could about his subject: he wished to discover how Nelson won the Battle of Trafalgar and set about finding out. Besides collecting books to supply the background for the battle, we began to visit the British Museum and the Public Record Office together. This was fun and interesting for me also: reading through the ships' logs and private letters, the story is told to you. Sometimes the facts contradict themselves and like detectives we followed up the clues until quite suddenly we came across a letter which made the whole picture clear. As we took notes from the captain's and master's logs, Dudley noticed that at sea the calendar day began at twelve noon, not at midnight. The Admiralty changed this system just a few years later.

When studying the published positions of the ships at Trafalgar, Dudley realised the positions were misplaced by twelve hours, so he set to drawing up his own maps of the ship's positions and their manoeuvres at certain times during the battle. Once published, his work was accepted and acknowledged to be correct. All subsequent biographies of Nelson used Dudley's work. We met Admiral A.H. Taylor, who was an authority on Trafalgar, having made a lifelong study of the battle as his hobby. He helped and encouraged Dudley tremendously. We also met the marine artist Colonel Harold Wyllie who knew everything there was to know about square-rigged ships, the ships-of-the-line and all the ins and outs of them and he helped Dudley with many details about the *Victory*. As a young man he saw the last of the sailing warships change to steam. In 1925 the Society for Nautical Research launched an appeal and raised £125,000 for the reconstruction of the *Victory*. They commissioned Harold Wyllie to supervise the masts and rigging, since it was obvious only he knew sufficiently enough to undertake such a task. For the previous fifty or more years the *Victory* had become virtually a hulk in Portsmouth. She had been built on and stripped off again, had lost her original masts and spars, and had three short stumps sticking up forlornly from her deck. There was a danger of her being destroyed and there were not many people left who knew how she should look. Harold Wyllie accomplished his task and the *Victory* is now a museum piece.

In the *Victory* Museum close by the ship there is the magnificent Trafalgar panorama painted by W.L. Wyllie, Harold Wyllie's father.

As our library grew, it became obvious that it would be difficult to live on board a yacht unless it was large enough to hold all Dudley's books. Besides wanting to move away from London, we really wanted to leave England and find a place with a warm climate and low cost of living. We considered Spain, Majorca or Italy. A place not too far from England, from where we could return every so often to do the research for other books.

But at this time we were still hankering after a boat in which to cruise and why not the Mediterranean? Besides size being one problem, bad weather was another. One drenching of salt water over Dudley's precious seamanship manuals, hard to replace, would be an expensive loss.

If bad weather was one problem, so hot sunshine was another. Yachts in the Mediterranean have crews to pour buckets of water on the decks several times a day, and put out awnings to fall over the yachts' topsides almost to sea level to keep them cool, preventing the wood shrinking and the seams opening up. Our yachting was strictly do-it-yourself and relying on our authorship earnings only, we could see that we would be spending most of our time in the Mediterranean busy with boat maintenance and have no time to write books.

All this was going through our minds when we visited Italy for the first time in the summer of 1958. When we arrived in Santa Margharita we were enchanted with its steep hills dotted with houses and gardens descending to the rocky shore and sea. The houses were painted pale ochre, salmon, pink and blue; many had false windows and panels painted on them and all had shutters at the windows. One evening we climbed up the hills behind the town and walked through vineyards and then a farmyard to reach a vantage point to look down over the whole of Santa Margharita. The scene below us was beautiful, the sun was beginning to dip down towards the horizon and becoming pink in the haze which so often rests just above the sea in this part of the world. We sat and looked and as time slipped by we watched the lights come on one by one.

Dudley said "What I would give to have my yacht anchored down there!" We idly discussed our hopes for the future and vowed we would come back to live in Italy. However, we returned to London and to Nelson at the Battle of Trafalgar, which Dudley began writing in the autumn. It was due to be finished the following year, so that it could be published on 21 October, the anniversary of the battle.

In the evenings Dudley was virtually living in the year 1805: he had been reading Nelson's letters and thinking about him so much that quite suddenly one night he took the typewriter away from me and began typing for some time. When he finished Dudley turned to me, his face slightly flushed, and told me he had the most extraordinary experience. He had felt as though Nelson had been standing at his elbow while he described his character and personal appearance. He felt as though he had met and known Nelson. By the middle of March, with the delivery date due in one month, Dudley was writing hard and had written 95,000 words. But he still had not reached the actual battle. At the time he complained he felt as though he was running up a down escalator.

The first draft of the book was finished two months later and, running behind schedule, it was obvious there was not much time left for him to edit it. A month before we were due to go away on holiday in June, we borrowed another typewriter and Carol, my stepmother, came to help with the typing in the evenings. So there were the three of us, Dudley cutting and editing the pages chapter by chapter, while the two of us typed them. The book was given the title *England Expects*, taken from Nelson's famous flag signal to his fleet just as the battle against the combined fleets of France and Spain began: *England expects that every man will do his duty.* Finally it was finished and we were ready to go on holiday. Since Dudley was working in the Foreign Department at *The Evening News*, he often spoke on the telephone to Corrado Pallenberg, the paper's Rome correspondent. Corrado had already given us details of the cost of living in Italy, which had made us decide to spend our next summer holiday in Italy again. Having told Corrado we wanted to live near water, he had sent us a list of villages on lakes and coastal areas that he recommended us to visit. We were going to find somewhere to live in Italy.

CHAPTER THREE

The Reconnaissance 1959

Once again as the ferry reached the approaches of Boulogne harbour, the anonymous and blurred voice announced over the loudspeaker in French and in English, that drivers should now go below to their cars and all passengers on deck have their landing tickets and passport control tickets ready to be collected, "but please keep the gangways clear." As harassed looking husbands disappeared below while wives, panicking searched their handbags frantically for their tickets, and children asked innumerable questions, the distinct aroma of Gaulloise cigarettes drifted from the quays towards us. Porters waited in groups, ready to pour on board like pirates to seize the luggage of those few passengers who were travelling without cars. Then I was walking down the gangway and hurrying towards the vast open space where the cars, on leaving the ferry, were being assembled. As I waited for Dudley to arrive from the ship, the excitement mounted within me, for now we had really started out on our search for somewhere to live in Italy. Eighteen hours later we were eating dinner on the terrace of the hotel where we stayed the year before at Santa Margharita. The following morning we set out to visit house agents and began to collect a large and new Italian vocabulary: words for rent, furnished, unfurnished, with water, electricity, bedrooms, sitting room, kitchen and bathrooms. We were offered many apartments and villas, all of which were far beyond the price we could afford to pay. Santa Margharita was for the international set, not for us. Sadly we left Santa Margharita and drove to Lerici, just to the south of La Spezia and the first on Corrado's list. We remembered that Byron and Shelley had lived in the village early in the nineteenth century for a few years. The house agency was closed for lunch when we arrived, so until it opened, we decided to explore the castle above the southern end of the village. It was a fine fortification and one around which Dudley thought he could set a historical novel. Later, when we saw the house agent, we discovered the rents for his villas and apartments were also too expensive and we continued on our way south along the Via Aurelia, originally built by the Romans and which ends at Rome. That night we stayed at a place called Bocca di Magra, and here quite by accident we found a furnished apartment at a reasonable monthly rent. It was self-contained, but part of the hotel in which we stayed. We arranged with the hotel owner and her son, who spoke English, that we would return in two weeks' time to let them know if we wished to take the apartment the following year. We rather liked Bocca di Magra. The hotel was the only one there and except for July and August, we felt it would be a peaceful place. The river Magra passed in front of the hotel and beyond it to the south was the coastal plain stretching towards Viareggio and Pisa.

Only a few miles inland the Apennines rise sharply with their white marble scars which turn pink when reflecting the colours of the sunset. It was a place in which to stay if we did not find anywhere else during our brief three weeks' holiday. And once settled in there, we could explore further to see if there was somewhere else we might like better. The next day we set off southwards to visit Porto Ercole, which is just one hundred miles north of Rome. Porto Ercole, Monte Circeo and the Amalfi coast, just south of Naples, were three places strongly recommended by Corrado and we had read about all three before we left London. The few hints the guide books made about Porto Ercole and its brother village, Porto Santo Stefano, on the knob of land we could see half way down the leg of Italy, had made us think that this would be the right place for us.

We crossed the river Magra and entered Tuscany and the further south we progressed, the more enchanted we became. The soft rolling landscape meeting the Tyrrhenian Sea reminded me a little of the South Downs in Sussex, but in addition there were neatly arranged olive groves, the trees standing in lines which curved up over little conical hills, so typical of this part of Tuscany and looking like neatly sewn patchwork quilts. Inland, with the terrain rising more steeply, we occasionally saw a hill town perched high up with towers standing out sharply against the blue sky. In centuries past these hill towns began with a fortress with houses inside the fortified walls. But gradually as more houses were built outside the walls, they became hill towns. But in many of them the walls and the arches of the old gateways still stand today. The wheat was turning gold in the fields we passed and men and women were cutting hay. The women also were completely dressed in black, including black scarves tied round their heads, their faces deeply tanned by the sun. With them were creamy-white oxen: beautiful creatures with soft doe-like eyes and placid countenances. Standing in pairs, harnessed to little carts, they idly swished their tails across their backs. They became a familiar sight to us, for as yet few farmers could afford mechanical farm machinery, and instead of tractors, they used oxen to pull their ploughs and carts. So we fell in love with Tuscany with its blue sky, fields of gold and green and the pale silvery colour of the olive groves. The nearer we reached Porto Ercole, the more certain we felt that this would be the place where we would choose to live.

When we were nearly there we could see Monte Argentario standing abruptly out of the sea and on this mountain we knew, from reading the guide book, that Porto Ercole lay on the southern side and Porto Santo Stefano on the north. To seaward we could see the island of Giglio, its outline a smaller replica of Monte Argentario, standing in silhouette against the blue sea and sky. Monte Argentario itself might once have been an island, and we often referred to it as such. In fact it is joined to the mainland by two natural sandy causeways, which form a salt lake between. In turn, the salt lake is divided in two by a road which leads to Monte Argentario. The southern causeway has a long, curved sandy shoreline with beautiful pine woods running along its entire length just behind the beach. These same pines grow along the coast throughout this region, always close to the shore. They have a wonderful resinous pine scent and are inhabited by cicadas who sing from their branches during the hot summer afternoons. But when approached, they would all stop at once and we experienced the silence with the pungent aroma all around us.

The shoreline along the northern causeway also has a long crescent of sand, but has some houses along it. Close to where the centre causeway joins the Via Aurelia, there is the small bustling town called Orbetello, which is surrounded on three sides by water. Five centuries before, Spain occupied this region, which was called *I Stati Presidii*, and included the coastal plain stretching from Argentario to a few miles north of Talamone, towards Elba. They made Orbetello their capital and today it looks like a little Venice, with the houses reflected in the surrounding water on calm days. The town was completely walled and fortified at one time, but now only a little remains, including an impressive gateway on the east side through which all traffic from the Via Aurelia has to pass. We saw that Monte Argentario had twin peaks and the mass of the mountain runs in a north to south direction parallel with the Italian coast. We were looking at its eastern side as we approached, but later we discovered a beautiful semi-circular valley close to the western side and bordered by another lower ridge of hills which descended steeply to the sea. There were pink oleander bushes in flower along the side of the road and when we came to a fork at the end, a signpost told us that Porto Ercole was eight kilometres to the left and Porto Santo Stefano lay twelve kilometres to the right. We chose the left-hand turning, feeling sure this would be our future home. The road twisted carelessly round gently curving bends towards Porto Ercole while Monte Argentario rose upwards on our right. The land looked fertile and we could see little farm houses dotted here and there, with patches of golden wheat and ploughed strips of land as well as more olive groves. Suddenly on a hill to our left, we saw one of the three large fortresses which were built to defend Porto Ercole and, soon after, we spotted the second sitting on a hill beyond the village. The third fortress, we knew from the guide book, was low down, guarding the eastern entrance to the harbour.

Then we descended into Porto Ercole and we found our way down to the harbour. Alas, it was an anticlimax, for the approach and glimpses of the fortresses, had set our hopes high, but we were disappointed with the village itself. The high hills closely surrounding the village rise sharply to meet the craggy peaks of Monte Argentario, causing Porto Ercole to be in shade when the late afternoon sun dips behind them.

We stopped a woman to ask her if there was a hotel here and, before we knew where we were going, we had been ushered into a double room of a small home. But in this way we met our first Italian family. In a whirl of introductions in the kitchen, we met Mama, Papa, their two sons, Mama's sister whose husband worked in Genoa, Mama's sister-in-law who we never discovered was married or not and, finally, *Nonna* the mother of Papa, a little wrinkled old lady with the most beautiful pair of sparkling eyes. She never said a word, but seated round the large kitchen table and all of us drinking coffee and making conversation in our atrocious Italian, we all laughed and giggled, and *Nonna*'s twinkling eyes enjoyed it all.

We asked them about Porto Santo Stefano and they advised us not to go to that terrible place. It was a large and noisy town, not at all like their little peaceful and beautiful village. And for the first time, we saw the Italians' immense pride in their home town and land immediately around them. Indeed, it seems their loyalties are first their village, then their province, and finally their nation in that order. Nevertheless, we did visit Porto Santo Stefano the following morning. There were more pink oleanders flowering at the side of the road and the moment we rounded the last bend and saw the fishing port and a small boatyard stretched out before us, we knew there was no need to look further. We stopped to look at our future home: the town lay astride two bays, each curving inward with the hills rising above, but not overshadowing the town as they do at Porto Ercole. The headland between the two bays has a church and rows of buildings which rise one above another until suddenly they come to a stop at the fortress strong, square, squat and indestructible. We were thrilled to find such a splendid reminder still standing of the Charles V and Philip II conquests, five centuries before. Below us in the first bay the harbour was filled with fishing boats, yachts, two schooners and an ancient steamer in the process of being unloaded. We were told later that she came in regularly with phosphate from Tunisia. A wide quay passes round the harbour with the road while the buildings, three storeys high, were painted white with grey shutters, louvered to keep out the bright sunlight. Without exception, the roofs had the red terracotta tiles used everywhere in this part of the world. We drove down the hill, crossed a dried up stream running from a valley behind the port, passed a few large fishing boats hauled out on a slipway, where they were being caulked, and then the Post Office and Police Station before we followed the road round the headland as it climbed a little and then descended into the second, smaller bay.

There were a few rowing boats at anchor and, on the far side, the ferry to the island of Giglio tied up at the quay. This part of town was called *La Piazza*, 'the square', where we stopped and parked the car by the Bar Centrale, its tables and chairs outside and protected from the sun with blue umbrellas. There was another bar across the bay by the Giglio ferry and we could see villas, some painted pink as well as white, rising up the hills around the bay, each with gardens with orange and lemon trees and the narrow cypress pines standing like sentinels on guard. Date palms grew each side of the road and the Town Hall is here, set back in the middle of the bay with a flight of steps and a balcony above them on the first floor for official people to watch events with processions and parades on certain feast days. We saw shops and the pharmacy and noticed the 'Agenzia' next to the bar while sitting at a table and drinking a cup of coffee. Soon we hurried inside to ask about villas for rent. "How long for?" said the man.

"A month, two months . . ."

"Oh no," we said, "for years."

"Come back at half past three, and I will show you some villas then. In the meantime, I will look up the ones that are available on a yearly basis."

At a quarter past three, we could not stand waiting any longer and we returned to the Agenzia. Soon we headed off to look at two villas just outside Port Santo Stefano which we did not like and we pressed the agent to show us some others.

"There is one more on the hill above the town," he said and added doubtfully, "but it is a rather noisy place."

"Well, let's go and see it," we said with fear clutching our hearts, in case we did not find anything. We returned to the town and took a road which wound up and round, and then suddenly we were in the forecourt of the fortress. The agent turned the car and crossing the road, he headed up a track rising sharply directly opposite the fortress.

"This is Via Appetito Alto," he announced. Halfway along the road on the left Dudley pointed to a house, painted white with bright blue shutters.

"I hope it's that house," he said to me. But no, we went on past. Our driver faltered . . . stopped . . . and then called to a child asking which was the house of Signorina di Pol. "That one there," the child said pointing behind us, and so we retreated back the way we came, stopped and . . . yes . . . it was the house with the blue shutters.

We went through a gate with a little red tiled roof over the top, and down a flight of marble tiled stairs.

On hearing our footsteps, an old lady surrounded by many children popped their heads round the front door and we were greeted with a sea of faces. There was even a baby and with all these children around us, we were introduced to Signorina di Pol. Her house and its position were perfect. It was just what we wanted: it looked over the first bay with the large harbour.

We knew then what fun we were going to have watching the boats come and go. To the left there was the fortress standing on its platform above the town and to the right we could see the boatyard and the road climbing up to the headland of Punta Nera, around which we had driven to arrive in Porto Santo Stefano.

We noticed red geraniums were planted in the garden and a large olive tree was growing in the centre of a courtyard. The house was, in fact, split into two apartments. The Signorina's apartment was on the ground floor and the sitting room had French windows leading into the garden. Besides the sitting room there were three bedrooms, a kitchen and a bathroom. Water and electricity were supplied because the house had only been recently built. We had been warned that many houses in Italy, particularly in the south, have neither commodities. The *Signorina* promised to fit a water heater in the bathroom, which would give us hot showers. We saw that the cooking in the kitchen was essentially a make-do holiday arrangement with a little two-burner stove only. We would have to buy a refrigerator and a stove with an oven.

Cooking was with bottled gas. The rent was ten pounds or 20,000 lira a month and we were not sure if she then expected us to bargain, but trying not to look too anxious to clinch the deal, we said we had to go to Rome to see friends the next day, we would think about it and return on Monday to let her know, and all being well, we could then draw up a contract.

But we knew perfectly well as we climbed up the steps to the road, feeling intensely happy, that we would take that house.

The following morning we drove to Rome and reached the centre of the city at the same moment General de Gaulle arrived for his State visit, bringing the traffic to a standstill. Eventually, we found ourselves in the Parioli district and settled ourselves into a hotel. After lunch, a tremendous thunderstorm burst over Rome that forced us to stay indoors. We telephoned the Pallenbergs and arranged to meet them that evening for dinner. We liked Peggy and Corrado from the first moment we met them. They were a little older than us and as nice as their letters promised to be. Corrado was working in London as a journalist for an Italian newspaper before World War II where he met Peggy, and because he was an Italian citizen, they were separated by the hostilities during the War.

In Rome, Peggy opened her own literary agency, whilst Corrado covered Italian and Vatican affairs for *The Evening News*. He also wrote several books, including *Inside the Vatican* which describes the political and financial organisation of the Catholic Church. We shared similar ideas and tastes; they were exactly the right people to answer our innumerable questions. They were sorry we did not like Porto Ercole and staggered to learn we had already found a house in Porto Santo Stefano. But Peggy insisted we should go further south before making a decision and take a look at Amalfi, Positano or somewhere south of Salerno. She said it was like being in another country, as the character of the people and countryside were so different.

After dinner they took us on a tour round Rome and we never forgot our first impressions of this beautiful city, as we saw the Roman Forum, the Coliseum, temples and churches, all floodlit and standing peacefully in the Roman night. It was cool and Rome was already half asleep; and so we had all Rome's glory to ourselves. We met them again for dinner again the next evening, after a day's sightseeing by ourselves. Peggy emphasised again we should go south and Corrado persuaded us to look at Monte Circeo, as this was one of his favourite spots.

We left Rome early next morning and had lunch in Monte Circeo. This little village had a Spanish character and we could see why Corrado liked it so much. We liked it too, but we still felt Porto Santo Stefano on Monte Argentario was going to be the right place for us. We continued south and passed quickly through Anzio, modern and newly built after its bombardment during World War II for the Allied landing there. When we arrived in Naples we became lost in the narrow winding streets in the centre of the city, but by early evening we were driving round the Sorrento peninsular and came to Positano. We were overwhelmed by the beauty around us: sheer rocky cliffs plunged into the sea several hundred feet below and the mountainous ridge of the peninsular rose steeply above us with high crags and lush vegetation growing in the crevices, pointing upwards and hanging down in wild contortions. Unfortunately, the masses of rock and cliffs high above the sea, gave Dudley the feeling of vertigo, as if he was being drawn downwards into the sea, and he felt he could not live there.

We spent the night in Amalfi and, although it was beautiful there, we found the steep cliffs and towering mountainous terrain on which both Amalfi and Positano perched above the sea, very overpowering. We still preferred the graceful hills and mountain of Argentario and the working port of Santo Stefano.

The first thing we had to do once we were back in Porto Santo Stefano was to sign the contract for the house. The second was to obtain a certificate of residence. After that the remaining ten days of our three week holiday were free for us to enjoy. We visited the agent next morning, whom by now we knew as Signor Bracci and together we saw Signorina di Pol. We told her we would like to rent her house from 1st January 1960 and we arranged to meet at the agency that afternoon to draw up the contract. In fact, it was really quite simple, as the contract was already a printed form. Our names and agreed rent were written in and all that remained for us was to sign it. With us acting as interpreter, was Tibbi Wongher who, with his mother, ran the *Pensione Weekend*, the small hotel where we were staying.

Tibby was a remarkable character: he was born in Hungary and had French nationality. He could speak the language of his birth, French, English, Italian and German. He was interested in archaeology and geology, and loved finding pieces of Roman and Etruscan pottery. With plaster of Paris he made the pots, jars and little oil lamps complete again and had a fine collection in his room. He explained to us that we were responsible for the inside of the house, the plumbing and electricity. Also the contract renewed itself automatically each year if neither party informed the other they wish to cancel it three months before the end of the year.

The house settled, our next task was to visit the Town Hall and apply for a certificate of residence. In an official pamphlet from the Italian Embassy in London, we had read that in transporting our goods and chattels across the frontier into Italy, we must be able to show a certificate of residence to make the operation run smoothly.

At the Town Hall we met for the first time *Cavaliere* Metrano, who had been awarded with this title for his services to the Commune of Argentario in his position as Town Clerk. Our request appeared to set the office in chaos. It seemed it was difficult to give us a certificate of residence, in fact, it would be impossible. Before we could have our certificate, we needed a permit to live in Italy. We knew very well it would take three months for our application to be granted and that we had to apply for it through the Italian Embassy in London after we returned home. Certainly, we could not come back to Porto Santo Stefano again before our planned arrival at the end of December to apply for the certificate, by which time it would be too late. We had reached a deadlock.

Cavaliere Metrano cried: "But how can I give you the certificate? How do I know you are coming here again in January?" A fair point, but he had underestimated my husband, who was never at a loss for words. Dudley made great sighing sounds and casually mentioned that we loved Porto Santo Stefano; we had been to Santa Margharita, Portofino, Rapallo, Lerici, Viareggio, Castiglioncello (we had passed through on our way south), Monte Ciceo, Amalfi, Sorrento, Positano, to look for a place to live. But we think Porto Santo Stefano is the most beautiful. There was silence for two awful seconds and then pandemonium broke out. It should be added that when a couple of foreigners are in obvious difficulty with the language, people come from nowhere to help and by this stage of the proceedings, the *Cavaliere's* office was quite full. All these people repeated Dudley's pronouncement to each other in wonder and then more loudly and excitedly to each other. The crowd broke up, heading for the door to repeat it outside to others in adjacent offices. Groups formed and split to form other groups so that it reverberated throughout the Town Hall.

When order was restored, *Cavaliere* Metrano suggested we return next day and in the meantime, he would look through the regulations and see if there were not some way round the difficulty. We left the Town Hall feeling hopeful and despondent at the same time and spent the rest of the day on the beach wondering whether or not we would obtain the certificate we needed. The following morning, we duly presented ourselves at the *Cavaliere's* office, having rushed up the stairs to the first floor as soon as the Town Hall was open to the public. We looked at *Cavaliere* Metrano with eager anticipation: but he told us it was impossible to have a certificate of residence. He had discussed the problem with several people and it was suggested we could have a 'Certificate of Family' in which it would be stated the Pope family was living in Porto Santo Stefano as from today's or tomorrow's date, which was perfectly true. It would not matter if we went away and did not return until after Christmas.

He asked us to come again the following morning by which time he would have obtained the appropriate form and that we were to bring with us our birth and marriage certificates! We explained we had neither of these documents, but that our passports surely would be sufficient proof as they give our dates of birth and that my passport gives my maiden and married names.

Next day *Cavaliere* Metrano confronted us with a green form which, when he unrolled it, covered the whole of his desk. On this he began to fill in our particulars, name, address, age, place of birth, place and date of marriage. Then the names of our parents, our mothers' maiden names, place and date of birth and marriages, and so it went on until the form was complete and the *Cavaliere* sighed and commented about the bureaucracy of the Italian State. We sympathised and assured him we had bureaucracy in England too. But of course, he said: "When Italy was unified in 1861, we copied the English constitution and legal system."

Then *Cavaliere* Metrano smiled at us and said that if we came back the following morning, he would be able to give us the certificate. And so it was that we left the Town Hall the next day happily clutching it in our hand. Thus it was writ: *Commune di Monte Argentario, the family of Pope, living in this Commune from July 5th, 1959.*

We had only a few days holiday left and they passed very quickly. Suddenly it was the morning to leave and so we drove across the *piazza* by the Bar Centrale for the last time, round past the church below the fortress and into the larger bay, where the main harbour was. We passed the boatyard, crossed the little bridge and continued up the hill. At the bend we had one last look back: bye-bye Porto Santo Stefano. We'll see you again after Christmas!

We returned to our flat in Chancery Lane brimming with excitement and I found it was hard to stop myself from shouting over the rooftops that in another six months we would be off to seek a new life. The following Monday morning the office had a special quality about it that other first mornings after a holiday never had. I even felt like singing as the lift carried us up to the Editorial Department on the third floor of Carmelite House, I was excited at the prospect of our move to Italy and I was happy for Dudley to get away from the office at last. I went to my desk in the News Room and Dudley went on through to the Foreign Department.

As we parted to start our day's work, we gave each other secret smiles; we had decided not to divulge our plans until Dudley handed in his letter of resignation. The recognised length of time to give notice to one's editor was three months for a person in a position such as the one Dudley held.

At this point we did not have our residence permits to live in Italy and our whole scheme could yet come to nought. But our secret was nearly revealed when a colleague sidled up to Dudley in the office one day shortly after our return and hissed out of the corner of his mouth: "Porto Santo Stefano, eh?" Dudley only managed to grunt, "Uh?"

"Porto Santo Stefano, a nice little Tuscan fishing port?" he queried.

"What about it, then," Dudley muttered, "we were there on holiday last month."

"English author going to live near the fortress," he persisted. Apparently, some friends had stayed at the *Pensione Weekend* shortly after us and they had learned about our visit. Dudley asked him to keep it quiet until he handed in his resignation to the editor.

Life at the office continued as though everything was normal. Towards the end of August we began the paperwork for our emigration to Italy. We visited the Italian Embassy and came away armed with papers and pamphlets. We wrote to the Consul General and asked for the appropriate forms with which to make our application to the Ministry of Foreign Affairs in Rome, but which would be directed through his Consulate in Eaton Place. In reply we received four application forms and a request for four photographs of Dudley. There was a small space on the forms for wife and any children, and photographs were not required. Dudley stressed in his application that he was self-employed: he stated his annual income and the amount of capital we should be taking with us and to prove it would be sufficient to cover our living expenses for a reasonable period. This last point had to be confirmed by our bank manager and had to be sent with the application.

Dudley had also to state his reasons for wishing to live in Italy and this was harder to answer. We wanted to escape the rat race, the daily grind of work and the restraints of the British welfare state. The endless grey days and cold winters, stretching into the future. The cost of living in Italy at that time was very low, including our rent. We felt if Dudley was going to have a chance to become a full-time author, living in Italy might make it possible. Instead, Dudley wrote we wished to live in a tranquil and beautiful place, in an atmosphere to enable him to work, all of which Porto Santo Stefano appeared to offer us; and it would also give us an opportunity to study the Italian language and culture, a knowledge which one day Dudley might be able to use in connection with his work. We hoped this would be sufficient to allow us to live in Italy. We were warned that the answer to our application would take from ten to twelve weeks and, indeed, early in December, we received a letter from the Consulate requesting us to visit them with our passports to have them stamped with a visa, as we had received permission to live in Italy.

We were told we could import all our personal and household effects free of duty as long as we imported everything within six months of our arrival. We also discovered it would be very expensive to take our furniture: the cost of transporting it would be far more than its value. The apartment in Porto Santo Stefano was furnished and we hoped to add a few things later to make it more comfortable. We were given four other important pieces of information: we would be liable for Italian income tax, but would probably not start paying until we had been settled for two years or so. Secondly, that any amount of money could be brought into Italy without any difficulty. Thirdly, foreign nationals with a residence permit could buy property in Italy and finally they stressed it was most important that we register ourselves with the police within three days of our arrival in Porto Santo Stefano.

However, in England in those days there were Exchange Control Regulations on the amount of money that could be taken or sent abroad. Our bank had informed the Bank of England of our coming departure. Once we had left, our bank account would be blocked. This meant that no one could pay money into our account without permission from the Bank of England who would regard us as 'domiciled abroad' and we were given a file number. We also had to give the bank a complete list of all our assets, assurance policies and prospects in the United

Kingdom. We were thus 'domiciled abroad' but Dudley would be able to receive his royalties from his publisher who had his file number to apply for and gain permission from the Bank of England to make the payments without much delay. Although there was no double taxation agreement between Italy and the United Kingdom, the tax people told us at first we would be regarded as 'residents abroad'. If after two years we had spent eighteen months out of the country, we would then be titled 'domiciled abroad'.

This did not worry us too much because we were going to have a very modest income and tax avoidance was not one of the reasons we were going to live in Italy. We had to visit the National Insurance office too: Dudley had decided he would continue to pay National Insurance as a self-employed person, so that we would be entitled to the Old Age Pension. We also took out insurance policies against illness in Italy. At that time there was no national health system, though like America, there were various schemes which people could pay into, including a state one for poor people and one for civil servants. But for us, illness would be at our own expense. While all the bureaucratic paperwork was going on, the proofs for *England Expects* arrived and while checking for any more printers' errors, Dudley had to do the index. He also had to check the illustrations carefully and make sure the captions were correct. Harold Wyllie had given permission for several of his paintings to appear in the book, as well as one painted by his father. Our friend Colin Mudie, who later became a very well-known naval architect, drew a cutaway drawing of the *Victory*, a side view with most of the planking removed to reveal the interior of the ship.

Then there was a printers' strike, which not only affected us in the office, but it also delayed printing books. When it was over, *England Expects* was published at the end of November and appeared in the bookshops with a large number of other books, caused by the backlog of those delayed by the strike. As a result *England Expects* did not receive as much attention as we hoped. It was the best book Dudley had written so far and, for him, a new field which we hoped would lead to more historical naval non-fiction. A nice review appeared in *The Observer*:

"After surveying the naval situation leading up to Trafalgar, he gives an outstanding lucid and accurate description of the battle. The numerous individual ship actions are fitted into the general picture, without distracting the reader too much from the central theme of Nelson's ideas, his leadership and his heroic last hours. Mostly the author has shown good judgement in his selection of contemporary British, French and Spanish sources, ranging from Nelson's own dicta to the evidence left by captains of ships and other much less exalted eyewitnesses; and his excellent use of background material, such as the technicalities of handling and fighting the ships, the methods of communications, the customs and outlooks of the crews, allows even readers without previous knowledge of the subject to gain a vivid impression of the whole setting. This is no mean achievement, and Dudley Pope is to be congratulated on a very good book."

England Expects was published in the United States by J.B. Lippincott in the summer of 1960 and A.L. Rowse wrote a long article for the *Chicago Herald Tribune* in which he said Dudley understood sea power and continued: "What is more he knows how to write too – so well that his book is as exciting reading as a novel. Skilfully he weaves all the threads together, the personal as well as the naval, the characters and personalities of the commanders on both sides, Nelson's private life which was all too public – his touching devotion to Lady Hamilton and their child Horatia, his constant thought of them in his last days and hours . . ."

The book was also very well reviewed in *The New York Times*, the *New York Herald Tribune,* and in *Time* magazine. C. Northcote Parkinson in the *Sunday New York Times'* book review magazine, began with the praise: *"As a description of the Trafalgar campaign, Dudley Pope's book would be difficult to better . . . Mr. Pope tells his story with perception, with narrative skill and with a nice choice of words. . ."*

Friday, 6 November 1959 was our last day working at *The Evening News*. In the past few years we had said goodbye to colleagues who left before us, and it was the custom to have a collection to buy a gift for the departing colleague. A fair sum had been raised for us, so we had visited the London Silver Vaults to choose a pair of matching coffee pots with a little cream jug and sugar basin. It was truly a beautiful gift.

In the late afternoon almost everyone in the Editorial Department assembled in the News Room, with many printers and linotype men from upstairs there as well. We were overwhelmed by the number of people who came. There were speeches and Dudley gave his reply, thanking everyone for such a splendid gift and then invited all who could, to come over the road to the Feathers for a drink, it then being 5 o'clock the taverns in Fleet Street were already open, and as the last edition was ready for the presses to run, many old friends joined us there.

Now that our decision to leave had come into effect we were a little sad to say goodbye to our friends at *The Evening News*. During the presentation our minds went back to a certain Tuesday evening five years before when we had been the subjects of another presentation. For the following day we had married. I was excited to be setting out on this adventure, but a few doubts began to go through Dudley's mind, was it going to be a ghastly mistake? I was much more optimistic. I had absolute faith in him and was sure he would succeed in this attempt to earn his living as an author. We would be living in a wonderful climate: that between May and October we could make an arrangement to visit a place in a week's time and could be fairly certain to have a fine day. In Porto Santo Stefano we hoped to find peace and not be bothered by the telephone and the rush and urgency of London life.

It was obvious that Dudley was never going to be an 'establishment' person. When he was first in Fleet Street and a young reporter, he did go out drinking to keep up with 'the boys'. But as time went by he found he enjoyed drinking less and less. When meeting strangers at cocktail parties he found himself talking politely, while preferring to be at home writing his books. He sometimes felt he was regarded with suspicion when a stranger discovered he was a journalist and author. Someone definitely out of the ordinary and possibly eccentric. But to refuse to attend some of these functions is thought to be antisocial. Robert Graves has been quoted to have said that people are frightened of living abroad because it kept them out of the swim. On being asked what was the swim, he replied: "It's what drowns you in the end! Three quarters of your time in this country is spent talking, the other quarter is spent eating – you get no work done, writers think they'll get inspiration from the great dinners they eat with their witty friends."

In Italy, we found we were accepted at face value, and because we were foreigners we would be allowed to be as eccentric as we wished. We would not be expected to assimilate their customs so long as we kept within the laws of that country, naturally. As we made friends in Porto Santo Stefano we found they were, of course, curious and eager to know everything about British life. It is to be admitted we could have found the peace, freedom and the individuality we wanted in a small Cornish or Perthshire village. But for us, Italy not only offered a better climate, but something new and a challenge. In coping with all the formalities of going to live in Italy, the application for the permit and inventory in quadruplicate, we were excited with our plans and paid less attention to the amount of bureaucracy. Later an officer in the Customs House in Porto Santo Stefano, showed us his book of regulations and explained how the Italian Customs' regulations were styled after the British. Although we thought we were escaping the British bureaucratic life, there were a few occasions when we came up against the Italian.

When we returned from Italy in June, Dudley had approached his publishers to see if they would commission him to write two more books. He had already written the synopses for both and also drawn up a list of authorities he would need to do the research before our departure immediately after Christmas. Weidenfeld's readily agreed to both ideas. The first was about Admiral John Byng who was sent out too late to defend Minorca against a French invasion in 1756 with a small and badly undermanned squadron against a superior French force. The result of the battle was inconclusive but the French claimed the victory. Byng was recalled to face trial for cowardice and, although he was acquitted, he was nevertheless executed by a firing squad on the quarterdeck of H.M.S. Monarch in Portsmouth, an act of judicial murder to save the faces of the politicians then in power.

The second book Dudley intended to write was Nelson's battle at Copenhagen in 1801 and later his publishers also commissioned him to write a third book about a mutiny which took place on board the 32-gun frigate Hermione in the West Indies in 1797.

We had, therefore, the assurance of a few years' work ahead of us. The rest of November and most of December we were either at the British Museum or the Public Record Office. The martyrdom of Byng grew worse as we discovered the wicked machinations of the government of Lord Newcastle, revealed in letters we read and copied in the reading room at the British Museum. Since we did not have much time left, we had a great deal of the documents microfilmed and which we would transcribe later in Italy. During these last days, I was most often at the British Museum copying letters and official correspondence, while Dudley sometimes went to the London Library either to borrow books or return them. He also visited the Public Record Office to order all the naval documents he would need and most of these were put on microfilm.

Late in November our friends, Basil and Wendy Bowman, suggested they came with us to Italy. We had met them not long after we married when we lived on board *Concerto* in Southwick. Wendy, a tall willowy blonde always dressed with an elegance and style that was never matched by Basil, also fair but with a stocky build. Basil took part in motorcar rallies and Dudley had bought his first car from him. Basil then taught Dudley how to drive it and my husband's love affair with fast motorcars began. The first was a Morgan Plus 4, then a Porsche followed by an Aston Martin all bought from Basil's second hard car business in Hove, near Brighton. Now he offered to provide a van in which we could travel and carry all our possessions to Italy. They would stay two weeks with us and then drive the van back to England, calling in at Monte Carlo to watch the finish of the Rally, which takes place each January. Afterwards Basil would sell the van when back home. This was a wonderful idea and we readily agreed.

As Christmas drew nearer, most of the formalities of our departure were completed and our bank had our monetary matters in hand. We wanted to send our money ahead of us to the account we had opened in Porto Santo Stefano. But there was an irritating regulation which prevented the bank doing this until they had seen our travel documents, including the Dover ferry reservation for the van with its registration number and other details. Finding the right van caused some delay, but finally we were ready to leave immediately after Christmas.

In the last few days we packed furiously, went to say goodbye to Dudley's family on Christmas Eve, and spent Christmas Day with my family. There was some last minute packing, though most of the books already had been stowed in two large trunks. On Boxing Day, Basil arrived late in the afternoon with the van, and we began loading: first the trunks went in and then followed all sorts of cartons. The van became more and more full as the boxes were wedged and squeezed in and with a mighty shove we managed to close the back doors. From the windows the previous contents of the cartons could be seen: Echo margarine, New Zealand butter, Outspan Oranges and various makes of cigarettes.

It was going to be an uncomfortable journey with three of us sitting in front and the fourth behind, squeezed in among the boxes. It was decided that it would be safer for Basil to drive because the van was so heavily loaded, and Dudley would navigate for him. By now we were both feeling very excited and very nervous: each evening that last week we had had friends for dinner to say goodbye. And now we were feeling sad at leaving them. At least we had Wendy and Basil coming with us to keep us company over the first days. We said our last goodbyes and set off down the Brighton Road to stay the night in Hove.

It was pouring with rain in Brighton that morning with a gale blowing when we rose at five o'clock. The house was closed and locked up, and our overnight cases were squeezed in the van. We were going to have fun together and certainly our 'emigration' to Italy could not have been achieved in a nicer way. We reached Dover almost an hour too early, but a short queue had already formed and more cars joined soon after us. They all had skis strapped to luggage racks, a high proportion were Bentleys or Rolls, and a few Daimlers. There was also an Austin Omnicoach with, apparently, a load of food and cigarettes on board.

A British Railways man was there to marshal us into lines. But since there were so few cars we were organising ourselves without his aid. He wanted to chat and our humble Austin van was the obvious choice. Besides, Basil has a friendly face which invites a natter.

"Where yer going, mate?" he asked.

"Italy," replied Basil.

"Oh, Italy, eh. Nice place Italy, cho cho bimbo and all that!"

All of us were leading busy lives and did not listen a great deal to the radio, so we were not *au courant* with pop music. But later in Italy we did hear this song as we listened to the radio to try to get to grips with the Italian language. The cars ahead of us began boarding and soon it was our turn to drive across the ramp. To our horror, we saw that not only was the ferry rising up and down on the swells in Dover Harbour caused by the gale, but the ramp was a foot above the quay one moment and a foot below the next. The petrol tank of the heavily loaded van was only about six inches off the ground. Another British Railways man stopped Basil just as his front wheels were an inch from the ramp. "Now," he said, "when I say 'go', you go as quick as you can mate, or you'll damage your vehicle!"

"Go!" he said. We went, and with an almighty crash the van leapt from the quay on to the ship. Goodbye England. *Ciao* England. *Ciao Ciao bimbo!*

CHAPTER FOUR

Italy January 1960

After spending the first night on the road at Troyes we woke to find it was still raining. The wind blew so hard at times that it jolted the windscreen wipers away from the windscreen and buffeted the van so that Basil needed all his skill to keep it on the road. The rain stayed with us until late afternoon. We wanted to get as far south as possible in an effort to reach Porto Santo Stefano the following night. We did not stop for meals, making do with a few boxes of cup cakes that Wendy had brought with her. Basil remained behind the wheel, swearing he was feeling fine, but we stopped briefly from time to time for the rest of us to change places. By the time we reached Brignoles that night we found there was nowhere open to have a meal, so it was also cupcakes for dinner.

I had wakened that morning feeling distinctly nervous. Whereas Dudley was still worrying about whether we were doing the right thing, I was worrying about the Italian Customs which we would meet some time during the next day. The French Customs in Boulogne had shown initial interest in our van when we arrived, but waved us on when they learned we were heading for Italy. We set off early in bright sunshine after a good breakfast of fried eggs and by 9.30 a.m. we had our first glimpse of the snow capped Alps. At Fréjus we had to cross a temporary bridge as the original had been swept away by a terrible flood just a few weeks before. To the north-west of the village there was a swathe of mud and destruction seeming to be at least a mile wide where the flood water had cut through the valley. There was a railway line with a partly derailed train and upturned motorcars looking grotesque with their wheels in the air.

We reached the Italian side of the Customs at lunch time and we were first asked for our passports. Then the Customs officer did several circuits round our van, finally stopping at the back for some time. My heart was sinking, thinking the officer wanted the van opened so they could inspect everything. I was sure if we unlocked the doors, some boxes would fall out. In the meantime we and our Customs officer became diverted by a pantomime going on nearby. A flashy looking Italian descended from a huge American car with a little box in his hand. He then proceeded to line up the Customs officers and our man joined them. We realised he was going to take a photograph of them all and within a few moments, he removed something from the camera and produced the photograph he had just taken. This procedure was repeated six times more, since there were seven Customs men on duty that morning. Then the camera was inspected and the next moment the Italian was in a tremendous rage, he flung the camera into the back of his car, waved his arms and stumped into the Customs building. He obviously thought by taking a photograph of them all, he would avoid Customs duty but he was going to pay more than he bargained for. We had just seen one of the earliest Polaroid cameras.

Our Customs man returned to business: "What have you got in here?"

I stammered an explanation in my self-taught Italian: "We come to live in Italy . . ." hesitation, ". . . I have my things for the house."

"Where are you going to live in Italy?" he enquired. This was easy to answer. "Porto Santo Stefano."

"Where's that?" he asked.

"In the province of Grosseto," I replied.

"Ah, Grosseto. Ah . . . yes." We passed to him the Certificate of Family and the inventory with its wonderfully impressive stamps.

"You must take this inside," and pointed to the Customs building where the angry Italian had entered and even more angrily left some minutes later. Dudley accompanied me and we joined a queue which ended at a glass window behind which

sat a little man with glasses. Soon it was our turn. We handed in
our inventory and certificate and explained we had just arrived
to live in Italy. The man looked at the inventory and said: "But
it is in English. It should be in Italian. I cannot understand what
it says!"

"It is a list of our personal belongings, the Italian Embassy
asked for a list in English." He took down a huge book from
a shelf above him and opened it almost in the middle, and
glanced at the page quickly. He then closed the book with such
an angry gesture that dust flew out of it. We waited, expecting an
explosion, but instead: "All right, go away!"

We could hardly believe our ears.

At the car we met our Customs man. *"Va bene?"* he asked.

"Va bene!" we answered. Everything was all right!

We climbed into the van. He gave us an imperious wave. *"Buon
viaggio,"* he said.

"Grazie," we said.

At Imperia we stopped to buy some food for lunch. It was going
to be a long day's drive, and Wendy and I were determined not
to allow Basil make us go without food again. We reached Genoa
at tea time and it took us an hour to get through the city, as it
sprawls so much along the coast. We pressed on to La Spezia,
it was 9.30 p.m. and we stopped for a meal at a *trattoria* which
revived memories of our holiday: the different atmosphere of
an Italian restaurant with its wholesome and appetising smells
tinged with garlic and olive oil, the sounds of cooking and the
musical singsong Italian voices. All remembered now in a hazy
dimness which was the fault of the Italian electric companies.
The dark lighting and an oscillating, flickering light – all of
which we quickly became accustomed within a few days of living
in Porto Santo Stefano. There we discussed whether we should
press on to Porto Santo Stefano or start looking out for a place
to stay the night. We estimated we would arrive about 3 a.m.
in the morning; but it was really for Basil to decide: he chose
to drive on. Wendy and Dudley sat in the front next to him for
this last part of the journey while I was behind, hemmed in by
the boxes stacked around me. I dozed and then woke to hear

Dudley saying it was Viareggio and discovered I had a box of books about to fall on me. I pushed the box back and drifted off to sleep again. Pisa... more boxes to push back . . . Livorno . . . boxes again . . . Cecina said my husband . . . boxes . . . sleep . . .

"What time is it?" Wendy asked.

"Twenty past one," said Dudley after fumbling with a torch. Sleep . . . boxes falling on me again.

"Where are we?" I asked.

"Nearing Follonica," replied Dudley.

"When do we get there?" asked Wendy, and I heard desperation in her voice.

"Another couple of hours, I should think," replied Dudley. Sleep . . . boxes . . . Dudley, following the road map for Basil, murmured something about a bend and suddenly, we met a whole convoy of lorries, huge "trains of the road" trailers each carrying up to sixteen Fiat 600s, stowed in two decks, one above the other. The length of the convoy was astounding. Then it was Grosseto, the chief town and administrative centre of the province in which Porto Santo Stefano lies. I did not sleep anymore and I could just see through the window the dark shapes of the conical hills with the regimented lines of olive trees.

Then we could see the high hills of Monte Argentario with the pylons and their three sets of red lights flashing on the peaks. Soon we were driving through Orbetello and on the road between the two lakes. Then the sign, left for Port' Ercole and right for Porto Santo Stefano. We drove through the series of bends and suddenly we had reached Punta Nera and there was Porto Santo Stefano, with all the street lights reflecting in the sea along the waterfront. We could see the fortress in the moonlight above the town. We wound our way past fishing boats hauled up on the hard and up the hill to the fortress, before making the sharp left turn into Via Appetito Alto. We drew up by the house and found a rather nice cat sitting on the gatepost. Wearily we climbed out and took only what we needed for the rest of the night. A cold damp air hit us as we opened the door. We found the electric meter and turned on the lights. The cat came in too and we saw he was a beautiful ginger tom. Someone shushed him out, shut the door and we shared out blankets and allocated bedrooms. We fell into bed using up the last bit of energy to remove our clothes. A dreamless sleep came up and hit me.

We were awakened late next morning by a hammering on the front door which was so insistent, that I got up and opened it. There stood a young girl with black hair and face full of vitality. But I had barely taken in her appearance and noticed she was gesticulating with a small buff coloured envelope in one of her hands as she burst out with a torrent of words which I did not understand at all. On repeating whatever she had just said, I slowly gathered she was Carla Schiano, daughter of Linda. Signorina di Pol had already written to tell us that Linda would help me in the house if I needed any assistance, and that she also took in washing. Having established who Carla was, she gave me a telegram, which had arrived the day before and they were very worried because we had not yet arrived; they had accepted it and hoped it was nothing urgent. Retreating to avoid any further embarrassment, I rejoined Dudley in bed and read the telegram. It was from friends in Brighton, giving us a welcome and wishing us good luck in our new home. It was a kind thought and much appreciated.

Fifteen minutes later there was more hammering on the door and since I was the only one with a little knowledge of Italian, I got up again and answered it. This time there were two girls, one younger than the other and both smaller than Carla. The elder had curly reddish hair and we learned later she was called Paola and her younger sister was Ensa. She began by saying, "I am the sister of Carla," and finished with the word, "telegramma."

I replied I had the telegram.

"Ah, good," she said, and with grins on their faces, they bolted up the steps. Then I remembered, that these were the children who had been with Signorina di Pol the day we met her during our summer visit.

Later in the summer when Paola left school, she began working for us, coming six mornings a week to clean the house and prepare our lunch. There was one more sister we had yet to meet, called Elda, and it would seem appropriate in the English meaning, as she was the eldest, married to a boy in the Merchant Navy and they had a baby son, Sergio. There was also Carlo, the only son and adored by all his sisters and away at sea most of the time with his father fishing off the African coast in a trawler that only returned every three months. During the following days we met our neighbours and shopkeepers in the village. All curious about us, but very friendly and helpful. This was the beginning of the 1960s before Italy was swamped with tourists and most visitors to Porto Santo Stefano were families from Rome who owned or rented villas in the summer. Mothers, maids and children arrived in July to be joined by husbands and fathers for the month of August.

But our first day in Italy had begun: we opened the shutters and there before us was sunshine, blue sea and the beautiful view which had been in our memories for the past six months in England. It was even more beautiful than we had remembered, because then it had been summer and the air had been hot and hazy. Trees and shrubs had looked tired and dusty, and the grass on the hills around us had been brown and burnt up by the sun. Now the air was fresh and the visibility this first morning was so clear that from our French windows of our new home, looking east, we could see Monte Amiata, with a dusting of snow on its peak, and the rest of the southern end of the Apennine Mountains thirty miles away on the mainland. We could also see little farm houses, stuccoed white and pink, scattered on the bright green of the coastal plain. Further inland, the hills rose, higher and higher until they merged into the Apennines, the colour changing from green to soft blue. To our left beyond the fortress we could just see the Tyrrhenian Sea itself and Punta Talamone, from where the huge bay curved round to end at the northern causeway, one of the three which joined Monte Argentario to the mainland. Thus our view to the north and east was a large expanse of water with the mainland of Italy beyond, and it was most often the cause of much time wasted, as we never tired of the scene with its constantly changing light and clouds.

Immediately below our house, we looked down on the roofs of houses descending to the harbour, protected from westerly winds by the harbour wall, and the southerly winds by the mass of Monte Argentario itself. But we could not spend time gazing out of windows this first day: we had a van to unload, a house to air, food and also wood to be bought. The Signorina had made a few small improvements to make us comfortable, as promised, the water heater in the bathroom, a pair of glass inner doors inside the solid wooden front door, and a wood stove to keep us warm. While the men unloaded the van, Wendy and I visited the shops close by on Via Appetito Alto.

Everything was so strange for us during those early days, and there was so much to learn. The butcher's shop was called the *Macelleria* and depending on the animal's age when it was slaughtered, he had four kinds of beef: veal, steak, stew or soup meat. Liver and kidneys were available on Tuesdays and Friday afternoons which were the two slaughter days every week. Whole chickens were freshly plucked, and every *Macelleria* had a large meat grinder on the counter to mince your beef twice for your spaghetti *Bolognese* sauce. In early spring there was ten week old lamb, with the chops so tiny and tender.

Next door, the *Latteria* sold us milk from churns and we needed to take a bottle with us. The milk had to be strained to eliminate cow hairs and then heated to almost boiling point to be sure it was pasteurized. The *alimentari* sold groceries and here we found all sorts of salami sausages and different types and shapes of spaghetti, which we had not seen in England at this time. In the afternoon, when the van was unloaded, we all went down to the village to find wood. Italy has a little coal, but in Porto Santo Stefano only wood was used for heating. We noticed not many shops had windows, just wooden doors, and the wood shop, *la legnaia*, had double doors, opening on to the street. Inside, various sizes of logs were stacked up and to one side there was an electric saw and scales. We chose the size of logs we needed and the woodman filled up four baskets and put them on the scales.

"*Quintale!*" he exclaimed. We looked at each other and then the penny dropped. Of course, a quintal is equal to 100 lbs in English weight and is used in measuring grain. We emptied the baskets of wood into the van, which looked strange now that it was completely empty and we went off in search of more shops.

We went to *la verdura*, the vegetable shop and met Signora Gina, visited a *Commestibili* and, although also a grocery like the *alimentari*, it had a much larger choice of cold meats as well as salami and cheese. This one was owned and run by the Rossi brothers and became our favourite. They explained to us that we should go to *la cantina* to buy wine, taking with us empty chianti flasks. We had noticed several in the kitchen and made a note to bring them down to the village next time we came. Like the wood store, the *cantina* had double doors on to the street and inside were huge barrels of wine. A hundred lira filled a chianti bottle and the wine of Porto Santo Stefano has a wonderful golden amber colour with a fairly dry and delicious flavour. But it had one drawback, and that was it did not travel.

The wood shop, *cantina* and Post Office were situated by the main harbour, but most of the other shops were in the second smaller bay, close to the Bar Centrale, the most important place in the village where all business was transacted over cups of coffee or a Campari soda rather than in the office. In the summer, when Porto Santo Stefano was full of visitors, there had been chairs and tables in a large area outside, but now La Piazza was empty. The bar has a public telephone, which the Post Office did not have, and a television set for the clientele to watch the football matches. The bar also sold cigarettes, salt and stamps, all part of a Government monopoly. In a room set off to one side there was a billiards table.

But now in winter after five o'clock in the afternoon there were only men sitting in the bar playing cards and discussing the day's work and events, while their wives were at home with their children, preparing the evening meal.

The person most often seen in the bar serving coffee or drinks, was a charming woman with greying hair, who spoke English with a delightful Dundee accent. Her husband, a Scotsman called Jock, came to Porto Santo Stefano during the war with the British forces. He returned from Dundee to marry her after he was discharged from the army, and ran the bar with his wife. Everyone in Porto Santo Stefano loved him and how they rejoiced when they had a son. In the autumn of 1959 Jock died of cancer and to show their esteem, the whole village came out and escorted his coffin from the church to the cemetery in the Valley. He was remembered with affection and people continued to describe him to us and talk about him. So we returned home feeling a little bewildered by all we had seen and learned. We had already discovered many things and felt more like strangers than we had ever before.

On the last day of the year we decided to drive to Rome to see how modern day Romans celebrated the New Year. We had dinner at a little restaurant in the Piazza Navona where Peggy and Corrado Pallenberg had taken us in the summer. Afterwards we decided to explore St. Peter's Square to see if there were any celebrations taking place. We found the square dark and gloomy, deserted except for a group of eight policemen, the *Carabinieri*, standing in the middle. Later we realised they had chosen a safe place. We re-crossed the river Tiber and returned to the centre of Rome. Basil needed to go into a bar and while we waited for him outside two *Carabinieri* hurried up to us and indicated that we should go inside with them. The streets were absolutely deserted and we were puzzled. As it drew close to midnight there were numerous loud explosions of fireworks that echoed along the narrow street.

Two seconds to midnight two more policemen dashed inside, and within moments, all was explained: there was a creaking of shutters opening above to be followed by loud crashes of breaking china and glass. The Romans were celebrating the New Year by throwing their old china and glass down on to the street, a tradition which would bring them a prosperous New Year. But it was not only Rome that celebrated in this fashion. It would appear to be the whole of Italy and our drive back to Porto Santo Stefano was very tedious indeed. In every town we passed through to reach home, the streets were littered with glass and china and, in a few cases, also broken chairs.

In Orbetello we nearly knocked down a drunk, the only human we had seen on a street apart from the *Carabinieri* and in Porto Santo Stefano more glass awaited us. Next day it was reported in the newspapers that in Rome an itinerant firework vendor had slipped and fallen in an effort to escape the *Carabinieri*. He fell on the box of fireworks he had been carrying, which exploded and killed him.

New Year's Day was a holiday as in Scotland. It was very quiet down at La Piazza this New Year's Day, but on visiting the Bar Centrale for cigarettes, we did find a large proportion of the male population there playing cards. The doors were kept closed as it was cold.

The ginger cat we had seen when we arrived soon moved in with us: he strolled in at lunchtime and Wendy gave him some spaghetti. We discovered his name was Arturo and he considered the house as his. He had belonged to a family who had lived nearby and who then moved a few kilometres away to their new home. They had taken him with them but he preferred his old hunting grounds. He slept on the doormat outside the front door of the apartment above us, winter or summer. There was enough shelter there from the rain and wind and he could keep half an eye open on his terrain.

As Basil knew everything there was to know about motorcars and their engines, we wanted to buy a car before he and Wendy left. Dudley had set his heart on a second-hand Alfa Romeo which we hoped to buy at a reasonable price. We had bought some newspapers, expecting to find some cars advertised with their prices. We did see one Alfa Romeo for sale, but there did not seem to be any second-hand car dealers in our part of Italy.

However, we met Nino Malacarne, large and well-built, who had played for the Lazio football club. He had exactly the Alfa model Dudley wanted to buy: it was a bright apple green and looked well used. In fact, Nino had bought the car second-hand also, and we would be the third owners. Basil inspected the engine under the bonnet, checked under the front and rear ends, and by the time he had finished peering in and around the car, Nino had reduced the price quite considerably. We took it for a ride, Basil driving, taking the road that climbed steeply from La Piazza, which twisted and turned until it meets the T-junction to the west of the fortress. Here we turned right and headed away from the town. When Basil was satisfied with its performance we returned the car to Nino at the Bar Centrale, telling him we would like a little time to think about it.

A few days later we offered Nino L.100,000 (then £58) less than his lowest price and he accepted. To find him in the middle of the afternoon, we had gone to his place of work in the Valley, close to the harbour. There he and his partner had a large warehouse and written above the huge double doors were the words "Varoli

& Malacarne". Inside they stored and maintained the highly varnished Riva high speed runabout boats, which Italians love to use, particularly for waterskiing. Their owners came in August to play with them and they were stored there for the rest of the year.

At the warehouse, which they always called 'the garage', we were introduced to Nino's business partner, Chito Varoli, who invited us to his house. On passing through a pair of tall iron gates nearby, his car, an old Lancia, swept up a curving driveway which rose steeply and we suddenly came to a terrace, surrounded by a white stuccoed balustrade with a house facing towards the sea. The view was the same as from our house, though at a lower elevation. This was the Villa Varoli: the first villa to stand on this site was Roman, the lower walls and the cellar were still the original in perfect condition. On the terrace and behind the house near the kitchen door were pieces of dismembered marble arms, legs and heads and a torso lying scattered around with a few broken amphora , all possessions of former Roman owners of the villa. Before the Second World War the villa had had three stories and was bought by Chito's father with a vast tract of land stretching from the villa eastwards towards the top of Monte Argentario. It was bombed in 1944 and Chito rebuilt the villa with just one storey on the Roman foundations. There was a flight of eleven marble steps to the front door, a few broken in places and were all that remained of the villa's pre-war glory. Inside we were given a glass of whisky and we quickly got to know each other, speaking French in those early days. Chito was a small, shy man, with hair receding a little and turning grey. He had a fiancée in Rome, called Simonetta, whom we met later when they married. In fact, Chito spoke a little English which he had learned on a visit to Canada with an uncle.

His partner, Nino Malacarne, was a different person altogether. He was large and athletic looking, an extrovert as Chito was an introvert. Nino was happy go lucky and easy going whilst Chito took his life and work seriously. It seemed that after retiring from the Lazio football club, he had invested some of his savings with Chito and built the garage. They explained to us that we and Nino had to go to a lawyer to draw up the contract or bill of sale for the car. On signing the contract and handing over the cheque in front of the lawyer, the car would then be ours.

By the middle of January it was time for Basil and Wendy to return to England. One early morning we watched them drive down the road, turn at the fortress to descend down into the Valley. We went indoors and went to the sitting room window to wait for them to reappear at the far end of the harbour. We were feeling a little lonely as we saw the van pass the boat yard, climb up the hill and disappear round the bend on Punta Nera.

As the days went by, we continued to discover new things about life in Italy. We became accustomed to the coins and notes and learned early on when drawing cash from the bank, to have the amount in as low denominations as possible. The butcher, the vegetable shop, the Rossi brothers at the *Comestibili* and the Bar Centrale usually had enough change. But even the stamp counter in the Post Office had sometimes to find change by raiding the pensions section. One of the first things we became aware of and accustomed to were the noises of Italian life. Besides the noisy chatter, laughter from window to window, music and singing, there were the Vespas and Lambrettas, the scooters revving up as they sped along the narrow streets.

Most of the houses in Via Appetito Alto had no running water and there was a large communal wash house at the end of our road. Life began at daybreak with the loud braying of donkeys at the water tap by our gate, which awakened and frightened the wits out of our guests on their first morning with us. Our neighbours stopped there every day to give them water and also fill beautiful copper urns before climbing upwards to their vineyards and olive groves. But even earlier in the mornings, before light and if there was no wind, we were sometimes disturbed by the rattling of anchor chains, interspersed with shouting and cursing, as the fishermen weighed anchor, the sounds coming up directly to us from the harbour.

Then about five in the evenings while the donkeys returned for another drink at the water tap, the fishing boats returned to the harbour, rattling their anchor chains again, and shouting welcome to friends waiting on the harbour quay. We soon learned to go down there to buy the freshly caught little squid, *calamari*, which were so delicious fried in the frying pan.

Sometimes we walked down to the village by the rapid route, using the steps and narrow alleys from the fortress. It seemed all

Italians had beautiful voices and it was a joy to hear a woman singing in her house or to hear snatches of music from radios as we passed. The *alimentari* in our road was owned by Signora Santina and there I bought our bread daily and sometimes 100 grams of tuna fish from the very large tin can on the counter. These were the days before plastic wrapping, and our portion of tuna was placed on a piece of greaseproof paper and wrapped up. Santina could never change a lira 1,000 note and I realised why when I noticed my neighbours never paid for their purchases in cash. It was all written down in a small notebook until the wine and olive harvests were in near the end of the year, then the bills were settled. But the *alimentari* was a marvellous gossip shop and as I waited for my turn, I had the opportunity to listen and try to understand what was said. At first the people were a little shy to speak to us, but we greeted our neighbours morning and evening to try to break the ice as quickly as possible. We were the only ones on the street who had a car, and we were guiltily conscious that we were better off until they made us not to feel so.

We were conscious of stares too until we realised that it was the national habit to watch passers-by, particularly strangers, and just as they were curious about us, we were curious about their lives too. They were not staring at us because we were English. We could have been Italians from Rome or Pisa. Anyone not born in Porto Santo Stefano was a stranger.

As soon as we learned enough Italian to understand most of the things said to us, I realised we had been accepted just as we were. One day when alone in Santina's shop she said to me without any malice or envy in her voice: "You must be very rich!"

"Oh, no," I replied very startled. "What makes you think that?"

"You always pay for everything you buy," she said simply.

I explained that Dudley was an author, writing books. It had already occurred to us that people would think we did absolutely nothing all day long, but live in Porto Santo Stefano. I explained that my husband worked hard and the fact we had money depended on how well the books sold. Today we have some money, but maybe tomorrow we have none. We preferred to pay as we bought, so as not to owe money that perhaps we could not later pay. "Ah yes," she said. "That's life," and shrugged her shoulders expressively.

We also needed a radio, good enough to receive the B.B.C. overseas service. Here we enlisted the help of Tibor Wongher at the *Pensione Weekend* to act as interpreter, negotiating the price for us. After he finished we had a good German made radio for lira 15,000 cheaper than originally asked. Since it was a Saturday afternoon we could not go to the bank to get cash, so we planned to return on Monday. But the shop owner insisted on sending the radio up to our house immediately, *"subito, Signori"*, without even a deposit.

Since our visit in the summer, Tibby's mother had died of a kidney disease. Now the kitchen was in the hands of a young girl called Giovanna. She had blonde hair and a fair skin, as fair as any Swedish girl could be. At first she was very shy and blushed even when saying *"Buon giorno,"* to us. But very soon we saw that Tibby and Giovanna were very much in love and they married later in the year.

In the early days we returned home often to a cold house, as the stove had gone out. This was causing us several problems, it would burn well or not burn at all, or it belched smoke depending on the direction of the wind. It was a cylindrical iron stove with openings at the top and at the bottom, a smaller version of the kind found in an army barracks. Then to add to our annoyance, having got it going well, and putting on more logs to add to the blaze, the grating at the bottom of the fire would fall down into the ashes and all our efforts came to nought. Another problem soon became evident: the flue was a tube which connected to the chimney in the wall. The wood was green and we soon had water trickling down the wall. Corrado Pallenberg in Rome assured us this was a common problem and the solution was to get a mason to cut a larger hole in the wall just below the pipe connection, insert a drawer made for the purpose in which the water would collect. Then each morning before lighting the fire, we could empty the drawer. Later we bought a larger terracotta stove which behaved better, but we still had to use the green wood.

During winter days with the wind south-east – the *Scirocco* – the fire would not burn at all, so we went to bed early. There was another reason why we had early nights too: on days when the wind blew hard from any direction, and it poured with rain, the electricity failed. Visitors to Italy during these days would find a candle in a candlestick in their hotel room. Our electricity came from Terni in the central Apennines. Sometimes the breakdown was on the mainland and everything was blacked out. Other times it was only on Argentario: the electricity cables came through Orbetello, along the central causeway, and round the coast to Porto Santo Stefano, hanging loosely between poles. Whenever the wind blew over a certain force, perhaps the poles fell or the wires crossed, but the fuses blew.

Peggy Pallenberg introduced us to a wonderful invention called a 'priest', which was a bed warming frame which folded flat when not in use. There was a small hook on the upper part of the frame from which we could hang a small, metal pan. As long as the stove was alight, we could put a few red hot embers in the pan and shove the contraption into our bed. The frame held the upper sheet and blankets off the lower sheet and mattress by about two feet and the whole bed warmed up rapidly. But unlike a hot water bottle, it had to be removed before going to bed.

In all the shops and dairies the floors were swept and washed each morning and in summer, sawdust was thrown down to stop dust rising and mingling with the food. In April when the flies arrived, curtains made of beautiful beads and small metal links or with colourful plastic strips, came out to be hung in the open doorways. Even though these curtains swayed gently with the summer breezes, a few flies did still manage to get in.

As the seasons passed during this first year in Italy, we discovered the delight of eating fresh fruit and vegetables just in from the farms on the Maremma. How we loved the peaches and figs in summer, grapes in the autumn and at the end of the year, oranges and huge knobby lemons. But just in the first few weeks we discovered and enjoyed so many different things.

CHAPTER FIVE

The First Year – 1960

With Basil and Wendy's departure our minds turned to work, to start on the book about Admiral Byng. In those days Dudley preferred to write after lunch and on into the evenings if we did not have guests staying with us. That first year we did make the mistake of inviting too many friends before we left England because we feared we would miss them too much. Some mornings when we had no need to go shopping, we went for walks. But each day after lunch before settling down to write, Dudley began working on his notes. He indexed and entered references to them in a diary to keep everything in chronological order. These were the notes we made at the Public Record Office and the British Museum, and then those from the books borrowed from the London Library. Towards the end of the afternoon Dudley sometimes wrote letters to friends or, feeling restless, he would get up from the table and suggest we go out for a while. Sometimes we went to a bar at the far end of the *Piazza*, owned by Renato Chiodo whom we met the previous June. He had told us that during the War his motor torpedo boat had been captured near Malta. Renato had been taken first to Egypt and later transferred to England to a prisoner of war camp near Birmingham. Soon Renato's skill at football was discovered and on Saturday afternoons he was allowed to play for the local team as goal keeper.

One Saturday a talent scout for West Bromwich Albion saw him and after the match spoke to him. If Renato wished to stay in England after the War, he was promised a contract to play for

West Bromwich Albion. Indeed, Renato stayed eight years and when he returned to Italy to marry his sweetheart, he opened the bar on the quay with his savings. Renato had a very English looking moustache and a very reserved and sad manner. His wife helped him in the bar and they had a son, then twelve years old who was going to school in Grosseto. In the summer the chairs and tables were put outside, each table having a gay coloured umbrella with a notice on each which declared: "Here English is spoken."

Renato, in fact, came from Civita Vecchia, some sixty miles to the south and on the way to Rome. He was not a native of Porto Santo Stefano and did not feel happy there. It seemed that after his stay in England, he had never been able to fit himself back into Italian life again. His only dream was to return to England. Other days we used to call on Chito and Nino at their boat garage. Chito's English was improving as he had more practice talking to us. Our Italian improved slowly until eventually we were able to speak in Italian, while he liked to reply in English. Soon after Wendy and Basil left, Chito and Nino called to invite us to have lunch with them at Chito's home. There we met one of Chito's brothers-in-law, who lived in Cecina. Chito's mother and father had died some years before and he was their only son. But Chito had four sisters and they, or their husbands, were always visiting him. There were innumerable times when we were invited to the villa for a meal to meet them all, and we saw what a close knit family they were. We were not only made to feel welcome, but almost part of the family too.

One of our most pressing needs were some bookcases for our books, which were still in the trunks. A carpenter called Giovanni was recommended to us and he made us two bookcases, beautifully veneered with mahogany and varnished. He also made a letterbox for us, with a window below the letter slot. He painted it blue and the word *POSTA* was written vertically in white paint. It also had a lock. Giovanni was fair haired and slow speaking and came from Orbetello. Soon after we met him, he brought his wife and three-month-old son to live in Porto Santo Stefano, where he had found a new job in one of the carpentry shops. He augmented his income in the evenings with private work but, unfortunately, when his new employer discovered what he was doing, he forbade him to work anymore in his spare time with the threat of losing his job.

The highlight of each day was definitely when the post arrived. We had a post woman called Little Teresa: but she was large and strong, carrying the mail in a heavy tan leather satchel. Her day began at eight o'clock when she and two colleagues sorted out the post for their three postal routes. The letters were stamped on the back of each envelope with the date they arrived in Porto Santo Stefano. The bus brought the mail from Orbetello to the Post Office with the sacks stowed away in the luggage compartment at the rear, while the outgoing mail also left on the bus. About ten o'clock Teresa set off with her colleagues on the first of their two daily rounds. She turned left when she left the Post Office close to the harbour quay and walked round towards the church, to deliver the post to the houses in the *Rione Croce,* or the Quarter of the Cross and also in the *Rione Fortezza,* the fortress (including Via Appetito Alto). Here she had to climb up and down the steps in the alleyways until she reached our road. It was not surprising the Post Office had employed such a strong woman. Teresa usually reached our house each morning a little after eleven o'clock, depending on how many letters she stopped to deliver and people she met to have a gossip. Some days the letters would not fit into the box, or there was insufficient postage paid and she would need to ask us to pay her a few lira. So she would open our gate and call out in a loud voice, "*POSTA!*" In the afternoons she would be by our house again by about half past four, and if she was lucky and did not have many letters to deliver, she was back at the Post Office by five o'clock and able to go off duty. In a few instances, we found some of our letters went astray. In one case, my mother wrote from Australia to say she was coming to visit us. Not receiving a joyous reply, she then sent us a telegram. We suspected someone along the route fancied the stamps and took the letter. We did receive other letters that had been clearly franked, but had no stamps, and Teresa did not demand lira for these. Peggy and Corrado told us that if you wanted to be absolutely sure your letter was delivered, not to send it by registered post but send it without stamps, because the postman or post woman would be sure to hound down the recipient for payment before delivering the letter personally.

When our money finally arrived for the car, we met Nino outside the Bar Centrale in the *Piazza*. To our surprise, instead of setting off for the notary, he shepherded us into the bar where he bought three forms, the *Carta Bollata*, each of which was headed with a Government tax stamp. These forms are the mainstay of Italian bureaucracy. If anyone wished to write to any Government or local government office, whether applying for a passport, installation of water or electricity, drawing up a contract to buy, or sell a house, land or in our case, a motorcar, the contract had to be registered and thus addressed to a civil servant, the *Carta Bollata* had to be used. But there were some pitfalls: there was a margin with a vertically ruled blue line running down each side of the sheet of paper, and whatever was to be written had to be confined within the two margins. Should anyone be so careless as to squeeze even an 'e' over the blue line, the bureaucrat concerned, depending on how he was feeling at the time he was reading the form, could put it down to leave it for a while, or allow it to get 'lost'. At the notary's office, our names and the details of the car were written down by a clerk on one of the forms, and then copied on to the other two, including the price. Dudley and Nino signed their names and then the notary signed under a note that the above agreement had been drawn up in his presence, and his clerk signed as witness. Dudley then gave Nino his cheque.

But during all this something puzzling occurred: when it came to writing the price of the car on the contract, Nino had asked us what was the price we had agreed on. On replying the agreed amount, Nino had said, "No, no, no," and asked us again. We persisted on the agreed sum and Nino again repeated his question. We could not understand why he kept asking us the price. Later we learned that Italians put down a much lower amount than the real price in the sale contract, because the seller would later have to pay fifteen per cent tax on the sale. When the buyer hands over the cheque, the notary discreetly turns his back so that he does not see the real amount. At this point in the proceedings, Nino shrugged his huge shoulders and disappeared into another room with the solicitor. There was an argument, and after a while matters were settled between them.

As our house was built on a steep hillside, one part of the small garden was on one level and a small flight of steps led down to the lower part of the garden. My kitchen window looked out on the wonderful old olive tree in the centre of the court yard and had had its trunk split into four when it was young, so that as the branches grew up and outwards, the olives have plenty of sunlight to grow in the summer. Purple irises were planted around the old tree, while flower beds full of geraniums surrounded the whole area and flowered from spring until late autumn. Our next door neighbours, the Orsinis, told us the tree had to be at least 100 years old since Grandma Orsini could remember it growing when she was a child. Sometimes late in the afternoon we walked up the hill rising behind our house to find the sun again. The track was steep and narrow, lined with old stone walls, so that very quickly we were up among the vineyards. Some of them had a very tiny stone shelter, where the farmers would rest and eat their lunch at the hottest time of the day while their donkeys were tethered in its shade. Argentario had many tall signal towers high on the hills around the coast. But Chito Varoli also had one on his land overlooking the valley behind Porto Santo Stefano. We went out walking one afternoon to see it and found there were many pines and cypresses nearby. It had a solid door three metres up which was blocked by a fall of stones. There was also a chimney hole on one side and there appeared to be a cellar or dungeon beneath. Nino told us later that it was believed a tunnel linked Chito's tower to Orbetello. Other afternoons we would get in the car and take our favourite route along the Strada Panoramica, westward along the coast, to watch the sunset. This was the road, which begins in the valley by the harbour, winds up the hill, passing below our house and by the fortress to continue round above the piazza and shops on the quay of the smaller bay. Suddenly with the houses left behind, we would be in sunlight again, high up above the sea. Below us were cliffs, the blue sea and the islands of Giglio and Giannutri to the west. On clear days, as the sun began its descent towards the horizon we could also see the mountain peaks of Monte Cristo and Sardinia. At first they were lavender and then deepening as the sun lost its intensity, becoming dark silhouettes as the sun slipped behind them. On calm days the sea was silver and the colours of the sunset were reflected in the departing sun's path, rose, orange, pale pink, yellow and lemon. At this time, the road continued along the coast for five miles and this first year there were only a few villas standing in large grounds. Later a hotel was built here and many more villas as Argentario became more and more popular. Near where the road ended there stood the Bar Argentarola, which only opened during the summer holiday season. We liked to park the car here and sit and wait for the sunset. Immediately below us, sticking out of the sea like a broken tooth, was a rock and on rough and windy days we loved to watch the sea break against it. We soon met the owner, Signora Alba, who came to clean and paint her bar and plant flowers for the coming season. She was a very delightful and youthful grandmother, with her long black hair piled on top of her head. She pointed out to us the highest peak on the ridge of hills above us and explained this was called Argentarola, from which her bar and the rock below, took their name. Spring suddenly came in a way we had not been able to notice before, since we had always been too busy working in London to witness the smaller things of life going on around us. But it was certainly much more interesting to watch the lizards come out of hibernation, and see some finches, a few thrushes, blue tits and sparrows suddenly arrive in a cluster to chatter in our large olive tree. We also had one robin. In April for a few weeks there were thousands of swallows and swifts on their summer migration north from Africa, swooping and gliding above the harbour.

Late in February a letter arrived from C.S. Forester, the author of the Hornblower series of novels; he had just finished reading *England Expects*, which the publishers had sent him and enclosed an endorsement, or quotation, which could be used for publicity purposes.

Every summer, Forester, went to London and stayed at the Savoy Hotel. He had read *73 North* and had contacted Dudley at *The Evening News*, inviting him to tea. He had expressed surprise when he had learned that Dudley was busy with research to write a book on the Battle of Trafalgar as he toyed with the idea himself, but then rejected it, and said Dudley was a braver man than he was. At the time, this had given Dudley some misgivings.

In 1959, when C.S. Forester was in London again, we were both invited to tea at the Savoy and we also met Mrs. Forester. Forester himself was a small man and by this time was suffering from arteriosclerosis, but it did not appear to be affecting his mobility very much. During the conversation Forester let slip that he admired Dudley's work: he considered him to be his natural successor, and suggested that Dudley should think about writing sea novels in the future. Dudley always enjoyed reading the Hornblower books and was stunned by Forester's suggestion at the time. Yet early this year he began to think about a novel and drafted a few ideas which he thought could work out well. He began to find the idea of writing sea novels more and more attractive, as they would solve the problem he sometimes had with the background research which made gaps in the historical narrative, and with our small library it was hard to find the material.

Although this was the germination of the Ramage novels, Admiral Byng and then the mutiny of the *Hermione* would keep Dudley busy during the next two years. But when he did write his first novel, he had already planned it would be the first in a series. But at the time he said to me with some regret that he was afraid the novels would keep him away from his non-fiction work and the research into the past which he so much enjoyed.

When Dudley finished setting out all his notes for each chapter, he began his first draft of the *Byng* book. Some days in February were warm enough to take his typewriter, a small table and chair outside and write by the olive tree. But as soon as the sun disappeared behind the hill above us, it became chilly and necessary to come indoors and light our stove in the sitting room.

During March *Byng* was progressing slowly and Dudley had some grave doubts about the book. He felt the story was not going at all well: as he reached the battle off Port Mahon in Minorca, he was afraid the narrative was too flat, not having the tension and excitement of Nelson's Battle of Trafalgar. The difficulty was Admiral Byng had a very different character: he did not have the flair of Nelson; he was staid and cautious in comparison, and this seemed to make the book dull.

But once he was through this part of the book and nearing the trial, the narrative became easier, A month later, Dudley began cutting back the manuscript, taking out quite a lot of material and finished the first draft in early May, having taken fourteen weeks to write it.

We had decided to visit England as soon as I finished typing the first draft of the *Byng* manuscript. We would visit the Public Record Office and the Reading Room at the British Museum again to gather as much material we could both for the Battle of Copenhagen and also the mutiny of the frigate *Hermione* that took place in the West Indies, south of Puerto Rico in 1797. The captain and officers were killed and the crew sailed the *Hermione* to La Guaira on the Spanish Main.

Dudley also wanted to research a second mutiny that happened on board the *Danae* three years later in 1800. She was a 20-gun corvette, part of a flotilla based in Jersey, which was patrolling off the coast of France, near Brest. We had to go through the archives, make notes and put in requests for the ships' logs, muster lists and the minutes of the courts martial to be put on microfilm.

On the way home we also went to the French Naval archives at the Citadel in Brest for a few days, to see what documents they had on the *Danae*. Here we met Captain Marot, who was the *Archiviste de la Marine*. He was very helpful and quickly found all the papers relating to the *Danae* in a file with the name *Le Diable Lui-Meme* (*The Devil Himself*) printed on the front cover. The corvette had been built in France and called *La Vaillante*. She had been put into service to carry prisoners, many of them aristocrats, from the prison at Rochefort to exile in Cayenne, French Guyana. The ship was then captured and commissioned into the Royal Navy and renamed the *Danae*, only to return to the French flag after the mutiny.

At this time rebels in Algeria were agitating for independence and many bombs (*plastiques*) were exploding in Paris, so that security at all naval and military establishments was tight. Each day when we arrived at the main gate of the Citadel, we were escorted to the Naval Archives by two armed sailors. While we were with Captain Marot we noticed he occasionally turned to an English dictionary and, much to our delight, saw it was an original edition of Dr. Samuel Johnson's *"A Dictionary of the English Language"* that was first published in 1755. Captain

Marot and his two assistants helped us by copying out some of the documents, so that with Dudley and I copying as well, the work was completed quickly. On our last day in Brest we drove out to the end of the peninsular at La Conquet to see the headland off which the crew of the *Danae* had mutinied. Dudley took photographs including the remains of the little monastery of St. Mathieu nearby, to help him describe the area when he came to write the book many years later.

Work on the *Byng* manuscript resumed as soon as we returned home to Porto Santo Stefano. It now had to be edited and heavily cut, but during the two months we were away, Dudley had had time for reflection before setting out to reduce it from 200,000 to 160,000 words. We sent the typescript off to the publishers in September, but a few weeks later a letter came from Weidenfeld's asking for further 30,000 words to be cut. This Dudley accomplished in eight days and decided the book was the better for it.

But it was not all work: Chito and Simonetta had married in Rome while we were away and as the weather had become so hot in July and August, we went swimming with them some mornings with Nino and other friends who had a boat. Also, once a week we had a dinner party either at the Villa Varoli or at our house. We went sometimes to the outdoor cinema in Orbetello and one memorable film we saw was *Sink the Bismarck* , which we all enjoyed. Much to our amusement the whole audience jeered at Hitler and his Nazi perorations.

Peggy and Corrado Pallenberg came some weekends to stay with us: they had just bought land in Porto Ercole and began to build a house. Over the next year they came often to see the progress of the construction. Corrado loved the golden coloured wine of Porto Santo Stefano and often late on Friday afternoon Dudley would dash into the kitchen, slip all the raffia handles of the empty chianti bottles over his arm, by now a fair number, jump into the car to drive down to the *cantina* to fill them. All we had to do in the evenings during the weekend was to be sure there was a full bottle by Corrado's chair.

Family and friends visited us during the summer. We loved driving out into the Tuscan countryside to explore the hill towns either on our own or with our guests. In southern Tuscany many of them were built on early Etruscan settlements before the Romans came on the scene. Some of the buildings appeared to grow straight out of sheer rocky cliffs and most are sited at the fork of a small river. All of them were once fortified, the forked river becoming a natural moat almost round the whole town. Many of the old walls and gateways remain and many towers are still standing. San Gimignano is the most well known with thirteen, but did originally have sixty-two. Our favourite was Orvieto, also built on Etruscan foundations and whose thirteenth century cathedral can be seen from the west twenty miles away across a valley, with the beautiful mosaics on the western facade gleaming in the mid-afternoon sun. Sienna and Volterra were not far from where we lived either and we drove there many times.

Later, in his first novel, Dudley used Volterra for the name of his heroine, and the place where she lived. His hero, Lieutenant Ramage would meet Gianna, Marchesa di Volterra, on a shore close to where we were living on Monte Argentario. We also enjoyed the festivals that were celebrated in Porto Santo Stefano. There were many whole and half day holidays throughout the year, the majority of them religious or saints' days.

But Easter was the first festival, when we were wakened early on Good Friday morning with voices singing a most beautiful and moving lament. We hurriedly dressed and went down to watch the long procession which was led by a band and then several men carrying a large cross escorted by the priest, altar boys and choir. Behind, the villagers were formed up in two lines, everyone wearing black, beginning with little girls who gradually became taller and then followed by the women. Next came small boys and lastly the men. In the evening all of the houses in the village were illuminated with crosses or the Star of David in their windows. On Easter Sunday morning we were wakened by joyful singing with the band playing again and there was the same long procession with everyone wearing white. Red flags were hanging from windows and there were black and gold flags flying from the fortress.

The next festival was *Ferragosto*, the Feast of the Assumption of the Virgin on 15 August. On this day the four quarters of the town meet by La Piazza and have a rowing race across the bay and back in front of the Town Hall. Each quarter had a band with its team dressed in their quarter's colours, bearing the flags of *La Valle*, *La Croce*, *La Fortezza* and *La Pilarella*, and they met with a cacophony of sound on the quay. Our quarter's team was led by a donkey and rider, dressed in *Fortezza's* colours. The crews embarked and the race took place, cheered on by the large crowd. Finally the 4th November was Liberation Day, the day when Italians remembered the end of the First World War, when Italy fought on the side of the Allies against Germany. There was a military band with a contingent of the Navy and Air Force, who gathered on the quay with a large wreath to board the Giglio ferry for a ceremony at sea.

The grapes were harvested in the autumn and taken to the wine press. Our neighbour who lived opposite our front gate, kept his wine in huge barrels in the large cellar beneath his house. He pressed his grapes himself with his feet, leaving the squeezed juice for three days to allow the fermentation to begin and then poured it into his large barrels. The cellar was shared with his donkey while he and his family lived above. As the months went by he would catch Dudley on his return from some errand, and liked to lure him into his *cantina* and taste the maturing wine with him. The new vintage was always sweeter than that of the previous year's wine and Dudley never enjoyed this wine tasting.

Another time at a weekend, both Corrado and Dudley were invited into the *cantina*. The olive harvest soon follows and in October they were large and swollen enough to be picked. Our landlady, Signorina di Pol, had explained to us that our next door neighbour, Signor Orsini, would come with his wife and two young children to pick the olives, arrange for them to be pressed and share the oil with us. They came with broomsticks, a green umbrella and a sheet: Signor Orsini went up the tree with the umbrella, holding it upside down and hooked it by its handle on a branch to catch the olives as he pulled them off their twigs. Mama and the children, Rosella and Vincenzo were below on the sheet sorting and discarding the poor quality fruit. A second olive tree on the lower terrace was still too small to climb, but it had a good crop of olives also.

A few days later Signor Orsini returned from the olive press with eighteen litre bottles filled with a dark green sludge. He assured us it was a very good crop. Over the next weeks the sludge slowly settled down to the bottom of the bottles and a beautiful golden oil appeared above. Even though we also shared the oil with Signorina di Pol, we had enough for cooking and salads to last us throughout the year until the next harvest was in. The Orsini family were always kind: Signor Orsini took our rubbish each day to fertilise his garden where he grew vegetables and as the months passed Rosella or Vincenzo came with small gifts of eggs, beautiful artichokes and egg plants, apricots and grapes, and wine. His wife had an outside oven and when she baked, she sometimes sent Vincenzo round with a flat sweet bread spread with jam for us. We were helping Vincenzo with his English homework at this time, which we were very happy to do. But this did not last long because his teacher said he was making mistakes.

Later, we met a delightful Italian girl who was not very fluent in English. After discovering we were living in Via Appetito Alto, she realised with embarrassment we were Vincenzo Orsini's English neighbours, and we realised we had met his teacher. We had been using words which were not included in the lesson's vocabulary.

Towards the end of the year, Dudley began transcribing the *Hermione* material from the microfilm we had brought with us from London and he also wrote a letter to the Museo Naval in Madrid to enquire if they had any documents concerning the *Hermione* affair. He knew there was a large archive relating to Spain's possessions in the Americas in the museum and as soon as we received a courteous reply from Admiral Guillon, the curator of historical documents, we decided we should go to Spain to see what papers we could find about the *Hermione*'s arrival in La Guaira on the Spanish Main. Within a few weeks we set off to drive round the Mediterranean coastline as far as Barcelona and then inland to Madrid, arriving there early in December. The road deteriorated as we progressed and after Zaragossa we broke the Alfa's rear shock absorbers by crashing into a huge pothole. We found an Alfa Romeo agent in Madrid and left the car there to be repaired. Dudley then contacted the Naval Attaché at the British Embassy and his assistant very kindly arranged an appointment for Dudley to see the Admiral at the Naval Museum. The *Hermione* papers had been found, but they were stored in a castle somewhere outside Madrid. We arranged for them to be put on microfilm and then posted to us. We then spent a few days sightseeing and went to the Prado Museum while waiting for the car to be repaired. Our return journey was even more difficult as it had snowed heavily across the plateau between Madrid and Zaragossa and we arrived in France with the two rear shock absorbers broken again.

Christmas came and we bought an imitation tree, lights and decorations. The Pallenbergs had warned us when employing a maid, household staff are paid a thirteen month year. Paola later explained to me that she spent some of her monthly pay to buy sheets for her *corredo* (trousseau). When asking Peggy and Corado about this they explained that couples were often engaged for seven years before they could afford to marry. The girl had to have twenty pairs of sheets and her fiancé had to save one million and a half lira, about £900, to buy the furniture.

Thus our first year in Italy ended: we were slowly becoming more fluent in Italian and making new friends. On the last day of the year Dudley was able to note in his diary that he had written the first few lines of *Hermione* mutiny.

CHAPTER SIX

Italy Years 1961–63

Unfortunately, early in the New Year of 1961, Dudley learned he was not yet finished with *Admiral Byng*. In January a letter arrived from the American publishers saying they did not like the way *Byng* was done and suggested rewriting. Dudley had been afraid this might happen as he was not satisfied with the book himself. We sent a cable immediately to Weidenfeld's and within a few days we heard the manuscript was on its way back to us as they were able to retrieve their copy from the printers before they started setting it in type. Dudley settled down to sketch out the Byng story and began rewriting. Within a few weeks he had already finished the battle off Port Mahon in Minorca and by the time he reached the trial he decided the book was reading very much better. It also gave him the opportunity to amend some of his opinions that he had written in the book.

The revised manuscript was returned to the publishers some 200 pages and 68,000 words shorter at the end of April. Dudley also came to the conclusion that the delay in beginning the *Hermione* mutiny gave him more time to decide how he would construct the story from all the notes he had made during the research. *At 12 Mr. Byng Was Shot* was published in 1962 in the United States and in May it came out in Britain. The reviews were good, describing the scandalous affair of the trial and execution of Admiral Byng. John K. Hutchens in the *New York Times* said Dudley had written a fine book and Gordon Harrison in the *N.Y. Herald Tribune* wrote:

"Dudley Pope writes absorbingly of ships and the men who fought them. He writes too, with an effectively restrained anger of the political chicanery by which his unprepossessing hero was caught and killed. The sense of immediacy which is the product of thorough research and a lively historical imagination makes one forget the passage of two centuries . . ."

In Britain, there were good reviews in *The Sunday Times, The Sunday Telegraph,* The *Observer* and the *Sunday Express,* the last describing the Byng affair as judicial murder. But in spite of the reviews, the sales were disappointing. However, during the first six months in the United States Byng sold 3,200 copies and in Britain, 3,007, although Weidenfeld's were hoping for 4,000. But the book did not earn more than the advance royalties already paid. We had received a royalty statement for *England Expects* one year after publication in 1959, which also gave disappointing sales figures. The book had not sold more than the advance royalty payments, which we also had long since received. At the time Dudley thought that his publishers were not promoting or pushing the book enough. Fortunately, the sales in the United States were better and good reviews were still coming in, including one from *Harpers magazine* written by Garrat Mattingly.

With the combined income from both countries and the rights sold for translation for one or two of his other books, as well as a paperback edition of *The Battle of the River Plate* which was also still in print, we did have just enough to live on when we were in Italy.

A letter arrived from Lynn Carrick, Dudley's American editor and also a vice president at Lippincott's, telling us the news that he and his wife, Virginia, would be moving to London soon, as Lynn had been appointed Lippincott's European representative. They stayed until Lynn retired three years later. We had met them both in Rome for the first time when Lynn had come on a business trip the year before, and then they came to stay with us for a few days in Porto Santo Stefano. This had given Dudley the opportunity to discuss his next two books with him. Virginia always accompanied Lynn and helped him a great deal. She was very well read and enjoyed browsing through bookshops while

Lynn was at meetings with publishers. She sometimes bought books she thought Lynn might consider publishing in America and we learned that it was Virginia who found *Battle of the River Plate* in a bookshop in London, read and recommended it to her husband.

Arturo, the ginger cat who had greeted us the night we arrived in Porto Santo Stefano with all our possessions, suddenly became ill. We took him to the vet who suspected TB and to his surprise, we decided to try a course of penicillin injections. Unfortunately, Arturo became worse and it became clear the vet's diagnosis was correct and he did have TB. We were very upset, but there was no choice but to put him put to sleep. However, a few days later Arturo was back in our kitchen, having somehow managed to escape. That evening, feeling terrible, Dudley returned with Arturo to the slaughter house and waited with him until the end. There was no animal clinic in Porto Santo Stefano and most of the vet's work was to check the health of the animals arriving to be slaughtered. There must have been very few people in Porto Santo Stefano who had pets. We noticed our neighbours treated their animals well, but were not affectionate to them. Our neighbour, Signor Orsini, had a guard dog and he was just that and spent most of his life in the garden on a chain that ran along a wire strung up high from the front door to the gate. We learned the reason for this attitude to animals when we were taking Arturo to the vet for the penicillin injections. One day we stopped to buy some fruit at the *verdura* and there Signora Gina asked why I was staying in the car. So Dudley explained I was holding a sick cat in a basket and we had been to the vet for an injection. "Ah," she exclaimed, "just like a Christian!"

It seemed the belief in Italy at this time was that animals do not have souls. But I am sure Italians in large towns and cities who do have pets are just as besotted with them as people are elsewhere.

Visitors began arriving early this year and friends came and went that summer, but Dudley managed to continue with his first draft of the *Hermione* mutiny. He was able to reconstruct the events before and during the mutiny from the logs of the *Hermione's* captain and master, as well as from the minutes of the courts martial, when the mutineers were caught and brought to trial. Also we heard from Madrid on 17 July that the microfilm had been posted to us and we received it early in August, just as the first draft was finished. While I was transcribing and translating the microfilm, Dudley began writing a new draft of the mutiny, hoping to make cuts to reduce the length. One day, though, he broke off suddenly to spend a day to make an index of his Copenhagen notes. We had decided to go soon to Copenhagen to research the Danish side of Nelson's battle there in 1801. We left in September, driving through Switzerland and Germany and stayed with a friend, who not only lent us a car to visit places and buildings mentioned in the documents describing the battle which are still there, but also his small yacht, so we could sail in the Sound to see where Admiral Hyde Parker and Nelson had their line of battleships drawn up, facing the Danish battleships and defences. At the Historical Section of the Marine Library of the Danish Admiralty, we were met by the King's librarian and his assistant who greeted us with a large trolley loaded with a huge number of documents, some of which were written in the old Danish script, similar to old German. We were there for more than three weeks working with two translators as we needed the help of an expert who could read and translate the old script for us.

During the summer of 1961, many more yachts came into Porto Santo Stefano, some to be hauled out at the boat yard for work. Dudley enjoyed going down to the harbour in the late afternoon to see them all moored to the quay, meeting and talking with the people on board. Most of all he missed not having a boat of his own. He sometimes invited the skippers and crews to our house for showers and often we all enjoyed a meal together. We made many friends, some of whom we would meet again a few years later when we were in the West Indies.

A small ketch called *Tokay* sailed into the harbour, whose owner was running the boat yard with two partners. They hoped to attract more yachts to Porto Santo Stefano for repairs, renovations and conversions. We decided to buy her and Dudley surveyed the boat himself. He found a few things that needed to be repaired, including a few cracked frames that had to be strengthened. Up to this point the shipwrights at the yard had worked only on fishing boats and Dudley was not at all satisfied with the quality of the work. A battle of wills began between Dudley and Guido, the chief shipwright. One memorable day Guido stalked off with frustration, to complain at the office saying: *"Testo di ferro lui, testo di ferro lui,"* *[head of iron him]* meaning Dudley was the most stubborn man he had ever met. Guido was replaced by other carpenters several times, but eventually *Tokay* was launched in the middle of the summer. We then went sailing to the islands of Giglio and Giannutri not far from Porto Santo Stefano and later this area became the scene at the beginning of Dudley's first Ramage novel.

During all this time Dudley was still rewriting and editing the *Hermione* mutiny and with the strain of getting the boat the way he wished, it left him exhausted. He lost so much weight that our friends Chito and Nino noticed and they were so concerned they asked if there was anything they could do to help. Unfortunately, the struggle to get *Tokay* repaired made Dudley less tolerant to other frustrations he was beginning to find with Italian daily life. We were by now speaking Italian and able to follow more that went on, and discover things that were not so admirable. Small daily inefficiencies and the promise of *"domani"* [tomorrow] by tradesmen which were not kept began to irritate him more and incidents such as seeing a policeman kick a dog lying on its side with a broken leg did not help, although this was the only incident of animal cruelty we did see while we were living in Italy. From this point on Dudley became increasingly disenchanted with Italy and more and more he was criticising Italians. Eventually he told me he wanted to live on board a boat again. We could buy it in England and return to the Mediterranean with her. He began writing to several yacht brokers in Britain asking for details of yachts they were advertising in the yachting magazines and we put *Tokay* up for sale.

In the meantime, work continued with cutting and editing the *Hermione* manuscript. In early August Dudley had finished his corrections and rewrote some early pages. He also worked out a different way to rearrange the first part of the mutiny and, after more cutting and editing, the book was finished. But there were still the Notes and Bibliography to do, followed by the Public

Record Office references and the last of the Appendices. Finally, near the end of January 1963 copies of the manuscript were sent off to the British and American publishers with the title *The Black Ship*. The weather all across western Europe suddenly turned very cold with the temperature in Porto Santo Stefano falling to zero centigrade and then to minus two degrees. On the morning of 1 February we woke to find two inches of snow had fallen during the night for the first time in living memory. The passes through the Alps were blocked with snow, so we decided to delay a planned visit to England. At a loose end and not able to relax, Dudley decided to start the sea novel that he had been contemplating for some time. The story went well and by the time we set off to England later in February we took the first fifty-eight pages with us.

We stayed six weeks in England and during this time Dudley worked again on the *Hermione* manuscript, incorporating more cuts suggested by Lynn Carrick who, with Virginia was now installed in London. Barley Alison, the fiction editor at Weidenfeld's, read the first pages of the novel and enthusiastically demanded a synopsis for the rest of the book, which Dudley drafted immediately. Before we left England to return to Italy both British and American publishers had agreed to commission two novels. Later, the hero would be called Captain Ramage, and these first two books became the beginning of a series of eighteen books, all published with Ramage in the title and all set during the time of the Napoleonic Wars with some stories taking place in the Mediterranean and others in the Caribbean. But two years were to pass before the first was published.

In the spring of 1963 we spent many weeks in the boatyard painting and varnishing *Tokay*. Finally in May two Sicilians decided to buy her immediately. With the departure of *Tokay*, Dudley returned to writing the first draft of the novel, and by the middle of June the book was going well. He was happy with the way the story was developing, but commented he was not sure if it was good fiction.

The book begins with the hero, Lieutenant Nicholas Ramage, regaining consciousness from a blow to his head to find his ship sinking and he is the only surviving officer remaining alive on board. Nearby a 74-gun ship of the line is still firing broadsides into his ship to disable and then capture her. Ramage escapes to Monte Argentario with a few men to carry out orders to rescue some refugees escaping from Napoleon's army advancing down Italy, among them the Marchesa di Volterra. The novel ends with a court martial where Ramage, as senior surviving officer, has to justify the loss of his ship.

Dudley had to do some research to be able to describe Bastia and the coast of Corsica and found enough information he needed from Admiralty charts originally drawn from surveys made by ships of the Royal Navy during the eighteenth and nineteenth centuries which we had for *Tokay*. He also found more material in his copy of the Admiralty Pilot for the Western Mediterranean, which gives sailing instructions and small sketches of the coast, drawn by generations of ships' masters showing distinguishing features such as church towers, windmills, shapes of hills and mountain tops.

The arrival of the page proofs of *The Black Ship* interrupted work on the novel for a few days. Dudley continued to be unsettled and, for several weeks after, found it difficult to resume writing until one morning early in August he had a furious row with workmen who were noisily shifting sand outside on the road for the construction of a house near us. After he calmed down he began work again and wrote six pages that day.

Shortly after we went to a party and met Jane and Antonio Pallavicino, who invited us to visit them at their home at Capalbio, just a few kilometres south of Monte Argentario. We walked over their land and found a beautiful square tower called the Torre di Burano close to the beach. Dudley decided immediately to use the tower as the rendezvous, where Captain Ramage would meet the Marchesa di Volterra. On another visit to Capalbio we took photographs so Dudley could describe the tower while writing the book. He also decided to include a wrecked ship episode for an exciting ending.

Yacht brokers were still sending us details of boats for us to consider and among them were details of a cutter called *Golden Dragon*. The boat seemed large enough for us to live on board and we liked the look of her. We hoped to buy her and return to Porto Santo Stefano or perhaps, visit Malta or Greece. At times Dudley missed friends with whom he could have interesting discussions and arguments. He was always interested in international affairs and was often critical of British and American foreign policies. Yet when he was writing he also wanted to be alone. As he talked more of leaving Italy, I knew he would be happiest living on board a boat again, so that when he needed a change of scene, we could pull up the anchor and sail somewhere else. We hoped to find quiet bays where Dudley could write and move to busy anchorages when we wished to be social. This we were able to do after we sailed to the Caribbean in 1965. I was also very happy living on a boat, although I did not want to leave Italy. I am more tolerant and easy going, and apart from a thoughtless episode of cruelty to the dog, I could more easily accept the way things were in our daily life in Italy. At the time I was sad that we would be leaving Porto Santo Stefano and our friends we had made there.

We had decided to visit England in late September when *The Black Ship* was published and Weidenfeld's held a party for Dudley the night before publication day. At this time George Weidenfeld was publishing coffee table books and he wanted Dudley to write one and put forward several ideas. Dudley's mind was preoccupied with the novel, so he was not immediately receptive to the idea. But he did suggest *guns* would be a good subject for Weidenfeld's to commission someone else. However, at another meeting, George was very keen on the idea and persuaded Dudley to write the book for him and at a conference later, it was decided *Guns* would be the title. Dudley would have to deliver 50,000 words the following May, captions for the pictures in July and everything ready for the printer by October 1964. He also wrote a synopsis for *Guns* while we were still in England. Good reviews of *The Black Ship* appeared in the London newspapers as well as many of the daily provincial papers. They all described the dreadful events of the mutiny and Derek Jewell in the *Sunday Times* wrote:

"For his balance in making all this more than melodrama, Mr. Pope deserves another ring on the sleeve of his burgeoning reputation as our brightest young naval historian. His detective work is outstanding, as is his sheer literary feat of pummelling diverse source-stuff into tightly knotted narrative of suspense. Equally important, he cleverly weaves in social detail that has the ring of authority and enough salty clarity to give the least expert reader a sharp impression of the total setting."

While in London Dudley had arranged for a copy of *The Black Ship* to be sent to C.S. Forester and later in October he received a letter from him:

4 October, 1963
"Dear Mr. Pope,
THE BLACK SHIP came a day or two ago and I finished it – I finished a breathless first reading at any rate – last night. It's intensely interesting and I'm sure it will be successful. I can make some suggestions, too late I fear, for you to act on them in this particular case. It's a complicated story, and, in the nature of things bound to be a little repetitious because of the successive trials. You might have saved yourself a good deal of trouble by thinking out the book in considerable detail before you put pen to paper. It's the method I myself use; with a beginning and an end clear in your mind the next thing to do is to think out very clearly the stages from one to the other. The real advantage of this system is that it saves you occasional false steps. Now from the strategy we can go on to the tactics; you should do the same thing on a much smaller scale each day, running through your mind before you start work the passage you are going to write so that you get it straight and don't put B before A . . . There's one routine you follow which is perfectly acceptable to everyone but me, but I always try to avoid it. That is, start in the middle when a fresh subject is coming up and then going back to the beginning. It may be for dramatic effect – it seems a good starting point, but I always think the price paid for the dramatic start isn't equal to the cost of having to go back again . . .

. . . I can't think how I've come to be so pernickety, when I've enjoyed the book so much. I don't want you to misunderstand me – THE BLACK SHIP is very good indeed, and I read it with the greatest, very real enjoyment . . .

Yours,
CSF

Dudley replied to this letter on 10 December, when we had left Italy and we were living on board *Golden Dragon* in Oulton Broad:

"Dear Mr. Forester,

I was delighted to get your letter of October 4 which arrived as we were in the midst of saying farewell to Italy after four years to return to live in England for a while. Now we are settled down in our new home – a beautiful 47-foot sailing cutter sturdily built entirely of teak. Your comments and criticisms of THE BLACK SHIP were just what I wanted and one particular point you made is most valuable – that I tend to start in the middle when a fresh subject is coming up and then go back to the beginning. I have reread two or three of my books where I have done this, and was disagreeably surprised to find how confusing and unnecessary it is, and I shall never do it again! It was, as you suggested, done for dramatic effect, but seldom if ever achieves it – this is quite clear in retrospect . . .

. . . There is nothing more annoying when one is asked to criticise a book to have the writer making excuses for some of the criticisms: but I'll risk annoying you over your reference to planning of the book. As you say, it was bound to be a little repetitious in places, but the original basic outline of the story was considerably blurred because the book had to be cut by almost a third . . . and the result was that some sections had to be telescoped and others changed round. Normally I do follow the pattern that you suggest, working out a page by page outline of the story – rather like 'headlines' which appear on the right hand page of some books, a different one heading each page . . .

It is a pity they filmed once again the Bounty story, because I think the Hermione episode would have made a good film. As it is, I imagine no one is interested in mutiny films any more . . .

Incidentally, when doing research for Copenhagen, I came across some interesting sidelines on Bligh's character, both from British and Danish sources. None of them make him appear a very pleasant individual. . . . I am now busy . . . working on the novel . . . The first draft has worked out quite well, but on second thoughts I think I have crammed too many episodes into it – eight or ten whereas four or five will be enough. The trouble is, I think, I've written so much non-fiction, where the problem has always been that I have too much material for the contract length of the books, that I find it hard to write at a more leisurely pace. However, I suppose one should be thankful that the first draft of one's novel should suffer from having too much action rather than too little . . . Because Byng was not a financial success, despite excellent reviews, my publishers in the U.K. have come up with an idea for a large 'coffee table' book on the history of guns, ranging from cannons to handguns and very lavishly illustrated in colour . . . I shall probably do it, because the terms they offer are so good, and also because recent books on firearms have concentrated on handguns whereas there is a good deal of interesting material to be written and illustrated on cannon, and I shall concentrate on the interplay between design and warfare . . .

Again, very many thanks for your comments on THE BLACK SHIP. There was no need to apologise for the remarks you made because if one wants to improve as a writer an ounce of criticism from an expert is worth five tons of praise!

My wife and I join in sending you and Mrs. Forester our best wishes and trust that you both keep well.
Yours sincerely,
Dudley Pope"

When we went to see *Golden Dragon* we found that she was a beautiful wooden boat, built with teak. She was lying on the River Crouch and our friend Bill Fowler met us there. Bill and Colin Mudie, also good friends who had begun their early careers together before Bill set up his own office as naval architect in Oulton Broad. Bill was an east coast man from Suffolk, slow speaking, fair with wispy hair, small and agile, was always a good hand to have on board a boat. He surveyed *Golden Dragon* for us and found she was in good condition. The next step was the negotiations to buy her. But Bill did have one reservation: *Golden Dragon* was a cutter, having one mast with a large mainsail and two jibs, or foresails, and he wondered whether the mainsail would be too big for us to handle when sailing on our own.

When we signed the papers for *Golden Dragon*, everything had been accomplished that had been planned for our visit. We were ready to return to Porto Santo Stefano. Our friends, Basil and Wendy who had driven out to Porto Santo Stefano with us and our possessions, were aware of our new plans to return to England and live on board *Golden Dragon*. Basil prepared a van he would lend us, and we would leave our car with him for the next few weeks. We were going to leave Italy in the same style we had arrived.

During the next few weeks in Porto Santo Stefano we packed, burned papers, and sold our few pieces of furniture. Our landlady came from Rome to go through the inventory and the Orsinis, our next door neighbours, sent in a chicken, some wine and a cake. Our parting was tearful, but we hoped to return with *Golden Dragon* although, with plans to write a coffee table book on guns, our stay in England was likely to be longer than we had planned.

CHAPTER SEVEN

England 1964–65

We sailed *Golden Dragon* to Lowestoft from Burnham, motored up the River Waveney, and passed through Mutford Lock to enter Oulton Broad, where we were able to tie up alongside a wooden jetty at the yacht station. Our friends Patricia and Bill lived just across the road above their chandlery shop with Bill's design office at the back. Once a week, we had a hot bath, a delicious meal and an evening in their 'snuggery' – a small and cosy sitting room warmed by a large fire. During the first two or three months on board we were busy making a few changes down below and found a shipwright to do some joinery work. One of the most important things was to fit shelves into a locker to hold all Dudley's reference books. We bought a small diesel stove to keep us warm, and the copper chimney had just the right diameter to pass through one of the ventilators on deck.

Golden Dragon was built at the Wing-On-Shing Yard in Hong Kong in 1938 to a design by H.S. Rouse, who was living in the Far East at this time and had built her for himself. He shipped her back to England just before the outbreak of World War II, and *Golden Dragon* lay in a mud berth on the river Dart for five years. Her hull planking and deck were built with teak from Thailand and the heavier timbers, the frames and beams, were yacal, a type of ironwood. She was a boat built for heavy weather sailing, strong with fine lines. She would be our home for five years and would carry us some thousands of miles.

As with all boats, and particularly wooden boats, there is always work to do on board. If it is not mechanical, with a part to be replaced on an engine, or generator, there is always painting and varnishing to be done. Dudley was occupied much of his time with work on the boat. He was also suffering with back pain, which became more and more acute. After visits to specialists it was diagnosed as a slipped disc and for a few months he visited a physiotherapist at Lowestoft Hospital twice a week to have his spine stretched, in the hope that the disc would eventually slip back into place. This treatment was not successful and eventually he was fitted with a belt to support his back. Although the pain did ease during the next few years, Dudley suffered with pins and needles in his left leg for the rest of his life as a result of a pinched nerve.

However, he was never prepared to change his life style because of his back. Early in 1964, Dudley began to draw up lists of the illustrations he would like to have for the book on guns. He also wrote some material for the publishers to make up a dummy chapter, which they would use to sell *Guns* as a coffee table book to U.S. and European publishers and which, when published, would have the text translated into various languages. Dudley would not receive a contract or part of his advance royalty until all of the publishers were committed to George Weidenfeld.

Also, at the beginning of this year Dudley worked on the characters for the novel and began rewriting the first chapter later in January, but so many things conspired against him during the day, he could only work on the book in the evenings. He had still not settled on a name for his hero: he had tried several but was not happy with any of them. But late in January while driving to Lowestoft for one of his twice weekly appointments at the hospital the name came to him. Close to the Docks we always passed Roddam House, perhaps once belonging to a family connected with the fishing industry. Dudley commented what a good, strong sounding name it was: "Roddam, God damn, blast, damage, ramage . . .", then turned to me to ask what I thought of 'Ramage' for the Captain's name.

When we returned on board *Golden Dragon*, he looked the name up in a list of naval officers for the period and found there was a young Scots officer called Ramage. Finally, the name felt right and the second draft of the book was finished in July. Apart from a few more alterations, the book went to the printers in

October, and when it was published it had the title *Ramage*.

During this time we visited Harold Wyllie, still living in Dunkeld, and Dudley was able to find a trove of information about guns in his library. He also discussed his idea to write a book about the daily life on board one of the ships of Nelson's Navy. Harold Wyllie immediately offered to draw some sketches illustrating small pieces of equipment on board, such as the flintlock for the great guns, the fire engine, the belfry with the ship's bell and the different types of gun shot. Many years later this became Dudley's *Life in Nelson's Navy* with the sketches at the end of each chapter.

On 15 January C.S. Forester had written to thank Dudley for his letter of 10 December :

> Dear Mr. Pope,
> Your last letter reached me while I was enjoying complete idleness in Maui in the Hawaiian Islands, and the local Polynesian paralysis completely prevented me from answering it until my return. But it was a pleasant stay; at the moment there is one luxury hotel (where I stayed) and the rest of the island is still unspoilt, but the plans are made and within five years that two mile beach will be like Waikiki. But it is the best winter climate in the world, I think; at noon the sun is just too hot to sit in, and the sea is just warm enough to stay in permanently. And the middle of Maui is a 10,000 foot extinct volcano with a practicable road up it and ice and snow waiting for you at the top whenever you need a change.
>
> In April my wife and I are going on a high brow cruise round the Greek Islands, and then I'll be spending the month of May at the Savoy in London, and I hope there'll be a chance of our making contact.
>
> And I hope that the novel has worked out properly; artistically there's no need for anxiety about a correct length. Within very wide limits it can be any length as long as it's the <u>right</u> length in the author's judgement. Your taste will tell you that, and if it is episodic the episodes have only to move logically from one to the next as far as the concluding one – it's a little like planning the

composition of a picture, and taste is the only guide.
And my final hope is that the GOLDEN DRAGON proves to be
entirely satisfactory.
Yours very sincerely,
C.S. Forester"

In May we went to visit them at the Savoy Hotel and found
Forester in the middle of writing another Hornblower book. He
had a small technical problem which involved Hornblower in a
sailing manoeuvre with his ship. He read several pages to us and
wanted to know if Dudley thought it feasible. Dudley agreed it
was, and made a few suggestions while Forester wrote notes.

Forester liked the name 'Ramage' and Dudley sent him a copy
of the manuscript when it was finished. A lengthy correspondence
between them followed. The first letter came later in July when
Forester was at home in Berkeley, California.

13th July 1964. "Dear Dudley,
I hope you will think that this letter is good news. I liked the
book with a lot of reservations which I will explain and which
you can discount. Dorothy (that's my wife, with taste and lots
of experience) liked it with almost none. I suppose that's the
important part of this letter and I've put it first.

You have been very considerably (unless I'm completely self-
centred as I may well be) under the influence of C.S.F., which
must somehow turn me a little against the book – the best
explanation I can offer is that idiotically I resent someone else
doing what I might have done. (I have the feeling – I'd lay
odds – that nine reviewers out of ten will mention me and make
comparisons.) So I had to combat this frame of mind in order
to enjoy the story; but Dorothy had none of those feelings. I'll
answer your letter before going on with this discussion, as that
will deal with many of the points anyway.

There's no harm in Ramage having a persecution complex;
people do have these things and it's one of his facets and serves to
make him real as long as it doesn't put the reader off, not him,
but off reading the book. With physical descriptions I think it's
best to provide an outline for the reader to fill in himself, and that

you have done. It's awkward when a film version comes along, for then the character doesn't agree with the reader's mental picture. But that's a distant bridge. Dorothy actually asked me if the conduct of the court martial was to be believed. That answers your question; you may feel you have to strengthen the credibility. You leave me with the impression that you personally have a poor opinion of Italians, and I know you didn't want to. It's just bad luck, the result of course of the story – I don't see how you can remedy it without alteration of the plot, but minor modifications of phrasing might do it. But I shouldn't worry. When you talk about Hemingway's dialogue you're setting yourself a very high standard indeed. And I have to say that a good deal of the dialogue rang the smallest amount false to my ear. But it was not so much the Italians as the lower orders of Englishmen. And I can't make any helpful suggestions about it, and I'm sorry – I can only suggest you read those speeches again.

I liked your Nelson even though he has affected me differently – I feel you are entitled to present him that way although I wouldn't have done.

Now a real knock. I was left with the impression that the introduction of Jackson was deliberately contrived to gratify the American market. I feel sure I am right. It may be successful but I must warn you very strongly always to write to please yourself without a thought for the market. In the same way you shouldn't ever trouble your head about what reviewers say. Write as well as ever you can by your own standards, putting in only what appeals to you, and to hell with everybody else. Of course this is only my feeling, but I've acted on it all my life – I've never subscribed to a press service and I doubt if I read more than five percent of my reviews – I wouldn't cross the street to get hold of one, and the interest I have in them may be mercenary but it isn't artistic. I have never written anything for money; that is true in the sense that I have never modified anything I had in mind in the hope of making additional money. I'm under another handicap that I'm sorry for. You know that I'm in the middle of a Hornblower novel myself and I find it hard to be sympathetic, having so many of my own troubles. Hornblower had just broken open a captain's desk with a handspike fetched from a gun when I found myself reading about Ramage doing the exactly the same thing. So please understand why I am disturbed enough not to give Ramage all the care and attention he deserves – that's why I'm glad Dorothy has read him right through with only the one single criticism I've mentioned. You ought to know by now how self-centred writers are, and when they're actually writing (I did 20,000 words in the ship) it's very hard to get at them. I can wish you luck, and I can even predict it but you can see I haven't either the strength or the surplus sensibility to be enthusiastic. I'm sorry the Golden Dragon's voyage turned out to be abortive; mine in the freighter might have taken much the same course.[4] Running down Channel the lubricating oil for the diesels turned out to be contaminated and the engines started to seize and we only just made it into Falmouth. Even after three days there and a complete change of oil (ten tons of lubricating oil!) we had further trouble and several minor breakdowns – it's a most uncanny feeling to be adrift far out at sea and no engines. But I suppose it would be worse on a lee shore. It's very good news indeed that you're going to have a body-child after your six brain children. Conception is usually equally pleasant, but I don't know which I should choose if I were offered the choice between mental and physical parturition.

Please give Kay my very best wishes and accept my congratulations. One thing I was going to say and have just remembered. The newly finished book is always a disappointment to the writer – it's never as good as the writer hoped for when planning it. You'll see all this if ever you read 'The Hornblower Companion' if ever that's published.

Yours,
CSF."

Dudley replied at length to Forester on 25 July 1964:

"Dear C.S.F.,
Very many thanks for your letter, which arrived last night. There was no need to be so apologetic for your difficulty in reading Ramage through, as it were, with Hornblower's spectacles.

---

4   The Foresters returned home to the USA on board a freighter.

But first of all, I'm most grateful for your comments: they've been read in the spirit you meant them and are beyond price. Where you've suggested ways of improving the story (dialogue etc), I'm having another go. And my thanks to Mrs. Forester, too. I'll refer later to her reservation about the court martial. The only thing that disturbed me, naturally, was your feeling that DP has been influenced by CSF. How true that is, in the sense that no one writing fiction set at sea in Nelson's time could fail to be. Both publishers (UK and US) and myself knew that comparison with CSF would be inevitable; and in a way this is your fault! Before you think I mean that rudely, I'll explain why ! If one was writing thrillers set in the 20th century, one is in an 'open market'. One COULD say that Ian Fleming's 'James Bond' is a refined and sophisticated version of Mickey Spillane's heroes. One doesn't bother to because Spillane's heroes could also be said to be a rough version of Bulldog Drummond, and so on. There is only one hero who is both lawyer and detective – Perry Mason. But if someone was a lawyer by education, took up writing, and decided to use his expertise to write crime/law thrillers, then he'd be also open to the criticism that he's copying E.S. Gardner, even though his hero might be different in every characteristic The problem is that both you with Hornblower, and Gardner with Perry Mason, have had a complete monopoly in your respective fields. The reason has been in your case, I think, that there has been no one who has the unique combination of being a wonderful story teller and writer with the requisite background knowledge. Of the two things, probably the background knowledge is the most valuable . . . because it takes so many years to get that knowledge. In my own case I have only just written my first novel, as you know, yet I've been studying the period for more than 25 years – from childhood.

I should have told you, when we last met, why I wrote this first novel; it might have explained a lot to you . . . I have spent the last 15 years gathering as much material about the days of sail in what is loosely called 'Nelson's day' as I could. Much has been newly discovered, as you'll remember from the Trafalgar book, and Hermione. I've been collecting this material for my own interest, helped greatly by such people as the artist Harold

Wyllie, who re-rigged the Victory in 1925 and who is one of the world's authorities on rig and design . . . All this has been done in order to record life at sea in those days. For my part, my books are often criticised for being too full of detail; a valid criticism I know, but few people realise I put much detail in simply because I want it to get into print, so that it is recorded and available for future generations. But there is much material particularly that dealing with the type of life led by the men -- which is difficult to publish . . . the novel seemed a suitable 'vehicle'. The next few sentences are going to sound conceited, tho' they are not intended to be. With the exception of yourself, few people writing today have the foggiest idea what it was like at sea in a gale of wind in those days. The writing of naval history is in the hands of professors who never get to sea. As proof of this one need mention only Mattingley, whose Armada book was brilliant but which never quite came to life because he never really had those ships at sea . . . I've been lucky inasmuch as I learnt a bit about fear, the smell and sound of guns, etc. in the last war, and my hobby is sailing. Given that I know what it is like to be shot at and scared, know how to sail a fore-and aft rigged ship and in theory a square-rigger, and have accumulated a fair amount of background about life at sea in Nelson's day, using the novels as vehicles for publishing material seems a logical step. And of course it is, except for one thing; Forester/Hornblower is/ are unique. No one else has seriously attempted to write such books since the days of Marryat and his contemporaries. There is a similarity, in a sense, between Mr. Midshipman Easy and Mr. Midshipman Hornblower, but the former is not in print and that latter is much more sophisticated, and presumably due to those two factors your first Hornblower was not criticised as copying or deriving from Midshipman Easy. But had Marryat been writing when you started (and presupposing that the passage of time had changed his style), then I think you would have faced the comparison. Which is where I've come in, I think. I don't mean that there is any comparison between Hornblower and Ramage in terms of quality (I wish there was!) but there must be in terms of background. Ramage is a completely different type of person from Hornblower – not an exact opposite, naturally, but completely different. Whereas, for instance, Hornblower never reflects on social conditions round him (on shore), Ramage does. This is, I suppose, just me: Ramage doesn't do it in order to be different from Hornblower. Nor is Ramage bad at maths because Hornblower is very good: I am hopeless at maths, at card games, and have a bad memory. I lisp, I go off the deep end about silly things, I've felt in my time that 'everyone's agin me', and I've written a book on Byng. From that you'll see the gradual evolution of Ramage in my mind has followed an obvious pattern. I knew it was useless to make Ramage a different person from myself; after all, I know for sure my reactions to a given situation. And he being in effect Byng's son followed on from realising just how much family feuds etc. could and did affect service life . . . Referring to your comments. Mrs. Forester reacted to the court martial as I feared people might. In fact it is legally 'water-tight'. But I had the feeling that it was not too convincing unless the reader knew I d have made it water-tight. And, of course, there's no way for the reader to know. Anyway, I'll have another shot at that. The other reaction I had feared has come from you: the American Jackson. No, this wasn't put in for the U.S. market – I've found that there is no need for an American 'angle' to make a book sell in the U.S.A. The Trafalgar book proved that, and the reviews of 'The Black Ship' show that the critics hardly mentioned the American angles, of which the book provided plenty. I wanted a 'partner' for Ramage who could be critical without being put on trial, and also someone who would see things differently from a Briton. Also, for future stories, I wanted to enlarge on the various questions leading to the War of 1812. You may remember I dealt with the impressment of Americans at some length in 'The Black Ship', and it was as a result of that that I finally decided to make him an American who, as Ramage has already revealed, probably has a Protection in his pocket. This Protection is going to provide two important episodes in the third novel of the series. So, given that one wants a cox'n who can be critical or impertinent, see things differently, and be able to change nationality when needed, an American is the obvious choice, since their lack of formal discipline is well known. He was, incidentally, going to be called Jessup, after the

American captain of the Mercury in The Black Ship, but that looked rather obvious and he became Jackson – due to my habit of referring to odd strangers as 'Jackson'. The derivation you've probably guessed – 'Jammed like Jackson in the bread room scuttle'!! . . . If the Hornblower references in the MS annoy you, then please send me a postcard to that effect and I'll delete them. They were put in because Hornblower IS a 'real' person, and – this is hard to phrase, and sounds rather lame in view of your feelings! – as a tribute to the fact that you have made him a 'real' person: so real that someone else could refer to him in a book in that way, cursing the fact Hornblower wasn't around to help him (Ramage) solve the maths side of the problem. Anyway, it seems a poor way of thanking you for your help by writing such a long letter; but I'd sooner not publish Ramage than have you think he's a copy of Hornblower. My wife has read your letter and says she doesn't believe you think that – indeed, you only say 'under the influence of CSF' – and that it would be hard for anyone to write fiction of Nelson's day without being 'under the influence' since you are the only contemporary writer who (effectively) uses that period. I must now have another bite at the Ramage cherry in the light of your suggestions; and I keep my fingers crossed that the foregoing will go some way towards assuring you that there was no intention on my part to conjure with your brain child, and in addition, 'Ramage' would not have seen the light of day for several years had I not thought you had finished writing Hornblowers. But above all, I value the fact that you write to me frankly about your own thoughts, and can only hope that you have the patience to wade through mine.

Yours sincerely, Dudley Pope

P.S. About Ramage and Hornblower smashing up the King's furniture – no, people's private property! – with handspikes: does the handspike episode in Hornblower form an essential part of the story? If so let me know and I'll change it round in 'Ramage'."

A reply was received on 3 August:

"Dear Dudley,
I think the best piece of advice I can give you is not to worry; if

you're at work just go on working, and don't waste any of the precious energy on anything else – satisfy your own taste and judgement and don't think about anything else.

You certainly have a point when you remind me that I said I wouldn't write another Hornblower book. But I suppose I was like Omar Khayyam – was I sober when I swore? I'm sorry; but there's room in the world for both of us. The breaking open of the desk is an odd coincidence as regards time, but not in any other respect. A man looking for ship's papers is going to break open the captain's desk for sure, and a handspike is the inevitable instrument; it's such a logical thing to do that there's nothing surprising in it happening twice in the pseudo-history of the period, and I think anyone reading both books would accept that. The Hornblower references just made me smile – it's amusing that a fictional character should be used to strengthen artistic verisimilitude. You can see I'm following my own advice and not worrying. Looking through your manuscript again I changed my mind about Jackson. I realise that you were following the same system as I have advocated in THE COMPANION (sorry to keep quoting that but I learnt so much from that book!) with something demanding to be done you selected the most interesting and satisfactory character to do it; you didn't think of a character and wonder what you could give him to do. There are so many other things I could say, but I'm still hard at work; I'm writing this letter today because I'm up against a minor construction difficulty and taking a day off to give it a chance to resolve.

Ordinarily I never allow such a trifle like letters to come between me and my work; I might as well be in gaol during that three or four months. I'll send the manuscript to you today, and every good wish of mine will go with it. Writers are nearly always too self-centred to be good critics (I must have written that fifty times to literary editors who have wanted me to do work for them, but it's still true) but it doesn't make them less friendly. Yours, CSF"

C.S. Forester certainly seemed a little dismayed that *Ramage* was perhaps too much like his Hornblower novels. But he was very generous with his praise and his criticism was fair. Certainly

Dudley was under the impression that Forester would not write any more Hornblower books and he knew comparisons would be made.

Within ten days of this letter being written, we received shocking and very sad news from his secretary, Commander J.D.P. Hodapp, Jr, who informed us that C.S. Forester had suffered a stroke, but was in hospital and expected to recover. Much to our regret, however, he died a year later. Dudley had had much pleasure meeting him and valued his advice and encouragement. It was sad there would be no further exchange of letters between them, and it was not only a loss for us, but also for all his fans that there would be no more Hornblower books.

We also received the good news that Weidenfeld's had not only sold the rights to publish *Guns* to several European publishers, but also to Dell Books in the United States. Work could now begin in earnest and immediately Dudley completed his list of all the guns he would include in the book, starting with the earliest known and ending with those of the present day. He had already drawn up a separate list of those he wanted to appear as illustrations and now gave them to Ed Victor, his editor during the production, and who would arrange for them to be photographed. Dudley also borrowed books from the London Library, and was able to use the library at Lowestoft as well. He visited the Wallace Collection in London; the Museum of Artillery at Woolwich; the Imperial War Museum; the Armouries at the Tower of London; and private collections.

At the Wallace Collection, which had acquired many fine handguns and all their accoutrements, Dudley chose nineteen items to be photographed, most of which made beautiful colour illustrations. There were many conferences at Weidenfeld's to discuss the production of the book and the illustrations. By early August Dudley had begun writing the text for *Guns* while Ed Victor wrote that he would like the first third of the manuscript sent to Vesey Norman, who was Master of the Royal Armouries at the Tower of London, and who very kindly gave Dudley an enormous amount of help and advice.

We had decided to move closer to London as the journey from

Oulton Broad to London was too long, whether by train or car. Dudley had secured an offer of a berth in Wapping Basin on the River Thames, but we finally took *Golden Dragon* to the inner harbour at Ramsgate, which was non-tidal. We sailed late in September with Bill on board as crew. It was a fine night with a full moon and a good breeze which made it an exciting sail. We arrived off Ramsgate during the early hours of the morning and anchored to wait for the high tide before entering the harbour.

As *Golden Dragon* lay alongside the inner harbour wall with a few small yachts tied up outside her, we used a ladder to climb up on to the quay. The high street with shops was only a short walk away and there was a pub on the corner. A lovely old seaman's church is tucked into the chalk cliff on the far side of the inner harbour with the road above, rising up the hill and then descending into Pegwell Bay. Ramsgate is one of the great seaside towns of the nineteenth century, although early settlement began in the thirteenth century with fishing and farming. The construction of the harbour that exists today began in 1749 and was completed one hundred years later.

By the beginning of November, Dudley was near the end of the text for *Guns*: he was tired and afraid he did not have the time or enough material available from 1890 to 1945. He was always a perfectionist, and believed a task was not worth doing unless it was done well. He managed to find the material he needed at the Woolwich Arsenal, where the curator was very helpful. Before posting the last section to Ed Victor, Dudley even had to cut some of the text before it was finished in November. Ed Victor telephoned to say the manuscript was fine and it had been sent off to the printer. The next task was to sort the photographs that were now arriving at Weidenfeld's and then write the captions for them. He came down to Ramsgate and stayed two days with us so as to go through them all. Packets of photographs went back and forth in relays between London and Ramsgate and continued during the first of month of 1965. When the captions were finished, writing new chapter headings was the last of the work to be done. Early in January Dudley visited the publishers to look at the layouts for the introduction and the first three chapters.

Dudley continued to travel to London from time to time to see the layouts as the chapters continued to be set up. Whilst travelling to London by train one day, he sketched out the story for the next *Ramage* novel. There was good news also because a Swedish publisher was negotiating for the rights to publish a translation of *Ramage* and Readers Digest made an offer to publish a condensed version in one of their issues.

Our baby daughter was soon due, and from the beginning of January I stayed in London with my family. Going up and down the ladder to the quay was beginning to be difficult and I had to go the hospital more often for checkups and prenatal exercises. She was born on 17 February and Dudley came to the hospital with a camera and took photographs of her when only two hours old: he was excited and happy and I was overjoyed after waiting so many years. We called her Jane Clare Victoria while the proud father wrote in his diary a few days later that *"Jane is very pretty – no doubt about that!!"*

At the beginning of March we were all together back on board *Golden Dragon*. Living on a boat with a small infant was not difficult at all. We had bought a carrycot so it was easy to take her with us when going ashore. This cot fitted in a berth amidships which Dudley had closed off with a small-gauge fish net that could be unhooked easily and with the high bunk board, kept Jane and her cot safely inside whether we were in port or at sea. She was bathed on the saloon table in a plastic bath and her clothes, when washed, hung out to dry on deck with ours. Fortunately, by this time, disposable nappies were available and we had no need to wash nappies. Since the accommodation on board *Golden Dragon* was below the waterline, we never suffered with cold draughts and were always cosy during the two winters we were in England.

The last chapter of Guns was finished in early March and during a visit to Weidenfeld's Dudley learned that Pan had bought the paperback rights of Ramage to be published in two years' time. Then we received exciting news in a letter from Barley Alison:

"18th March 1965.
Dearest Dudley and Kay,
A book called RAMAGE (said to be a Hornblower-type novel)
has been chosen by the Book Society for June. What is the
organisation coming to since it changed hands? It is not even
by C.S. Forester, nor based on that interesting Italian traveller
whose Diaries Longmans are republishing . . . A first novel by
a man who has only written naval history put forward by that
rather new publishing firm in Bond Street. I am afraid the 5000
odd members may resign in a body.

Seriously, though, it is definite. They rang Halfdan [Lynner]
five minutes ago and we are all delighted. We shall have to
deface the jacket with a band saying BOOK SOCIETY CHOICE
but what of it?

Heartiest congratulations from us all and my love to Miss
Dudley Pope.
Love Barley."

When the finished copies of *Ramage* did arrive with the 'Book Society Choice' band on the jacket, Dudley had already written several chapters of the next novel. Lynn Carrick had retired and Sandy Richardson was appointed to take his place at the American publishers. We had already met him in London the year before and found him a charming, likeable man with a pleasant face, dark hair and medium build. Dudley hoped he would have a long publishing relationship with him as Sandy was about the same age. He was in London again for more meetings with publishers and we had dinner together one evening. He told Dudley he seriously admired *Ramage* and suggested we go to the United States for the publication. Dudley, jokingly, said we could sail via the West Indies to New York, since he had helped two young men plan their voyage to Barbados while we were in Oulton Broad.

We were planning to leave England after the publication of *Ramage*. But we had not yet made up our minds whether to return to the Mediterranean, or sail to the West Indies. However, we were making *Golden Dragon* ready for a long sea voyage: Dudley was thorough and meticulous with everything he did and the work on *Golden Dragon* continued until our departure in July.

We sailed from Ramsgate on 22 May bound for Newhaven, where we were planning to stay for two months. We were still within easy travelling distance to London, but a little further to the west. We would later continue to Plymouth, which would be our last port of call before leaving England. By the middle of June we had definitely decided to sail to the West Indies. Dudley ordered two spinnaker poles which we would use for running before the trade winds when we crossed the Atlantic and they were sent to Mashford's Yard at Cremyll, which lies on the other side of the Hamoaze across from Plymouth. Other last minute work would be done there also, including scrubbing off the hull below the waterline and applying two coats of anti-fouling paint.

One night in the pub near the marina in Newhaven we had met Captain Richard and Mrs. England who owned the last British trading topsail schooner, the *Nellie Byewater*, which had foundered in a storm close to Bolt Head on 27 December 1951. One of their daughters on board was lost along with another crew member, while seven were saved with Captain and Mrs. England. Because of many delays, they had set out on a voyage to the West Indies in December and while battling gales for six days in the English Channel, were trying to return to Plymouth. They were a sad and broken couple and when they discovered we were planning to sail to the West Indies with a baby on board, they implored me to reconsider our plans. Their terrible story shook me that night, but I did have complete faith in Dudley's seamanship and the seaworthiness of *Golden Dragon*.

We planned to arrive in Barbados during the third week of November, at the end of the hurricane season which begins in June. Dudley anticipated that at some point during our voyage we would run into bad weather and he had prepared *Golden Dragon* accordingly. Never once had it occurred to me that we would not reach Barbados safely. However their story stayed with me until we sailed from Plymouth, but once at sea standing watches and looking after Jane I thought very little more of it. We certainly must have talked about the tragic loss of the *Nellie Byewater* and

---

I know Dudley would have pointed out that their vessel was old, having been built in 1873, and that it would be unusual to meet such a bad storm on our way to Spain in July.

Weidenfeld's had arranged to have the party to launch *Ramage* at the Royal Thames Yacht Club a few days before publication day and Dudley learned they had plans to print 22,500 copies. We went up to London the day before, leaving Jane in the care of her grandparents for the evening. Afterwards, we received the following letter from Barley, written on 31 May:

> "Dearest Dudley and Kay,
> So glad you liked the parties. That powerful Book Society and Bumpus 'eminence grise' (Bendor Drummond) loved you both AND the book which is encouraging. I am not surprised you are boggling at RAMAGE II right now. I doubt whether you will be able to settle to him until about 18th, i.e. after Ramage I has actually come out and been reviewed. Why can I only see Jane for a couple of minutes if I come down? I shall certainly agree to no such arrangement. I expect her to give me her undivided attention, smile, quirk, scream etc . . . for my amusement whenever she is not actually asleep. Can I propose myself for a Sunday in June? 20th or 27th for instance? I would like to come down by car, lunch on board and drive back around 6.30 or 7.00 if that was (sic) not too much trouble. Let me know at your leisure.
> Love to you all 3.
> Barley.

Barley was becoming a friend as well as being Dudley's fiction editor. In spite of rude and furious letters Dudley wrote Barley at times, often caused by a misunderstanding, and the equally forthright replies he received from her, the friendship endured until she died in 1989. Barley was petite and at this time had short dark hair with a striking silver streak across the centre of her head from her brow. She was five years older than Dudley and her experiences in World War II included driving ambulances and vehicles with the S.O.E. in Algeria. She then transferred from Algeria to the British Embassy in Paris in 1944 and later had the distinction of being the first woman in the service to hold the position of Third Secretary with full diplomatic status. Later, she worked in the Foreign Office in London before going into publishing. Barley's interests ranged far and wide, from her needlework; the plants in her garden; and her large circle of friends in the political and publishing world. Conversation flowed from Barley, always interesting and humorous, particularly when relating some disaster that had befallen her. She loved children, talked endlessly of her niece, nephews and god children and, I suspect, our Jane also, as she became a close family friend.

The reviews began appearing on the first Sunday in June, with one in *The Sunday Telegraph* which said Ramage had taken the 'mantle of Hornblower". We found others in *The Observer* and *The Sunday Times*. More followed in the daily newspapers and weekly magazines. On 13 June the *Sunday Express* had *Ramage* at No.2 on their best seller list. The book was published in the United States three days later and many reviews in the American newspapers did compare Ramage with Hornblower. There was also a fine review in the *New York Times* by Orville Prescott. Shortly after we received a cable from Sandy Richardson to tell us that they had sold the paperback rights for *Ramage* to Pocket Books.

It was such a relief that there would be paperback editions of *Ramage* both in Britain and America within the next two years. We hoped at last, with the novels, we were assured of a better income. All Dudley's naval histories had been well reviewed, but none of them had been on the newspaper bestseller lists, or generated very much income, selling little more than the advance royalties we received. Perhaps, at last, with the Ramage novels our income would improve.

One morning at the time though, I remember he was feeling sad at the thought that he would probably be writing a series of novels rather than naval histories in the future. Dudley enjoyed the research and discovering all he could about his subject, but unfortunately the books earned only just enough for us to live on. He was always thorough and meticulous with his research and when the time he took to produce a book was taken into account, they were barely profitable. Moreover, he still had Nelson's Battle of Copenhagen to write and other material already in his files for several other naval histories.

While at Newhaven, Jane had all her necessary vaccinations, and we had several shots as well for tetanus, smallpox and typhoid. We also had begun stowing stores on board and bought a variety of tinned and freeze dried food for the voyage, with plans to buy more in Gibraltar and the Canary Islands Then there were the jars of strained baby food for Jane and her powdered milk. There was some difficulty when the disposable nappies arrived on the dock: Dudley was furious when he saw three huge cartons containing 1,080 disposable nappies and he could not imagine where they could be stowed. I told him to go away for an hour or so and leave it to me. I was able to stow two thirds of them in Jane's bunk, some under the mattress and the rest wedged around her carrycot while the last third went under our mattress. When he returned he was mollified to see all the nappies had disappeared and all was well until early next morning, when I brought him his first cup of coffee in bed. Unfortunately, he had forgotten the mattress was now a few inches higher, and as he sat up he bumped his head on the strong, wide beam above the bunk. He subsided stunned to his pillow! This was a story he loved to tell against himself for some years to come. But it was not long before the nappies were really useful when changing the engine oil, or cleaning the oil and diesel fuel filters! They absorbed all the drips and were good for mopping up oil spills in the drip-tray under the engine. By the time we reached Gibraltar in September we needed to buy another three cartons.

We left Newhaven on 16 July with a fair north-east wind for the first few hours, but later it went west, forcing us to beat to windward and making our trip longer. By the time we reached Start Point the next day we missed the tide, so we decided to go into Dartmouth for the night. Next day with no wind we motored round to Plymouth. We came alongside at Mashfords to dry out for the men to scrub and paint the bottom. One side was finished that day and the rest the day after.

We met a doctor who had his yacht at Mashford's yard and

he set us up with a medicine chest. At the chemist he wrote out prescriptions for the antibiotic Penbritten, three ready-filled syringes with morphine in case we had a major injury on board, antihistamine and many other useful items. Fortunately we had no need to use any of these things during our voyage. Our day of departure was set for 24 July and in the early afternoon our crew arrived who would sail with us to Lisbon. We cast off all the lines holding us to the shore and moved out to a mooring buoy, while we stowed the last minute things and prepared to sail. Dudley wrote his first entry for the voyage in *Golden Dragon's* log book, which all registered vessels are required to keep on board:

21.50 Slipped mooring
22.00 Hoisting main, yankee and jib.
22.35 Log streamed at west end Plymouth breakwater.
Course 215.

The log was fitted to *Golden Dragon's* stern and a long line and rotor streamed astern in our wake, recording the miles run. The Walker log is a simple aid to navigation, and we recorded our progress every twelve hours in the log book.

We had no particular feelings as it seemed just like any other ordinary departure and I found it hard to believe we were really on our way at last. But I found it particularly reassuring when we passed two men in a small boat fishing near the breakwater at the entrance to the Hamoaze, who wished us a "good trip". We were bound for La Coruna in northern Spain.

CHAPTER EIGHT

Cruise to the Canary Islands: July–October 1965

Sunday began with sunshine and a fair wind, but later in the morning the sky gradually became overcast. Dudley was afraid a frontal trough might be approaching and just before dark the wind increased. Later in the evening we were hit by strong squalls just as we were abeam of Ushant, the most westerly point of France. *Golden Dragon* was hard pressed and it became difficult to hold her on course until we managed to reef the mainsail and drop the jib. Once the reefs in the mainsail were tucked in and with the staysail, *Golden Dragon* handled the conditions comfortably to make it an exhilarating sail. This was how she had won her Royal Ocean Racing Club races, when she could be hard pressed in heavy weather.

We felt tired and a little disheartened until it was remembered that Ushant was one of the worst places in the world for bad weather. I was worried at first how I was going to look after Jane if we continued to have bad weather, but after dawn the wind eased and we hove-to for breakfast. By midmorning, the reefs were shaken out and it was fair sailing again. Later we were surrounded by dolphins, three or four leaping together close to and ahead of our bow. The first three days at sea are the hardest as the body adjusts to the new rhythm: the noise of the sails and sheets as well as the movements of the boat, makes sleep difficult. Jane was happy in her carry cot and slept well. I was able to keep regular feeding times and take my turn on watch at night.

Next day was beautiful with a hot sun in a sky with only a few scattered clouds, but when the wind died, we lay becalmed. A tunnyman, like a great green dragonfly, passed us close astern, his rods rigged with several lines from each rod. He held up a fish and we exchanged it for half a bottle of whisky, which was all we had on board. Dudley never drank at sea and discouraged a drink in the evenings at 'happy hour' as he felt it blunted the awareness of those on watch.

The light winds continued all the way to La Coruna. On our seventh and last day at sea we had a close call with another fishing boat which came up astern without any running lights, nor anyone on deck. I was at the wheel and there was just enough wind fortunately to turn *Golden Dragon*, while the rest of the crew appeared rapidly to handle the sails. Off La Coruna the log read 594 miles when we hauled it in. After the bad weather off Ushant, we had experienced fair winds and fine sailing, except when becalmed in the Bay of Biscay. As we approached La Coruna the engine would not start, so we sailed into the harbour and anchored off the Real Club Nautico at lunch time.

General Franco came into La Coruna with his motor yacht a few hours after we arrived and the harbour was patrolled all day and night by a guard boat. We discovered it was a fiesta and the General had come to see the bullfight. Since it was also the weekend, Dudley went on Monday morning to see the Immigration and Customs authorities to report our arrival. It was always necessary when entering and leaving port to visit the port authorities for entry and clearance papers for your vessel and crew, whether it was a small yacht or a large merchant ship. Thus when Dudley went ashore with the ship's papers, he wore his grey trousers and navy blue reefer jacket and carried his yachting cap (with clean white cover) under his arm. In other words he dressed officially as captain of his ship. As a result he was always met politely and the formalities proceeded quickly without any problems.

In Spain the forms were large and for naval vessels as well as merchant ships. Among the questions asked to be entered on the form were "How many torpedoes the vessel carries?" and "How many coffins?"

The auxiliary engine in *Golden Dragon* had a mind of its own, sometimes it started and ran without difficulty. In La Coruna a mechanic diagnosed a blocked fuel line. We emptied the diesel tank, it was cleaned and a new fuel line was installed, using plastic tubing since we could not buy the thin copper fuel lines ashore. The engine was running when the man left, but later it stopped. The following day a large motor yacht called *Mac Owl* came in and, in desperation, Dudley went over to ask the captain if he was willing to lend his engineer. The captain and engineer were Norwegian and they both came to help. They quickly spotted that the fuel lines were installed the wrong way round and, after changing them, the engine ran perfectly.

The Belgian yacht *Hierro* also arrived with Annie and Louis Van de Wiele on board. They had already sailed round the world in *Omoo* and we had on board a copy of the book Annie wrote about their circumnavigation, which was called *The West in My Eyes*. We invited them to tea and asked Annie to sign her book. There was so much to talk about and too little time: they were anxious to be on their way as they were first visiting Morocco and the Cape Verde Islands, before crossing the Atlantic to sail to the West Indies. Dudley sent them off with a copy of *Ramage* and we arranged to meet again in Barbados, or Grenada. We also had on board three other books about cruising around the world: Dr. Roger Pye's *Red Mainsail* describing his voyage on board *Moonraker*; Miles and Beryl Smeeton's cruise on board *Tzu Hang*, which was designed by Rouse who designed *Golden Dragon*, and also built in Hong Kong; and Eric Hiscock's *Around the World in Wanderer III*. We read them all during our crossing of the Atlantic, comparing their descriptions of sailing to the West Indies with those we experienced.

We sailed on 5 August bound for Lisbon, there was a light wind and we were not clear of La Coruna before the engine stopped. We sailed on and when Dudley looked later, he found there had been a fuel leak and most of our diesel was in the bilge. We passed Cape Finisterre in bright sunshine and came close to the shipping lane between Europe, the Mediterranean and Africa. We sighted many ships including the liner *Oriana*, which crossed ahead of our port bow. Two days later the wind picked up and veered to the north-west and gave us a grand sail with the wind on our quarter. Unfortunately, at this point our crew were running out of time and needed to return to England, so we bore away and ran into Leixoes, getting into port after dark just as the barometer began falling and the weather became squally.

Next day a harbour man, carrying a large five-fold green form came on board and we were formally entered into Portugal when the form was completed. With the departure of our crew for the airport, we found a small yacht basin where we could tie up *Golden Dragon*. We sailed from Leixoes the following evening: our fuel tank was refilled and we were both feeling confident and cheerful. It was a beautiful moonlight night with a calm sea, but early next morning we ran into a fog bank lying along the coast, forcing us to sail further offshore to avoid it. We continued southward running in and out of the fog until, just before dawn three mornings later, we were fortunate enough to sight a flashing light ahead. Dudley was able to take a quick compass bearing before the fog set in again. It was Cabo da Roca, the headland close to Lisbon and the westernmost point of Europe. As we sailed past, the wind freshened clearing the fog away and we then had a fine sail into the River Tagus in bright sunshine. We furled the sails and as we were about to motor into port, saw a large square-rigged ship sailing in. As we turned towards her to take photographs, we saw she was the *New Endeavour* which we had last seen in Ramsgate. We motored up the Tagus to the yacht club basin and were turned away. We then saw another dock with a large sign saying "Foreign Yachts", but were chased away by the crew on a dredger. We then went into the Doca Pedroucos, the dock for fishing boats. It looked very new and was almost empty except for one fine yacht moored to the quay, which we soon discovered was *Foxhound*, a very well-known ocean racer in her day.

We stayed a few weeks in Lisbon where we managed to have the engine's gearbox removed and repaired. We also found a sail maker who repaired *Golden Dragon's* jib and made us two awnings. These would keep the sun off the deckhouse and cockpit and make it cooler down below. We found it hot in Lisbon and since we were going to the tropics, would find it even hotter in the West Indies, so the awnings would be necessary to make living on board comfortable.

A large box of mail awaited us at the Post Office, with news of continuing good sales of *Ramage* and more reviews. There was also a letter from Admiral Lawson "Red" Ramage, USN, who had just read the book, and a long correspondence ensued between the Admiral and Dudley for many years.

We visited friends in Lisbon and were overwhelmed by much kindness. We were lent a car and went to Sintra, a drive which took us through pine forests high up in the hills not far from Lisbon. The beautiful old houses are painted in pastel colours, with many of their facades partly covered with decorative blue and white, or pink and white tiles. Also, at Sintra we visited the National Palace of Pena which stands high above the town. We enjoyed our visit to Lisbon, and discovered some quarters still with their old houses painted in the same pale pastel colours and tiled facades like those in Sintra. The balconies on the upper floors above the street had flowers hanging in baskets. But we had to say our farewells and on 2 September, late in the morning, we motored down the River Tagus, hoisted the sails off Cascais and began the next leg of our voyage to Gibraltar.

We had a good sail that afternoon and night, but close to dawn the wind died. As the sun rose, in a cloudless sky, we could see Cape St. Vincent's striped cliffs in the distance ahead. As we drifted in light airs, Dudley soaked up the atmosphere for his second Ramage novel in which Captain Ramage would have a small role in the Battle of Cape St. Vincent, when Sir John Jervis defeated the Spanish fleet on St. Valentine's Day in 1797. We crossed Lagos Bay where, Dudley realised, Admiral Jervis had anchored his fleet after the battle and put 2,300 Spanish prisoners on shore and marched them to the Spanish frontier. There were plenty of ships rounding Cape St. Vincent, even more than we saw off Cape Finisterre, as the main north-south shipping lane runs close to the coast. Many passed inshore of us, among them several large tankers and a Turkish passenger ship. Later the wind returned, blowing hard from the north-west and late in the afternoon we decided to go into Portimao. Suddenly, about 7 pm as we neared the harbour, dozens of small fishing boats in gay colours appeared, all steaming in circles and towing dinghies with their bows hauled up almost on board their sterns.

The wind continued to blow hard for several days, but the fishing fleet went out each night. On the evening of 6 September, we weighed anchor for an overnight sail to Vila Real de Sant' António. We had a fine run through the night but lost the wind just before dawn. Later in the morning, we finally hove-to near the entrance buoys to wait for high water. There is a sand bar at the entrance and we feared *Golden Dragon* would not have enough water to cross it. The harbour of Vila Real was no more than a river with a strong current that changed direction with the tide. We were able to pick up a mooring buoy at Mason and Barry's yard, where we had more mail waiting for us. Among the letters we received was one from Virginia Carrick giving us the sad news that Lynn had cancer and had been in hospital for an operation. We were both very upset to learn that a good friend was so ill, his treatment was not successful and sadly he had only one more year to live. Lynn had overseen the publication of Dudley's first five books in the United States and Dudley had valued his editorial comments and advice.

We sailed in the morning three days later with a good westerly wind bound for Gibraltar. Off Cadiz at midnight we saw some fishing boats and as we passed Cape Trafalgar in moonlight, the cliffs looked eerie and ghostly as if wanting to give the impression they saw the battle.

In one of his novels many years later, Dudley gave his hero Ramage a small part in the Battle of Trafalgar when Nelson defeated the combined fleets of France and Spain on 21 October 1805. Just before dawn we saw the light of Cape Spartel which was our first sight of Africa. As daylight slowly came we heard the day break that morning: the air throbbed with barely discerned noises coming off the land and with the offshore breeze came the aromatic scents of sage and other herbs. The land was dark against a lightening sky and as the sun rose we saw the Atlas mountains that rolled away southwards from the North African coast. In the early morning sunlight we also saw Tangier, white and odd looking in the distance, seeming to float between the sea and sky.

On the north side of the Strait was the high land of Spain and shortly afterwards, we sighted the Rock of Gibraltar, so impressive and larger than one expects. The Gibraltar Police came out to meet us as we approached the harbour. They guided us in to one of the destroyer pens and as we came alongside they were already on the quay waiting to take our dock lines. A boarding officer joined them and they came on board. After descending the companionway ladder to come below, they found Jane in the quarter berth and tickled her in the stomach.

Our friend Bill would soon join us in Gibraltar to sail with us to the Canary Islands and Barbados. His wife, Patricia, unfortunately stayed behind to look after their business at Oulton Broad. In the meantime, we had a month to prepare for the next leg of our voyage and take on more provisions and nappies. We met Charlie Rodriguez, who was the very helpful agent for the port and we gave him shopping lists for stores (food) and bonded stores (liquor). He arranged for everything to be delivered to the boat, as well as finding us a sail maker. Ashore it was heartwarming to meet people so loyal to Britain and proud of their heritage. We were only too aware that the Rock was a Citadel, a place for siege and war. We found many delightful alleyways named after army terminology, harking back to wars in previous centuries.

Dudley began wondering how he could finish his second Ramage novel on time, some hundred pages of which he had drafted while we were in England. He liked to keep to the delivery date written in the contract with his publisher, but it was a flexible arrangement and he was never hurried to deliver on time. For a few days he did consider staying in Gibraltar for the winter to finish the book, but when the yachts *Dorothea* and *Odd Times* came and tied up near us and both were also bound for the West Indies, we continued with our preparations for the Atlantic crossing.

A very strong gale blew from the south-west which kicked up short, steep waves in the outer harbour and came into the destroyer pens, making all three boats pitch wildly. We moved behind another quay which gave us more protection and a few days later, while visiting the dentist, we bought a copy of *The Daily Telegraph*. There was a story about the gale and we read that a friend in command of a large yacht had gone aground on the coast of Corsica. The paper also had a weather chart and we saw that Hurricane *Carol* was out in the Atlantic and at about on our latitude. However, the Meteorological Office in Gibraltar assured us the system was now a depression and filling in. Bill arrived soon after and on 3 October we motored out of the destroyer pen in the early afternoon and hoisted the mainsail and jib in the outer harbour. It was blowing a brisk Levanter, (an easterly wind), and we reached over to the north African coast to avoid the strong current in the centre of the Strait. We were off Tangier after dark and Cape Spartel by midnight. Bill and Dudley had rigged the yankee on one of the spinnaker poles, and with a clear night and moon, we eased the sheets for a straight run out into the Atlantic.

However, Dudley noted down in the log book the details of the weather forecast the met office at Gibraltar airport gave him: *3 October 1965: Forecast: Low off Cape St. Vincent. Low between Madeira and Gibraltar filling and probably going N. Low 52 N. 22 W. front may come S. Winds: E at first (variable) SW light, going NW-NE."*

Unfortunately, our fair wind did not last the night. As we rounded Cape Spartel the wind veered south-east and became light. We took down the spinnaker pole and, during the last part of the night, cloud began obscuring the stars. It looked like an approaching frontal trough. By the afternoon it became squally with heavy grey clouds and rain, and we could just discern a long swell. Earlier in the morning a small bird, like a wren, visited Golden Dragon and then we sighted a whale. At noon a large brown owl flew round the boat and first settled on the forestay and then the boom. As the weather became even more miserable during the evening, we first dropped the staysail and then the jib.

The wind stayed south-west all that night and next morning. The barograph began rising, but then levelled off. We had hoisted the jib during the morning but Dudley was afraid there was another front approaching. The swell was still very long, coming from the west but later it was being crossed by other swell waves from the north and north-west. For the next eight days we experienced a series of squalls and gales: the Canary Islands lay to the south-west and the wind headed us from that direction, forcing us to beat to windward, tacking first south and south-east towards the African coast, and then west to north-west out into the Atlantic. On our fourth day at sea we had our first gale and hove-to under the staysail only during the night with the wind gusting to 40 knots. At daybreak the wind was still strong, but later in the morning we were sailing again when the wind veered to the west and dropped to a light breeze. We hoisted the mainsail and jib and, for the rest of the day, could lay our course to the Canary Islands, which were then 520 miles away. However within twenty-four hours *Golden Dragon* was hard pressed again with a double-reefed mainsail in heavy seas and squalls. Later, the wind increased with gusts to Force 8 and we had a second gale for the next thirty-six hours. Fortunately the heavy rain tended to flatten the sea a little, but at times it was impossible to look forward in the squalls as the rain cut our faces like knives. By the afternoon the squalls became less and by evening we were sailing on our best course for the Canary Islands. Life on board improved for two days and we were able to dry some clothes.

On our sixth day, an oil tanker passed us in the morning while we were sailing with a clear sky and a few small clouds. During Dudley's watch that night he reported he saw a moon rainbow. The following morning the wind died so we dropped the mainsail: I repaired a seam while Bill put on a patch and Dudley steered *Golden Dragon* under power to charge the batteries. Some threatening clouds appeared towards sunset and the barograph began falling, but it remained calm all night. Two days later and our ninth day at sea the day began well, but by early afternoon we had dropped our mainsail and foresail and were hove-to under the small storm jib as we experienced our third gale.

We stayed dry and comfortable down below – even though we had had spray over the whole boat for many days. When the squalls began again Bill had brought his laundry down below and it was drying in the fo'c'sle. A little later Dudley thought the wind was easing and took a look outside. There were enormous waves with breaking crests. As *Golden Dragon* dropped into the troughs we lost sight of the horizon all around, but she rode the sea comfortably like a seagull. We had now been beating to windward for nine days; it was not at all frightening during the times we were hove-to with the worst of the weather. Dudley and Bill alternated between excitement and fascination: they were scientific, timing the intervals between the foaming crests of the waves and estimating their heights. We also had a handheld anemometer which they held up into the wind to check the wind speed.

With the continual bad weather Jane had remained in her cot. Just before we left Gibraltar we had lashed it to the handrails in the saloon, so she could be with us at all times. The cot swung with the movement of *Golden Dragon* and she was as happy as a cricket, although she was teething with her first two teeth and was fretful at times. She chirped and waved her arms, and made a parrot crowing noise drawing in her breath. She also peeked over the edge of the cot to see us, but the continual movement was too much for her to sit up. Her rattle rolled and rattled in her cot when the motion was more violent. During the worst of *Golden Dragon's* rolling it took two of us to lift her from her cot to feed and change her nappies – one to lift and the other to give steady support.

We also needed two pairs of hands at times in the galley. I made large stews with the tins of meat and vegetables. We ate using bowls rather than plates, and while one person held them to stop them taking off into the air, the other poured the stew. To sleep in our bunks at night we wedged ourselves with plenty of cushions and rolled up blankets. Lying hove-to, *Golden Dragon* drifted slowly at one knot to the north-west. At times the waves hit the hull with a thump and with the rolling through sixty degrees, it felt as though we were on a swing at the end of a yo-yo.

In addition to the wind and sea, there was the continual noise of all the pots and pans in the galley which rattled as we rolled, even though I had wedged small towels everywhere I could.

We were now picking up *Radio Islas Canarias* which had cheerful music and was good for our morale. At dawn on our tenth day at sea, the barograph was rising, but there were still some threatening storm clouds and overcast sky. The wind had eased enough to take down the storm jib and hoist the double-reefed mainsail, staysail and jib. After a rain squall the sky began to clear and we were soon shaking out the reefs. We also hung out some clothes to dry, principally various pairs of Bill's trousers. The log on the stern was now reading 725 miles all to windward. But our spirits fell again one day later, as we had more heavy weather which continued for another two days. We were sailing with the mainsail reefed again and it was our eleventh day at sea. Bill was on watch at one in the morning and went aft to check the reading on the log. He then had trouble with another pair of trousers. A very large sea came on board, soaked Bill and half-filled the cockpit and some came below. Dudley and I jumped out of our quarter berths, rushed up the ladder and heard Bill say somewhat lugubriously: "I feel the time has come to heave-to." The seas were rough and the wind squally, blowing a near gale.

We hove-to for another twelve hours and then began to re-hoist the sails to get under way. When we came to drop the storm jib we found chafe had made several holes and some of the hanks near the top of the sail were worn through. We also found more hanks on the staysail and slides on the mainsail had chafed through and they had to be replaced before we could hoist them and get under way. Lanzarote, the northernmost of the Canary Islands was just forty miles to the south and, although we still had a swell, the wind allowed us to steer the course for the islands. That evening Bill began mending the storm jib, it was our twelfth day and last twenty-four hours at sea.

At noon next day Lanzarote was on our port beam and, as Dudley said, "where it should be!" We sighted Tenerife next morning at dawn, although it was mostly obscured by thick cloud. As we approached the harbour of Santa Cruz that evening, we had difficulty finding the entrance as there were many tankers anchored outside at an angle to shore. We also discovered later, we had sailed through a huge amount of oil.

We were finally anchored in Santa Cruz de Tenerife at ten o'clock that night by the yacht club. We had been sailing to windward for thirteen days over a distance of 1,038 miles. Next day a Swiss boat called *Seewolf* arrived in Santa Cruz, also from Gibraltar and had experienced the same weather as we had. A year later, when we met a Lloyd's insurance broker visiting Grenada, Dudley mentioned that we had sailed through the tail end of Hurricane *Carol* that had been in the Caribbean and then turned north-eastwards to re-cross the Atlantic. He told us that *Carol* had been very costly for his syndicate as they had had to pay out a huge amount of money for damage to property they had insured on the southern coasts of Portugal and Spain. The hurricane had never filled in as predicted in the weather forecast

Ramage at sea . . .

. . . amongst the islands . . .

. . . and The Bitter End.

Happy and content: Dudley, Jane (Victoria), and Kay

Golden Dragon   Playtime on the Atlantic

Finally ashore: Le Pirate, Marigot Bay, F.W.I.

given to us just before we left Gibraltar. This accounted for the heavy swells, squalls and gales we had had for so many days, when we changed sails to hoist the storm jib and then later lay a hull without any sails at all . . .

As we had tacked, beating to windward, each north-westerly tack away from the African coast brought us back closer to Hurricane *Carol*.

A few days later, a yacht called *Marion* from Stockholm came in and later *Lost Horizon* from Madeira with James Dobbs on board, whom we last saw in Oulton Broad. Also moored at the yacht club was a folk boat called *Saltpetre* belonging to Lillegard and Per Arnessen from Norway, who had been living in Santa Cruz on board their boat for a few years. Friends in Tenerife came with our mail and invited us to visit their home a few days later. They lived at Puerto de la Cruz near the Orotavo Valley, which we drove through on our way to their house on the other side of the island.

Tenerife has startling high peaks and deep verdant valleys. After almost two weeks at sea it was wonderful to see the tropical flowers: the red hibiscus, the white angel's trumpet, which hang down like bells, the brightly coloured bougainvillea and tulip trees with their beautiful red flowers. On terraces climbing up and down the hills, there were acres and acres of bananas, the fruit green and hanging down with a deep purple flower at the bottom of their stalks.

As we drove higher and higher we went through pine forests and saw many eucalyptus trees, whose trunks had a peeling bark. Another day, Per and Lillegard drove us up Mount Tiede, the dormant volcano, to the Las Canadas crater just below the peak at 6,200 feet. It was a place of such desolation that we felt we could have been on the moon. There was a fantastic assortment of lava rock, which had cooled and frozen into molten shapes. The old lava streams were still visible at the peak, white in the bright sunlight. The film *One Million Years BC* was being made at that time in the crater and we saw the actors and actresses, the men with long beards, all with long hair and dressed in furry animal skins and 1965 dressing gowns.

The hurricane season was still not over in the Atlantic either. On 20 October we bought a two day old *Daily Telegraph* with the weather chart and could see: *". . . ex-hurricane Elena in 35 degrees W and 38 degrees North, moving NE and filling, with a low between Madeira and Spain."* It was just the same conditions that we had had when we sailed from Gibraltar – only we had Hurricane *Carol* . . .

But the time to leave came closer; by the beginning of November the Caribbean hurricane season would be over and it would be safe to continue our voyage. We had our storm jib repaired and new canvas dodgers made on which Bill painted *Golden Dragon's* name before they were secured each side of the cockpit. The stores we ordered were delivered, including a stalk of bananas which were already ripening, but a second with hard, unripe green bananas arrived on the day of our departure: Our last day in Santa Cruz was busy: we took on board all the water we could carry and then Dudley and Bill scrubbed *Golden Dragon's* waterline to remove the oil stain, while I stitched the tabling on our yankee jib. Lillegard came over with brown bread, baked longer to keep it fresh longer and stayed to help us stow things on board. We were ready late in the afternoon with our two anchors up and stowed on deck and sailed amid waves and farewells from Lillegard and Per on board *Saltpetre.*

We headed south along the coast of Tenerife with a good wind and then sailed out into the Atlantic, with the islands fading astern as nightfall approached. In Dudley's watch, from three to five in the morning, he saw a comet which was like a soft, long feather painted in Chinese white. This comet was the Ikeya-Seki, discovered in July 1965 independently by two amateur astronomers, Kaoru Ikeya and Tsutomu Seki. It was bright and from where we were in the Atlantic near the Canary Islands, we saw it close to the northern horizon several more times just before dawn.

CHAPTER NINE

Voyage to BarbadosNovember 1965

We were now running with the trade winds bound for Barbados; with one jib set to starboard and the other to port. Dudley and Bill rigged a self-steering system with the jib sheets leading to the tiller. If the wind filled one sail more than the other, the sheet pulled the tiller over and with the rudder turning to port or starboard, the correction would bring *Golden Dragon* back on course. Shot cord was added to the tiller on one side to dampen the motion when wind gusts jerked the sheets. We quickly settled down to a comfortable routine.

While we were crossing the shipping route to the Cape Verde Islands we kept 'book' watches of two hours each. One of us on watch could read and every ten minutes or so go up on deck to check the horizon for lights of ships. We also secured our bright paraffin Tilley lamp on the coach roof. There are regular shipping routes across the Atlantic Ocean from Europe and Africa to the Americas, as well as those running down the eastern and western seaboards both sides of the Atlantic. When we sailed from Plymouth to Gibraltar, we had met some ships when we entered the sea lane off Portugal. When we were clear of the Canary and Cape Verde Islands we were sailing the old circular trade wind route taken by ships before the age of steam. Dudley had a manual on board among his navigation books, which gave all the shipping routes round the world. We would not cross another until we came near to the West Indies, when several routes converged and then we would keep watches again.

It was warm and we had the portholes open, but with the lively movement, they had to be fastened back to stop them banging. The deck stayed dry as the waves came up astern to pass under the hull, first the stern rising on the wave and then the bow, causing *Golden Dragon* to pitch lowly and occasionally roll. The trade winds and following seas became more calm as we sailed further out into the Atlantic, but strengthened again as we neared the Antilles. Everything in the galley was firmly wedged again with towels, and the noise we had was mostly the sound of the sea rushing past, the sails occasionally flapping and the thump of one or other of the sheets on deck as they led aft and the creak of the tiller. As soon as it was light, Dudley and I had coffee, Bill had tea or coffee and Jane had her first bottle of milk. Then Bill and Dudley made their daily tour round the deck to check the sheets for chafe as they wound round the winches to lead to the tiller, and to make sure there were no shackle pins lying on deck, warning of a sheet, or spinnaker pole, about to come loose.

Many mornings Bill cooked breakfast and often washed up, while I swept out and cleaned the boat below. During the mornings, Dudley and Bill were busy with 'make and mend', going through all the various things to repair. After our first week at sea we also began scraping the varnish work on deck, which had begun to turn yellow and peel. In the afternoons we relaxed, often sitting on deck just looking, watching the clouds and the sunlight on the sea. Dudley's favourite place to sit was right aft in the helmsman's seat, which had a comfortable back to rest against. We loved catching sight of the flying fish as they left the crest of one wave ahead of our bow and skimmed above the water to land into the next. In the sea their pectoral fins are folded at their sides, but once the fish take flight they open out horizontally to become wings. In a book on marine life we discovered later that the tail fin has a lobe which they use to beat the water to reach a speed of forty miles per hour before taking flight. Once their speed falls to twenty-five miles per hour they drop back into the sea again. We saw the most flying fish when a brisk trade wind was blowing with a fair size sea running, although even in light winds our bow wave sometimes brought the fish flying out of the water. One morning, early in the voyage, Bill woke Dudley with a huge smile on his face. He had three large flying fish in the bucket. The first had landed on the deck near him with a bang which made Bill think a sheet had parted. The second landed on the foredeck and the third came through the companionway as he was below filling the paraffin lamp, just missing Dudley in his bunk. Later we found five more and Bill was appointed fish chef. He measured them to discover the ratio between their unfolded pectoral fins and bodies to allow them to fly and the largest was over thirteen inches long.

Jane had a sleep every morning after breakfast, but by the middle of the morning she was awake again and becoming restless, pressing her face against the netting over her cot, anxious to join in the fun. When the weather was calm enough, I took her on deck with a cup of orange juice and sat with her in my lap in a shady place under the boom for a drink and gurgle session. We soon had too many ripe bananas, so we had them fried for breakfast and baked as deserts at lunch and supper, as well as taking them from the stalk to eat when we were feeling hungry. We finished with a large banana custard when they became too soft. We then had to wait a long time for the second stalk of green bananas to ripen, but by then we had eaten all the other fresh fruit bought in Tenerife.

We had a brisk trade wind the second day at sea and *Golden Dragon* ran 141 miles, but the next day the wind eased so much we had to take down the running sails and their poles. We turned on the engine and ran under power as it was a good opportunity to charge our batteries. Towards evening, a gentle trade wind returned, but it was strong enough to hoist the sails again. It was then that Dudley and Bill found the screws in the fittings at both ends of the spinnaker poles had worked loose and needed some urgent repair, using bolts, jubilee clips and wire strops which we fortunately had on board. We were then able to shackle the clews of the two jibs to the end of their poles. After that they were inspected daily as we continued to have problems with them. This particular day had also begun badly when Bill was cooking the breakfast. He had the eggs and bacon on a plate in the oven to keep warm, while waiting for the tomatoes to cook in the frying pan. Just as he opened the oven door to put some tomatoes on the plate inside, *Golden Dragon* rolled unexpectedly. With the door open, the stove swung down and the plate shot out scattering its contents on to the floor. Unfortunately this happened a second time and Bill burnt his hand as well.

As the wind died later that morning, one of the jibs became wrapped round a crosstree and badly chafed the sixth panel. We lowered both sails and spinnaker poles since we were losing the wind, and while Dudley steered under power, Bill and I repaired the jib, making two patches, using an adhesive tape made for quick repairs to sails and sewing it down. Then, of course, that evening with the wind returning, Dudley and Bill found they had to do more repairs to the spinnaker poles. We continued to have light and variable winds for the next two days, blowing easterly at two to three knots. But sometimes the direction changed from east to south-east so that we decided to re-rig the sheets leading to the tiller, so that it was easier to alter course. We also re-rigged Jane's carry cot, so it could be unclipped and taken outside and put in the shade under the boom when the weather was fine. By the fourth day at sea the log astern read 445 miles. Bill did some laundry with sea water and then waited for some rain to rinse it. He was lucky, because dawn the next morning began with half the sky filled with black clouds to the horizon and the other half looked thundery. After breakfast we were rolling with no wind and then there was torrential rain.

The disappointing progress made us get out the cruising books to find out the weather conditions *Wanderer III*, *Omoo* and *Tzu Hang* had during their Atlantic crossings. *Wanderer III* had nearly a week of light and variable winds and then two days of dead calm when they sailed from Las Palmas. Then they found the trade winds and reached Barbados in twenty-six days. *Omoo* had brisk trade winds for a week after leaving Las Palmas, then had light and variable winds during the middle passage of the crossing and took twenty-three days. The voyage of *Tzu Hang* was much the same and took twenty-four days. Thus encouraged, we put the books away and went on deck to find the wind had come up and soon we were sailing at seven knots. Early in the afternoon of our fifth day at sea the log read 535 miles and we discovered we were ten miles inside the tropics, having crossed the Tropic of Cancer at 23 degrees 27 minutes North. The trade winds remained for a few days in the east-north-east blowing a brisk five to six knots, the following seas became quite spectacular with noisy crests, which were not quite breaking. Taking the sun sight in the late afternoon was difficult for Dudley with *Golden Dragon's* lively motion. To shoot the sun in the western sky with his sextant, he needed to stand at the bow, which rose and fell like a seesaw as the waves rolled under the hull. When the moon became full and then waned, rising and setting later and later, Dudley could take moon sights in the morning and the sun at noon standing amidships where there was less movement and the sun was not yet hidden by the sails. It was not necessary to take sights every day as we had a long way to go, but Bill and I liked seeing our daily progress on the Atlantic chart.

When the pitching and rolling was not too much, Jane was able to play and crawl on the cabin sole aft by the quarter berths and the companionway ladder. We covered the area with a blanket and cushions in case she was rolled over and instead of playing with her toys, she was intrigued with the locker catches, the sea boots and a bucket stowed behind the ladder. When Bill was sitting there wiring a spotlight and had the bosun's drawer open, Jane had a terrific game pulling out the torch batteries, their shiny, golden sides being so irresistible for her.

The sixth day at sea we had run 632 miles: we got out the atlas to see where we were in relation to places on the continents. We were now south of Mexico and Egypt and more or less on the same latitude as Mandalay. The bread we had brought from Santa Cruz was beginning to mildew on the outside, but was still edible. Our meals took on a huge importance and we did have a good variety of food to try to avoid them becoming boring and repetitious. While the fresh tomatoes lasted I sometimes stuffed them with tuna fish mixed with mayonnaise. When we could no longer eat the bread, I began baking, not only bread but flapjacks made with oatmeal, butter and golden syrup; Melting Moments, a soft biscuit with an almond flavour; rock cakes and scones which we ate for our afternoon tea.

My little paraffin stove with two burners and a small oven, hanging in gimbals to swing with *Golden Dragon's* motion, handled it well. We had bought delicious oranges, lemons, grapefruits, melons and apples in Tenerife and also plenty of potatoes, onions, cucumbers and tomatoes which kept well in our little gas refrigerator. Because of the pitching and rolling this did not stay as cold as it did when we were at anchor, but it was cool enough to keep all the produce fresh until we had eaten them all. Of course, there were also the bananas. I greased all the eggs with Vaseline to insulate them from the heat before we sailed. Sometimes we chose the day's menu together. For breakfast we had eggs scrambled or fried with tinned bacon and fried tomatoes, or kippers or tinned sausages and tomatoes, or pancakes with syrup. As well as the stuffed tomatoes with tuna we also had the choice of tinned meats, liver pate or fish which we ate with cucumber, sliced onion, tinned beetroot and other tinned vegetables, such as peas or green beans, followed by fresh fruit. Sausages and mash potatoes were always a favourite for supper, but also we had tinned chicken and beef stews, steak and kidney or chicken pies with pastry on top which always baked well. We also had tins of roast beef, whole chicken and ham, which we tended to open on special days, such as when we entered a new time zone or passed the halfway mark on the chart. When the fresh fruit was finished, we had the choice of tinned fruits as well as tinned puddings, to finish our midday and evening meals.

The best distance run so far was on our eighth day at sea: 164 miles in twenty-four hours. We had sailed 929 miles and had 1,890 miles to reach Barbados. I complained that it was dark late in the morning, which reminded Dudley to adjust the clock on board. We had now sailed west enough to be in Greenwich -2, two time zones and the clock was put back two hours. The following days the wind began dropping until at times it was only blowing a light breeze.

With the calm weather Dudley was able to refill the water tank with some of the extra water we were carrying on deck. We had used 28 gallons in ten days and still had 78 gallons remaining. Bill and I washed our hair this day and Bill did his laundry, hanging his on the port side while Jane's was to starboard. Jane's hair was washed more often during her daily bath and she had had a manicure the day before amid much protest. I had been wearing a bikini for some days and Dudley was often shirtless. Of course, we had all our clothes on board while Bill came with a limited supply, bringing only what his kitbag could carry.

We were now scraping off the old, weathered varnish on deck during the mornings and one afternoon Bill began drawing. Sitting in the helmsman's seat aft, he drew the view forward with the twin jibs on their booms and then did a drawing of the galley. In the meantime, Dudley was delighted to find a copy of *The Sunday Times* which had been used to wrap around the green stalk of bananas to delay their ripening.

As we sailed out into the Atlantic the clouds settled into a regular daily weather pattern. In the early morning there were rows of tiny fluffy, cotton ball shaped trade wind clouds, all in line with the direction of the wind in a great circle all round the horizon. As the hours passed the clouds grew larger and larger until, by afternoon, they were all over the sky, sometimes obscuring the sun.

Another phenomenon we noticed out in the tropical Atlantic was that high altitude clouds came up from the west in the late afternoon, often causing a ring to form around the sun and giving us pale yellow sunsets. This at first made us fear bad weather was approaching, but by nine o'clock in the evening, when going out into the cockpit to check the weather conditions, we found all the clouds had gone and there were millions of stars visible all over the sky. Bill and Dudley were still reading the cruising books and had found Dr. Pye described the same phenomena in his book *Red Mainsail*. Some evenings Dudley and Bill discussed changing *Golden Dragon's* rig – from cutter to ketch – which would make it easier for us to sail her by ourselves. They loved to argue about the merits of their preferred rigs: Bill loved the old gaff rig, while Dudley would only have the modern Bermudan. We also listened to the radio in the evenings and could still pick up the B.B.C. Light Programme.

On our twelfth day at sea, we were half way across the Atlantic; we had sailed 1,442 miles and our position was 18 degrees 05 minutes north and 36 degrees 44 minutes west. We still had a fairly good wind of 5 knots and were making good progress in bright sunshine and a calm, blue sea. We had a special menu this day – melon and kippers for breakfast, salmon and newly baked bread for lunch, while Jane celebrated with a jar of Heinz turkey and vegetables, and there were flapjacks for tea and chicken for supper.

Two days later, we had sailed another two hundred miles. After fixing our position on the chart Dudley told us that if we continued sailing at our average speed, we could reach Barbados in ten days' time. Early one morning, during this part of the voyage, we sighted our first Tropic bird. It had a fat body, a long forked tail and snipe-like wings with black upper edges. It flew with a jerky movement at times and tried to land on our mast, fanning out its tail. The lovely weather continued and the Tropic bird visited us again. While scraping the outside edge of the bulwark forward at the bow, Dudley also noticed two pilot fish had joined us. They have wide blue and white vertical stripes and keep close under the bow. But they regularly whizz ahead about six feet, radius out to the side and then return to the bow seemingly unaffected by *Golden Dragon's* bow wave, unless they are swimming just beyond it. During the last week of our voyage we also saw a large whale which approached us on the port side and apparently went under the boat, because we saw a patch of lighter green water to starboard. But the whale must have continued to dive deep because we did not see it again. The winds began to be light and variable during the next few days, and in the middle of the night a loud bang made us leap from our bunks to rush on deck. *Golden Dragon* had simply hove-to with a very light wind. We hauled her round with the tiller and began sailing again.

Five days later, our seventeenth day at sea, the wind was still light and towards evening high dark, clouds began building up as though warning of bad weather. There were heavy rain squalls all that night that kept us up opening and closing port holes and hatches. We took down the twin running sails and hoisted the mainsail and a jib when the wind veered to south-south-west the next morning. Slowly a close reach became a beat to windward and at noon we changed jibs, taking down the yankee and hoisting a genoa for sailing in light winds. By evening there was so little, we ran the engine for a few hours and steered south until we found some wind. The sky looked menacing, but the night turned out to be fine. We were on watches for the first time for two weeks and Dudley reported seeing many meteors with long, fiery tails in the southern quadrant of the sky during his turn at the tiller.

The next day was Jane's nine month anniversary and she had discovered sucking and blowing through her teeth. Her two upper teeth were now joined by a third lower tooth, and the fourth was just beginning to come through next to it. She also began to hold up her arms with hands clasped over her head like a victorious boxer. She had trouble becoming adjusted to the changes of the time zones, as we had now put the clock back three hours and she was waking early.

With the light and variable winds and *Golden Dragon's* slower progress, Bill was fussing about how long the voyage was taking. He was, of course, worried about leaving Patricia alone to take care of the business at home. Barbados did still seem a long way away. We continued to keep watches, sailing with the mainsail and jib in the light airs, but fortunately the trade winds returned within another twenty-four hours. There was trouble again with the spinnaker poles when we began hoisting the twin running sails and more repairs were necessary.

As we drew closer to the West Indies we began to pick up short wave U.S. domestic stations loud and clear, but found there was more advertising and self-publicity than actual news bulletins. On the twentieth day at sea, we could finally move from the chart of the whole East and West Atlantic and use the Western Atlantic Coastal chart for plotting our course. Our latitude was 16 degrees 03 minutes north and the longitude was 48 degrees 10 minutes west, making us 640 miles from Barbados. The next day we put the clock back one hour for the last time, so that Greenwich was four hours ahead of us. We were now in the time zone of the Eastern Caribbean and we had already begun keeping watches again. Early one morning during this last part of our voyage we saw a flock of petrels flying low over the waves, ahead of *Golden Dragon's* bow. It is possible they were Wilson's Petrels which are oceanic birds, flying far from land and at certain times of the year are sometimes seen in the West Indies.

The trade winds also increased now that we were in the western Atlantic and not too far from our landfall. We were sailing more than one hundred miles a day with *Golden Dragon's* motion becoming very lively. The swell made taking the afternoon sight difficult for Dudley with the sails getting in the way of the sun as well. The French merchant ship, the *Saint Claire Deville* of Dunkerque passed us close to leeward on her way perhaps to Martinique and the crew on deck waved when they saw Jane in Dudley's arms. Seeing this ship really told us Barbados was not far away and I was sorry we would soon be there. We were having a wonderful voyage in our own small world, completely self-sufficient and part of me did not want it to end. I could have stayed at sea a little while longer.

In the afternoon of our twenty-third day at sea we had a strong east wind and fairly heavy sea running, first lifting our stern and then the bow. Suddenly we saw some fins sticking out of the crest of a swell astern and then were surrounded by at least two dozen dolphins, playing around us. We were making six knots or more and riding on the waves, while the dolphins swam under the boat and often dived ahead of us. After the noon sight that day Dudley had marked our position on the chart; we were 320 miles from Barbados and we had our last full 24 hours at sea. We picked up Radio Trinidad and enjoyed the music and listening to a most amiable young woman who was working without a script.

On our last day at sea, Dudley expected to see Ragged Point lighthouse just before dawn. If the visibility was good the light should be seen from twenty-one miles. We had kept book watches all night, with Dudley on deck between three and five a.m. Bill followed for the next two hours. At eight, land was sighted ahead and when I came up on deck shortly after, I saw the lighthouse to starboard, and with his sextant Dudley determined it was seven miles away. I had been on deck with Bill for a while earlier that morning, but neither of us saw the light before dawn. We sailed along the south coast of Barbados without having to change course and began to drop the sails off Needham Point, before turning into Carlisle Bay at Bridgetown. The coast looked very green and as Bill commented it was rather like the Isle of Wight, because we could not see any palm trees, only pines. We anchored in front of the Aquatic Club and finally did see some palm trees. The Customs and Immigration officers soon came out in their smart launch and uniforms: the formalities did not take long and it was obvious they were used to yachtsmen and their families coming in from an Atlantic crossing.

A boat called *Symphony* was there with Ed Shute and Patrick Blackwell on board. They were delivering her from Porto Santo Stefano, which was where we last saw them. *Lost Horizon* with James Dobbs was also there and he told us it took him twenty-three days from Tenerife. Reporters came out and took photos of us and later in the afternoon a man brought out a large cardboard box of mail from Ian Gale, the Editor of *The Barbados Advocate*. He was still the correspondent for *The Evening News* and before leaving England Dudley had written to tell him we were coming to Barbados and to ask if he would accept and hold our mail. There was also an invitation to dinner that evening.

When we went ashore the first thing we felt was the humid heat, and were also intrigued by the wonderful watery notes of the little tree frogs, which we could not see. But we did see for the first time the tall croton bushes, with their large colourful leaves, mottled yellow and green, red, and deep crimson.

The next morning, we took a taxi to the centre of Bridgetown. Our photographs and story were on the front page of Ian's paper and tourists recognised us in the street. A Canadian stopped Bill and me to congratulate us; in a shop Dudley bought two island cotton shirts, and when the manager recognised us, he gave Jane a present of a blouse. We saw many island schooners in the Carenage, but there certainly was no room there for yachts. We returned to the Royal Barbados Yacht Club for lunch, but it was too formidable with our bags of shopping and a baby in tow. We had also bought some fruit and avocado pears from a street seller, so only Dudley went in to sign the visitors' book. We then went down the Club's garden to the beach, climbed a wall and went to the Aquatic Club, where we had lunch. We ordered hamburgers and chips, which came with pieces of avocado pear, and all for under $3. The next evening Ian and his wife, Margaret, came to supper on board *Golden Dragon* and while we were sitting in the cockpit in the dark, a yacht came in under power at a furious speed and anchored. Next morning, we discovered she was *Rose Rambler* with our old friend Humphrey Barton on board with his two girl crew. Hum was working on something in the cockpit and as we came alongside, Dudley said in a loud voice: "What do you think you were doing, coming in to anchor like that last night?" Hum's head jerked up and then his face was wreathed in smiles: "Bill! Dudley! Kay!" and without a pause said, "Run out of cigarettes, old boy, the girls needed hairdos. They are ashore now at the hairdressers!"

Bill left that afternoon to fly back to England and we were sorry to see him go. He was always the perfect crew, an experienced sailor, always calm and fitted in so well.

Barbados is one of the few coral islands in the Caribbean, almost all the others being of volcanic origin. The island lies on its own out in the Atlantic some sixty miles to windward of the rest of the island chain. From Trinidad and Grenada northwards to Martinique the islands are known collectively as the Windward Islands, while the Leeward Islands begin at Dominica and extend to the Virgin Islands.

One afternoon after Bill left, Ian and Margaret took us for a drive around the island. We saw low and pleasant rolling hills and for the first time many trees so different from those in England: mahogany, ficus, papaya, breadfruit and mango and the casurina pines. The bright and dark greens of all the foliage contrasted so vividly against the deep blue of the sea. There were also large areas of sugar cane, much of it still on the original plantations with their old derelict stone windmills. But when the cane is cut these days it is taken to be crushed at the factory to become sugar molasses and then to the distillery for the popular Barbados Mount Gay Rum. We had read that the first farmers to settle in Barbados came from England in 1625 in the merchant ship *Olive*, but saw a plaque that said the first settlement was founded in 1605.

The east side of the island was much cooler with the trade winds blowing always on the coast. The air was filled with spray from the Atlantic waves rolling in and breaking on the coral reefs. We could see why the visibility was bad and why we did not see Ragged Point light before dawn when we were approaching Barbados on our last day at sea. We enjoyed seeing the various colours of the bougainvillea flowers, purple, lilac, red, fuchsia, pink, orange, white and yellow. The poinsettias were just beginning to bloom for the Christmas season with their bright red leaves around tiny yellow flowers. Another day, Ian and Margaret took us to the

Annual Show, where we saw members of families all decked out in the same colour. Iridescent green was popular that year and the children looked like bridesmaids ready for a wedding. We saw a group of horsemen and women playing a game of musical chairs. In the vegetable and fruit section of the show, there were horse radish, sweet peppers, and pimentos, egg plants, carrots, squash, ginger both dried and fresh, potatoes, cassava, dasheen or eddoes which are the large edible root that comes from the elephant's ear plant, also known as taro; yams, corn on the cob, and pumpkins. At the prize giving the largest pumpkin was not the winner, but the one considered most attractive.

Among the fruit we saw for the first time was the large grapefruit, called ugli fruit, and papaya, known as pawpaws in the islands. There were limes, lemons and oranges, plantains and many varieties of bananas, among them the small finger bananas, the apple bananas with a pink skin, as well as the long lacatans which are exported to England. In the livestock section there were the tropical breed of sheep with black bellies that have hair instead of thick wool, goats, cattle and pigs. There was a photographic and art show, and we were amazed to see the variety of goods made in Barbados. In an exhibit of the Barbados Industries we saw shoes, handbags, and clothes made from Sea Island Cotton grown in Barbados, house bricks and tiles, cigarettes, paint and, of course, the Barbados Mount Gay Rum. From the coconut came copra, oil for margarine, soap and body lotion, the coconut meat to eat and the milk to drink. The Bajan accent sounded soft and musical to our ears, and the people had a charming way of speaking. In the market and in stores I was asked: "What do you wish for, mistress?"

During our last week in Barbados Dudley got out and read the first 100 pages of his second Ramage novel which he had written before we left England. He now wanted to begin writing again and felt he could not delay work on it much longer. During the voyage he had noted down an idea for a Ramage story based on the La Guaira part of his book *The Black Ship*.

The anchorage at Bridgetown for yachts is an open roadstead where, during the months of December to April, large swells occasionally roll in to make it uncomfortable for living on board. The island trading and commercial vessels had a quay to come alongside in the Carenage, but we had seen it was not suitable for yachts. We were sorry to say goodbye to Margaret and Ian, who had invited us to come to their Christmas dinner. But Dudley wanted to reach Grenada before the Christmas trade wind began blowing hard, making it more difficult for just the two of us on board to sail *Golden Dragon*. We set sail for Grenada in the afternoon of 16 December with the mainsail and jib set. We had a broad reach with more sea than wind and later hoisted the staysail, booming the jib out to port. At daybreak, the following morning we saw Grenada on the horizon ahead of us.

CHAPTER TEN

Grenada 1965–68

As we approached Grenada we could see the high land in the centre of the island had sharp, craggy peaks, covered with tropical rain forest which reminded us of Tenerife, the hills and valleys covered with the rich green foliage and surrounded by the azure sea and sky. As we sailed along the south coast we saw deep inlets like fiords, the hillsides thickly wooded with shrubs and trees, and far inside, mangroves grew in the shallow water. Within a few months, these inlets would be our favourite anchorages.

The yacht anchorage in St. George's was in a lagoon just to the south of the Carenage and also almost completely surrounded by steep hillsides. There were bananas and coconut palms growing near the shore with breadfruit, mango and papaya trees behind them. At a higher elevation there were young mahogany and teak trees. On the northern side of the lagoon the houses began on the outskirts of St. George's, and behind a low promontory we could see the town with a church at the top of a hill which rose from the Carenage. On the seaward side of this hill there is a fort guarding the entrance to St. George's which has an advantageous view along the coast to the north and south, and also the hospital built lower down on the south side. The buildings around the Carenage have red roofs and are painted white. But elsewhere they are often built with a warm red brick, which had originally come from England as ballast in merchant ships. These were put ashore leaving the holds empty to receive the barrels of sugar molasses to be shipped back to England. At higher elevations on the island, bordering the rain forest, there are nutmeg and banana plantations, and also cocoa. The pods of the cocoa beans turn from green to yellow, orange, red and finally purple when ready to be harvested. We later saw some beans laid out in the sun to ferment, giving off a strong pungent smell, reminding us of our days in Italy in late summer with the smell of pressed grapes at harvest time. Some sugar cane is still grown on the island for the rum distillery as well as sugar for use on the island.

There were bright colours everywhere in Grenada, as well as the flowers, the Grenadians were always decked out gaily, red being a favourite colour and even the buses, painted green, red and yellow with names on the rear, such as "Humming Bird," and "Victory B". It was not uncommon to see a bed on top of a bus, oil drums or anything else. In town, women balanced large bundles of wood on their heads or a stalk of bananas, or a bucket of fish on their way to and from the market. At the Carenage sometimes we saw a huge turtle, alive on its back, being wheeled away in a cart and there were always wooden trading schooners tied up at the quay, some loading rum and other merchandise to smuggle on a night run to Venezuela. We learned new phrases used by the Grenadans: 'the bus left me' (I missed the bus), 'gone to come back', 'doan mash it up man' (don't break it), 'it caught a hole' (a sock or shirt had a hole), 'give a person a drop' (a lift in a car), 'to wait on someone for something', 'doan humbug me man,' or 'he vexed me, man', and 'I go to catch them books, man', meaning the books were going to be fetched.

At our berth at the marina we were awakened each morning by the harsh braying of donkeys, sheep or goats bleating, cows lowing, cocks crowing and dogs barking. After sunset we heard the chorus of tree frogs. We found *Hierro* anchored in the lagoon and just before Christmas we went for a drive with Annie and Louis, climbing up through the rain forest and over the high ridge in the centre of the island, where we passed the crater lake of the dormant volcano. Every valley seemed to have its river or stream running down to the sea, where sometimes we saw women washing their clothes using large boulders in the water. By Pearls airport an aeroplane took off and then a man on his donkey crossed the runway. We picnicked on a deserted beach on the east coast in the shade of the palm trees where two young boys found us. They climbed one of the trees to pick some coconuts, which they cut open with machetes, charging 10 cents for each one. For the first time we drank fresh coconut milk, and as the nuts were large but still immature, the flesh inside was a soft jelly and very sweet. The sea broke on reefs some hundred yards out and the noise frightened Jane at first. The wet sand from extra large waves that rolled in occasionally bothered her because it was cold and the sand moist against her skin.

We stayed in the marina of Grenada Yacht Services, always known as GYS, until early in the New Year of 1966, joining in the social life and making new friends. In the middle of January, *Golden Dragon* was hauled out on the slip at the marina to scrub off the hull below the waterline and painted with a coat of anti-fouling paint. As soon as we were launched back into the water, we left St. George's and sailed to Prickly Bay, on the south coast of the island. There was quite a large community of young families and retired people living in houses on the hills surrounding Prickly Bay, many of them from Britain. Just behind the beach we found the Calabash Hotel, owned and run by Brian and Aminga Thomas. They had four young children, often in the charge of Norah, a young Grenadan woman. In the late afternoon many families came to the beach after the heat in the middle of the day, so Jane always found friends to play with.

During the three years we stayed there we also met many interesting people who stayed at the hotel during the winter holiday season. One guest, Jack Frye, swam out to *Golden Dragon* from the beach and we invited him on board. He told us about his plans for building his new yacht and two nights later he invited us to dinner at the hotel. It turned out to be a very amusing evening because we shared a table with Dudley Moore and Peter Cook, both of whom were in *Beyond the Fringe* at the time. Jane came ashore with us and spent the evening with Norah and the Thomas children. There were plenty of fish in the bay and sometimes, especially when friends came by, we hung our paraffin lamp over the side on a boathook to attract the jacks and pompano. With rods and line we caught many and they soon went into the frying pan. We hired a young Grenadan boy called William, who was only sixteen years old at the time, but already a good worker and the years he was with us he was busy keeping up *Golden Dragon's* paint and varnish work. He was a quiet and tactful boy and loved going spear fishing with Dudley, whom he called 'Skip.' There were some days when he did not appear, through illness or the need for him to take care of his family's plot of land. We gave William one of our folding bicycles that we had brought with us from England, so he could cycle out to us in Prickly Bay and, later, to Caliviny Harbour which became our anchorage for the months of the hurricane season.

Dudley now had to resume writing, but before returning to the second Ramage book, he fulfilled his promise to write the second of two articles for Purnell's *History of the Second World War* magazine published weekly in ninety-six editions. While we were in Ramsgate he had already adapted one from his *The Battle of the River Plate*. For the second article he condensed and rewrote the battle in his book, *73 North*, between five destroyers escorting convoy JW 51B to Murmansk and a German battle group of two battleships and six destroyers. As soon as this article was finished and posted he began writing the next Ramage.

It was not long before a cable came to the Calabash from Sandy Richardson at Lippincott's asking how the next novel was progressing. Dudley had still not drafted a complete synopsis for the book and so he quickly did this and sent it off. The book, which would be called *Ramage and the Drumbeat*, with Ramage in difficulties off the eastern coast of Spain, but when he eventually reaches Gibraltar, he is sent with orders to warn Sir John Jervis that the Spanish Fleet in Cartagena will soon be sailing to break the blockade of Cadiz. Commodore Nelson joins Sir John with his squadron and the stage is set for the Battle of Cape St. Vincent. Dudley had all the background material he needed as we had sailed past Cape St. Vincent in a light wind and stayed several weeks in Gibraltar. Ramage sails from Gibraltar with a 'Levanter' blowing and runs into a full gale while trying to reach Sir John Jervis, just as we did in *Golden Dragon* when we ran into a series of gales on our way to the Canary Islands.

Work on the book went slowly because Dudley found it hard to write during the day. With a small child on board who was becoming noisier and more mobile, I was spending more time ashore on the beach with her. Dudley's work was also interrupted by trips ashore in the dinghy to the Calabash jetty. There were the trips to collect William early in the morning and return him ashore in the evening when his day's work was finished. Then there were the trips to take Jane and me to the beach, one in the morning and the second when she woke from her afternoon nap. She was too small at the time for me to run the dinghy on my own as I had to hold on to her: it would not have been safe running the outboard motor and coming alongside the jetty at the same time. At the end of the afternoon when William went home, Dudley sometimes stayed with us on the beach, met and talked to the hotel's guests, or went snorkelling. In spite of his frustration and while working out the details of Ramage's role at the Battle of St. Vincent, Dudley decided to draft a long technical article on preparing a yacht for an Atlantic crossing for the sailing magazine *Yachting World*. Later it was published in four parts. He then persuaded me to write about the provisioning of *Golden Dragon* and an account of our Atlantic crossing, which also appeared in the magazine in several instalments.

After this short break, Dudley did manage to make some better progress with the book. In early July he received a letter from Barley Alison complaining that the second Ramage had not yet arrived. But by this time the book was going well and Dudley was worrying it was going to be too long. The first draft was soon finished and while I was typing the manuscript, during Jane's afternoon nap and in the evenings after she was tucked away in her bunk, Dudley went through it again, listing the contents of each page to see where he could make some cuts.

While we still had *Golden Dragon* at the marina in St. George's at the beginning of the year, I had often gone with a friend to the beach in the afternoons, either at Grand Anse or a little beach close by. Jane picked up small shells she found on the sand and, like all babies, put them in her mouth. This drew our attention to how diverse and beautiful they are, so we began keeping them. The little beach nearest to the marina was closed off from the sea by a rocky barrier reef with a shallow pool inside which had many colonies of hermit crabs. There were thousands of little shells crowded together under rocks, each having a small crab tucked inside. At the marina we soon met Maurice Nicholson, the skipper of *Eleuthera* who was a keen shell collector. Maurice was interested to see what we were finding and recommended a book to help us to identify everything we found. So our passion for collecting seashells began. While snorkelling some afternoons, to have a break from writing, Dudley carried his spear gun and sometimes returned with a lobster. He also began to collect seashells eaten by octopus and left in piles outside their holes on the reefs. We did learn to use scuba later on and had all the apparatus on board. But we very rarely took it with us on our shelling expeditions. The equipment was heavy and needed to be rinsed off afterwards with fresh water, and a plentiful supply of water was not always available. Jane was later able to snorkel with us. She was floating in the sea from a very early age, wearing inflatable arm bands and by the age of two and a half had a little snorkel mask. At first she tended to swim under the water and come up for air like a little dolphin, but by the age of three her lungs had grown to give her enough buoyancy to stay above.

Until we bought a car we had to take *Golden Dragon* round to St. George's every few weeks to fill up with diesel, petrol for the generator and outboard engine, and grocery shopping. We were able to get water in Prickly Bay. Buying a car was not a complete solution because it was second-hand and had its own problems. On a visit to St. George's we met Fred and Joan Georgeson from California, who became part of our lives. Fred retired when he sold his wine business and they went to England to have their boat *Alano* built at Falmouth. They cruised in the Mediterranean before they sailed to the West Indies and now they chartered *Alano* for the twelve weeks of the winter season between Christmas and Easter, carrying two guests up and down the island chain to help pay for the expense of keeping up *Alano*, and give them a little more income. Joan became the adopted grandmother for Jane, whose own grandparents were far away in England and Australia.

We also met Frank Casper, who had just sailed round the world on his own. Frank was originally from New York where as a young man he worked for Thomas Edison on storage batteries. He became a good friend, popping in and out of our lives for many years. After his circumnavigation he cruised the Caribbean every winter and each May sailed across the Atlantic to Mashfords Yard at Cremyll, where *Elsie* was hauled out, her bottom repainted and yearly maintenance carried out. He then sailed slowly south to the Canary Islands to re-cross the Atlantic in November. Frank was a very good chess player and played with Fred Georgeson when *Alano* was in port. Frank always won and, much to Fred's irritation, would never explain the moves he made to checkmate him. Later on, Fred taught Dudley to play. So the general rule was Frank beat Fred and Fred beat Dudley.

Later that summer we received a letter from Sandy Richardson with the news that he was leaving J.B. Lippincott to go to Doubleday, one of the largest publishing houses in New York. This was a severe blow for Dudley as *Ramage and the Drumbeat* was nearing completion and he would have a stranger dealing with all the editorial details. But in September, once installed at Doubleday, Sandy wrote offering Dudley a two-book contract. He indicated that Lippincott's sales of *Ramage* had been disappointing, and at Doubleday Sandy could use the company's larger sales resources to do a better job. After considering Sandy's offer, Dudley wrote to Virginia Carrick to ask her for advice. Her reply came seventeen days later in which she said three things: Dudley should leave Lippincott's, that he needed an agent to represent him in all his future dealings with publishers, and that it should not be difficult to obtain the release. Dudley wrote to Lippincott's the day after receiving Virginia's letter, asking to be released from his contracts with them for *Ramage and the Drumbeat* and one other future *Ramage* novel.

A letter from Joseph Lippincott came in reply two weeks later, saying he would like to discuss the release and that Bob Hill, the new editor who had been appointed in Sandy's place, would come to Grenada and hoped Dudley would be satisfied with his explanations.

In the meantime, Dudley received a message from George Weidenfeld through Barley Alison that Doubleday was a 'book factory', too big and not the right publisher for him. Unfortunately,

Dudley did not pay enough attention to this advice and some years later came to regret his decision to follow Sandy to Doubleday. George Stevens took over the correspondence from Joseph Lippincott and letters passed between them during the next three months. It caused him much anxiety and distraction from his work, and as Dudley became more angry, so did the tone of his letters. There was a rancorous exchange in which he claimed he was being victimised while Stevens accused him of making threats. Bob Hill did come to Grenada in the middle of December. Dudley found him very pleasant and they talked on the beach almost all day, but there was no explanation as to why Sandy had left Lippincott's. It appeared Hill thought the tone of George Stevens' letters was wrong, and he confirmed Ivan von Auw would be the best agent for Dudley. He also warned against book factories and did not consider Doubleday the right publisher for the Ramage books. This last comment did put a seed of doubt about Sandy in Dudley's mind, but he was so angry with Lippincott's at this point that he continued to press for a release. Bob Hill's comment about 'book factories' also made me a little uneasy and uncertain. It was the second time I had heard this phrase during this contention with Lippincott's: Barley Alison had also warned Dudley, but the rift with Lippincott's had become so great now, that there was no way Dudley would climb down and agree to stay with them. At the time the idea of going to a large publisher seemed attractive, which would have more resources to publicise and push the sales of Dudley's books. Besides, Sandy Richardson had become a friend and we both trusted him at the time.

Near the end of the year, Dudley sent copies of all the correspondence to Virginia, who commented that George Stevens had messed it up. His letters had provoked Dudley and made him more angry. Virginia consulted Ivan von Auw at Harold Ober & Associates, who became Dudley's agent, and also with Donald Newborg, a family friend, who was also her lawyer. Early in January 1967, Virginia wrote to say that Lippincott's were expecting Dudley to come to New York rather than continuing with letters and telephone calls from Grenada. Dudley flew to New York late in January and the final negotiations were concluded, on condition Dudley withdrew his allegations of victimisation. Before he returned home to Grenada very relieved it was all over, Sandy offered Dudley a contract for two Ramage novels and one for the account of Nelson's battle at Copenhagen, the research for which we had done some six years earlier while we were still living in Italy.

Late in August, during the 1966 hurricane season, there was suddenly a full warning issued for the islands of Dominica, Guadeloupe and all the Leeward Islands. This was followed in September by Hurricane *Inez* which crossed Guadeloupe and killed twenty-two people. With all this hurricane activity, we sailed *Golden Dragon* to a deep bay further to the east, where we would have perfect shelter from any storms. Our hurricane anchorage was in Caliviny Harbour, a circular basin at the inner end of Chemin Bay. It was partially closed off by a long sand spit, but there was enough water to navigate through a channel and we found very good holding ground inside to anchor.

The eastern side of the bay was part of Westerhall Point, a peninsular of land that was being developed and already had some attractive houses built there. There was one home close to the water inside Caliviny Harbour with a jetty and we soon met the American couple living there. They had a small fishing boat on a mooring nearby and we were invited to use their shower at the bottom of their garden and close to the jetty. So often in the Caribbean, wherever we went we received many kindnesses such as this; to have showers and obtain water.

We also met the owners of the development of Westerhall Point, who were both architects. Beres Wilcox designed the exteriors of the houses and landscaped the gardens, while Kari designed the interiors. They sold their parcels of land with certain guidelines and designed most of the houses that were built there. They had a fine collection of Caribbean seashells and very soon we were going out together every Sunday with a picnic to a beach by car or with our dinghy if the place was inaccessible by road. Beres was often as stressed by his work as Dudley was with his and we had a day of relaxation together with their two sons and Jane, snorkelling and collecting shells.

While clearing another piece of land the Wilcoxes owned, they found the remains of an old fort on the point of Fort Jeudy, which Dudley discovered had a historical reference in an 1861 copy of the *West India Pilot*, which claimed Count D'Estaing had landed there in 1779 with 3,000 French troops. However, other accounts say D'Estaing attacked Hospital Hill in St. George's. Grenada was first settled by the Governor of Martinique, who landed with 200 men in 1650. The indigenous people living on the island, the Carib Indians who came originally from South America, did not take kindly to the settlement. There were many skirmishes until the final battle, when the Caribs were driven to the northern end of the island where they committed mass suicide by jumping off the cliffs into the sea at a place now called Sauteurs. At the end of the Seven Years War Grenada was ceded to Britain at the Treaty of Paris in 1762. After the rebellion in America when Britain lost her northern colonies, a naval war broke out between France and Britain and this was when the French forces invaded and occupied Grenada in 1779 under the command of Count D'Estaing. But four years later, at the Treaty of Versailles in 1783, the Independence of America was recognised and Grenada was returned again to Britain.

We had by now bought another car which was not quite as old as the first. But it was always necessary to have a passenger in the front seat to hold on to the door to prevent it from flying open when rounding a bend in the road. *Alano* joined us in Calivigny and Fred was always happy to go with Dudley to shop in St. George's and collect their mail. But there was one occasion when there were other difficulties: the car would not start and some men cheerfully gave Dudley a push. Then a tyre burst and, not finding a wheel jack to raise the car, the same men held up the car while someone changed the wheel.

We stayed in Calivigny until the middle of November. During this time *Alano* had joined us; while Fred was painting and preparing *Alano* for the next winter charter season and Dudley was working on his book, Joan and I went to the beach with Jane most afternoons. Sometimes when it was very hot, Dudley also came to go snorkelling and look for seashells. Jane was approaching her second birthday at that time and was swimming well with her inflatable arm bands. She was also talking in whole long sentences, but the problem was we could not understand what she was saying. With her sharp young eyes though, she was good at finding seashells as we walked along the beach.

Ramage and the Drumbeat was not finally finished until early in 1967. It was then that we received a letter from Barley Alison telling us she was leaving Weidenfeld's and asked us to book a room for her at the Calabash hotel at Easter. However, before Barley's visit, Sandy Richardson came to Grenada and also stayed at the Calabash. He was joined by Ivan von Auw, who brought the new contracts with Doubleday and they went through the details with Sandy, sitting in deck chairs under the coconut palms on the beach with cool drinks in hand. Ivan insisted on several changes and when Sandy agreed, Dudley signed them. That evening we were all invited to dinner on board *Alano* where Fred and Joan gave us a splendid dinner and produced two bottles of champagne. As Ivan flew back to New York, Barley arrived from London. She told us there was much unhappiness at Weidenfeld's and another member of the staff had already resigned. Barley was making plans to have her own publishing company. During the remaining days of her holiday we took her to our favourite beaches. Barley had collected seashells on a beach in the Oman, so she was thrilled to go snorkelling and collect shells with us.

Near the end of April we left Prickly Bay with William on board for a holiday cruise. We sailed in company with *Alano*, anchoring for the first night in Halifax Harbour on the west coast north of St. George's. Next day we sailed northwards to Bequia, stayed one night and then sailed on to Cumberland Bay in St. Vincent. We continued northwards to St. Lucia and then reached Fort de France in Martinique, where Fred and Joan had charter guests to pick up. We remained there for several days, enjoying the large town, French cuisine, bread, patés and cheeses. Fort de France also has a wonderful fruit and vegetable market, with a section at one end for flowers. Here we saw the beautiful bird of paradise flowers, anthuriums and ginger plants with their bright orange, red and purple colours.

We then began a leisurely cruise southwards to return to Grenada. Leaving Martinique we sailed in company with *Alano* to St. Lucia and after clearing Customs in Castries, we sailed together to Marigot Bay. Inside the entrance there is a narrow strip of land lined with a row of coconut palms which partly closes off a circular lagoon beyond where we dropped our anchor. The surrounding hillsides are steep and completely covered with coconut palms. There was one large house overlooking the entrance and two hotels close to the water's edge on either side of the bay. The only sound to break the peace at night, was the faint thrumming of their generators. After *Alano* left with their guests we stayed several more days, snorkelling, and enjoying the atmosphere. We bought a fish trap made from split cane and as the days passed we lived on the fish we caught and collected shells. Dudley photographed and sketched the bay and later used it for Ramage's action against the privateers in his next novel, *Ramage and the Freebooters*, adding this idea to those he had already noted down for this book.

We reluctantly left St. Lucia and continued south to Kingston in St. Vincent, where we took water on board and went shopping. The anchorage was an open roadstead in those days, but being on the lee side of the island, was fairly sheltered. We found Kingston a pleasant town with wide streets, old stone houses and cobblestone pavements. We sailed next to Bequia, the first of a group of islands and islets called the Grenadines which are administrated by St. Vincent, and anchored in Admiralty Bay. Here we lingered for a few more days, enjoying visits ashore. We found the semi-circular bay a well-protected anchorage, lined with palm trees and houses at one end.

Compared to the other Windward Islands with their high, craggy peaks of several thousand feet and rain forests, Bequia is a small island of just seven square miles and the two highest points are less than eight hundred feet. But in the early nineteenth century the island had nine sugar plantations and also grew coffee, indigo for its dye, and some cotton. During the last quarter of that century a whaling station was established on Petit Nevis, a small uninhabited island less than a mile from Friendship

Bay on the south coast of Bequia. As a result, boatbuilding also flourished on the island and the old traditional wooden boats are still built on the beach under the palm trees in Admiralty Bay, all done by eye without line drawings. Many men still depend on the sea for their livelihood, working on board trading vessels and fishing boats.

While we were still in Admiralty Bay, the fishermen often rowed round the anchorage in the early evenings and came to offer us lobsters at eighty cents a pound. We then sailed the short distance to enter the Tobago Cays where we anchored in the lee of Petite Rameau, a tiny islet with a pretty beach. We found the water amazingly clear and a beautiful jade colour, because the sea bed was covered with many pale green stones. The Tobago Cays are a collection of many reefs and islets with the larger islands of Mayero and Union a short distance to the west, while Palm Island and Petit St. Vincent are to the south. On the eastern side there is a long reef which protects the whole area from the Atlantic Ocean beyond. The reefs and channels inside can be picked out by their different colours: the deep water a beautiful dark blue, which turns to turquoise as it shoals, becoming pale blue and then aquamarine where the water is very shallow, while the dark brown areas warn the coral heads are very close to the surface.

The water around Grenada was never so clear, and in April as the hurricane season approaches, heavy rains begin falling in Venezuela and other countries bordering the north-east coast of South America. As the Orinoco River floods a huge tongue of muddy water flows out into the Atlantic and drifts northwards with the current around Trinidad and reaches Grenada before the sediment has completely fallen away. The rain begins in late May in Grenada and the rivers on the island also bring more sediment down to the sea. William really enjoyed snorkelling and spear fishing with Dudley, always keeping close, but a little behind him. We also snorkelled in shallower water looking for shells, enjoying the variety of corals and the smaller reef fish darting in and out among them. The hard corals grow to huge sizes, some round with a pattern like a human brain, others smaller clumps like cauliflower heads. We saw beds of finger corals and the large branching staghorn and elkhorn corals, just like the huge antlers on the animals they are named after. The colours range from dark brown to a lighter orange brown, light beige and a yellowish green, with the fire coral which can burn a finger if touched, a mustard yellow edged with white. There were also the soft corals including the sponges and gorgonians, in the shape of tall tubes and large vases and the more delicate yellow or mauve sea fans, waving slowly in the current. Among all this are the fishes, black and yellow, or yellow and blue, green, orange and black, some an iridescent blue sheltering close to the coral and sea anemones.

Soon we had to continue southward to return to Grenada and Cariacou was the last island we visited. This island is part of Grenada and we were able to do our customs and immigration entry formalities at Hillsborough before we returned to Prickly Bay. Cariacou is seventeen miles north-east of Grenada and is a quiet rural island, twenty-one miles long and twelve miles wide. It has been said there are as many goats and sheep as there are people, about six thousand, living on the island. There is a large fishing fleet of small sailing boats and, like Bequia, traditional wooden boats are built at Windward on the north-east coast. We anchored for two days in Tyrrel Bay at the south end of the island where we were completely alone, without any sign of habitation. When we went exploring with our dinghy into a small lagoon at the northern end of the bay we found a wooden schooner abandoned in the mangroves.

With all the accumulated mail that had arrived during our absence, Dudley did not begin working again until the end of the month, when he read through his Copenhagen notes and two days later wrote the introduction for the book. Also, as ideas for the plot took shape for the next *Ramage* novel, Dudley began writing a little of it each day. For a while he tried working on both books, but early in September, with the novel developing well, he put Copenhagen to one side. The novel was published in England with the title *Ramage and the Freebooters*, while in the United States it was called *The Triton Brig*. Ramage is at Spithead during the Great Mutiny and he is ordered to sail his new command, The Triton Brig to the West Indies.

Fred Georgeson lent Dudley a book on alcoholism published by Alcoholics Anonymous (A.A.) and was able to help Dudley a great deal on the subject because Fred was an alcoholic himself. He regularly attended their meetings whenever he could join a group. The chess games with Fred gave Dudley the idea for Captain Ramage to have a drunken surgeon on board and order him to play the game with Southwick to keep him occupied when not on duty[5]. Our voyage across the Atlantic in *Golden Dragon* gave Dudley the material for his description of sailing in the trade winds and he chose the name *Triton* for the brig because of the trumpet triton shells we were finding in Grenada. The privateers' base in the book was the bay in St. Lucia which we had visited during our holiday cruise.

We returned to our hurricane anchorage in Caliviny with *Alano* in August when the season became active. In the evenings when we visited each other for a meal, Fred and Dudley still played chess before dinner, while afterwards all four of us played Scrabble to continue the great championship that began in Caliviny a year earlier.

We had been discussing for some time the choice of either moving ashore to a house or buying a larger boat. Dudley worked at the saloon table on board *Golden Dragon* and the only way to go from aft to forward was to pass him at the table. Jane was now two and a half years old, but she was too young to understand not to talk to Papa when he was working. In early October a wooden ketch came into St. George's which was for sale and we drove over to see her. We liked the look of *Varuna* and, although she was hardly any longer than *Golden Dragon*, her accommodation was perfect for us. She had been built in Argentina with hard woods and her design and wider beam would give us that extra room we needed. Early in 1968 we received a letter from the lawyer representing the owners of *Varuna*. They offered us good terms to buy her, giving us a mortgage, for which we would have to make two annual payments over the next five years.

---

5   Two years later Dudley received a letter from the U.S. Navy Drugs and Alcohol Prevention Program asking permission to publish this episode about Bowen in their literature.

Dudley was completely 'in love' with *Varuna* but I did have some doubts which irritated him. I was instinctively against committing ourselves to repay such a large sum of money and, although our income did looked secure at the time with contracts for two more Ramage novels both from the British and American publishers which would shortly be signed. But Dudley certainly did need a place where he could write in peace. The main stateroom had a door that could be closed and with a skylight overhead and plenty of portholes, it would be perfect for him. The second thing which worried me was that *Varuna* also had electrical equipment and mechanical systems which we never had before on Golden Dragon or any other previous boats. There was the radar, an auto pilot, generator, refrigerator and freezer, all of which we would have to learn to run and maintain in good repair.

The first draft of *Ramage and the Freebooters* was almost finished at the end of the hurricane season, when he had to fly to London for the publication of *Ramage and the Drumbeat*, which had been selected as the Book Society's Alternative Choice. During the visit he was invited to the *Bookseller* lunch at the Reform Club to celebrate publication day.

While in London, Dudley met Peter Janson Smith who was now his literary agent handling all the negotiations for the rights in his books in Britain, the Commonwealth and all other countries, apart from the United States. Peter drew up a new two-book contract with Weidenfeld's for the next two Ramage novels, the fourth and fifth in the series.

He also visited *The Evening News* to see his old friend John Gold, who was now editor of the paper. John asked him to return to England and become managing editor of the paper when the post soon became vacant. Dudley refused without a moment's thought and John remonstrated that he should at least talk to me first and made the telephone call. The Thomases had invited Jane and me to stay at the Calabash Hotel while Dudley was away, the hotel being closed for two months for pre-winter season maintenance and renovations.

I was completely stunned by John's call, but I knew there was nothing that would persuade Dudley to return to England to work again on *The Evening News*. He had managed to be a full-time author now for almost eight years and I would never think of suggesting we change our present way of life. Besides, I loved my life on board *Golden Dragon* and neither of us had any desire to return to live in a cold and rainy climate again either. When John put the telephone down, he turned and said: "You knew Kay would say no!"

While we lived in Italy we had driven to England for the publication of Dudley's books and stayed with friends, so the trips cost us little. But once we were in the West Indies, although he did not go often to England for promotion and publicity purposes, he still stayed with friends and the publishers paid his air fare and any other extra expenses. Later, when Barley Alison became Dudley's publisher, he stayed at her house in London.

Early in January 1968 we met John and Elaine Steinbeck, who came to stay at the Calabash Hotel. On many mornings we were able to spend some hours with them on the beach, Dudley talking with John while Elaine and I had fun with Jane, while trying to listen to the conversation. John Steinbeck had just been on a trip to Vietnam to write a report for Newsday magazine on the war and while there he visited his son fighting on the battlefield. When alighting from a helicopter, he had stumbled and hurt his back. This was giving him a great deal of pain and they had come to Grenada for Steinbeck to rest and recuperate, staying at the hotel. Some nights he could not sleep and, needing reading material, he asked to read Dudley's books and any others we could lend him.

John talked of his visit to Vietnam and also of his long trip to Russia in 1948 with the photographer Robert Capa. They visited many cities including the ruined remains of Stalingrad, which he described in his *A Russian Journal*. Steinbeck was never an admirer of the Russian regime, he was always much more concerned with the human struggle and the terrible suffering of poverty.

It was while they were discussing their writing methods, John confessed that receiving the Nobel Prize was the worst thing that had happened to him. It set him such a high standard which he felt he could not attain in the books that followed. When talking about their daily work habits, he was horrified by the number of hours Dudley wrote each day. He suggested Dudley should reduce the hours and see if he produced better quality work, needing less time to revise and rewrite the following day. Dudley gradually did this and found it gave him more time for reflection and sifting through ideas for his next day's work. Sometimes, he could only work at night when a combination of things on the boat conspired to keep him from his writing.

Elaine Steinbeck visited us on board *Golden Dragon* late one afternoon to see our growing shell collection. While all the shells were out on the table a coffee bean cowry went up Jane's nose and, fortunately, came down again. Elaine called it the nasal cowry and we sent a postcard to John Fearnley whom we had met at the Calabash Hotel the year before and was also a good friend of the Steinbecks. We told him about the cowry's adventure and that Elaine and the Smithsonian Museum were making offers for it. John Fearnley was a theatrical producer in New York where Elaine had been a stage director.

We had received news from London that *Ramage and the Drumbeat* had been on the best seller list at either number three or four for the past six weeks. It was published in the United States in January and Elaine, back in New York, wrote to us on 1 February and enclosed a full page advertisement from the *New York Times* book section for *Drumbeat*. Dudley was happy to see Doubleday were promoting his book. Elaine wrote:

"Dear dear Popes: How we miss you! It all seems like a golden dream. New York is nice too – and for once we have time to enjoy it. John and I take long walks no matter what weather – and have been to the ballet – and up to the Metropolitan to see the new Monet. Everything is good but the news. It's hard to believe that the Viet Cong actually held the American Embassy in Saigon for six hours. The Ramage ad is a splendid full page from last Sunday's Times book section. Not many publishers stake a whole page for one book. Good for D & D – Doubleday and Dudley. I have a shell show for any who drop in. I had

great fun cleaning the good-luck fighting conch. And, Kay, I've asked our favorite book shop to seek out a copy of 'Cowries of the World'– and will send it on when found. Fearnley was in for a drink and we gave him a run-down on the Calabash and you. He sends his greetings. He is off tomorrow for St. Thomas, and then will take a freighter through the Canal up to San Francisco. You added so much to our wonderful holiday. So many thanks for all kind favors – and the pleasure of your good company. Do let's keep in touch. xxxx to Kay xxxx to Dudley xxxx to Baby Jane."

Early in February 1968, when *Varuna* returned to Grenada between charters, the skipper took Dudley out for a sail. He was convinced she was the right boat for us and spent two days inspecting and surveying her. Everything was agreed for the sale and we could pay the deposit. A week or two later Dudley flew to New York to meet the owners of *Varuna* and had dinner with them one evening. Arrangements were made to draw up a contract giving the conditions of the sale, which a few days later they all signed. *Varuna* would be available for us at the end of April at St. Thomas in the Virgin Islands.

Dudley had finished *Ramage and the Freebooters* and took the manuscript with him. When he had lunch with Ivan von Auw and Sandy Richardson they both said the third Ramage was a vast improvement on previous two. They had only three or four pages of suggestions for small changes to give him.

In another meeting with Sandy, they discussed plans for future books, while Ivan von Auw drew up the new contracts for the fourth and fifth Ramage novels. There was a tragic event which shocked America that year of 1968: on 4 April Martin Luther King was shot dead and that night Dudley told me there were many police sirens on the streets of New York.

Once back in Grenada, Dudley made the few changes to the manuscript suggested by Sandy and Ivan, and he wrote to tell Barley he had dedicated *Ramage and the Freebooters* to her.

A few days later, he received a letter from Weidenfeld's which began *"Ramage three reads magnificently"*. At the end of April we moved *Golden Dragon* to the boat yard in Prickly Bay, leaving her in a safe berth. We set off to St. Thomas taking William with us,

Varuna had had her last charter and we could take possession of her. Our plan was to return to Grenada with our new home.

CHAPTER ELEVEN

The Virgin Islands and Culebra 1968–1970

The Virgin Islands are a group of nearly one hundred small volcanic islands and islets with many coral reefs, extending over an area of about fifty miles. The three large islands of St. Thomas, St. John and St. Croix were Danish until the United States purchased them from Denmark in 1917. The British Virgin Islands, called the B.V.I. by all the inhabitants, are divided by the Sir Francis Drake Channel, with the two large islands of Jost van Dyke and Tortola on the north side and the smaller islands, Norman, Peter, Salt, Cooper and Ginger on the south side. The large island of Virgin Gorda, or the Fat Virgin, lies across the eastern end of Drake Channel, and Anegada is almost fifteen miles to the north. Unlike the rest of the Virgin Islands, Anegada is a low coral island, only a few feet above sea level, and surrounded by reefs and a long horseshoe reef extending towards Virgin Gorda, on which many a ship has foundered over the centuries. Tortola was first settled by the Dutch in 1648 who were soon displaced by British buccaneers, but by the beginning of the18th Century the islands were administered with Anguilla from St. Kitts as part of the Leeward Islands by which time a few English settlers had planted sugar. The first early settlement was in Tortola at Road Town, but in 1741 the B.V.I. had a Lieutenant Governor who set up his capital at Spanish Town on Virgin Gorda.

By then both Tortola and Virgin Gorda had thriving Quaker settlements, but rainfall in the region is always uncertain and with hurricanes as well, some years were disastrous for the plantations. By the beginning of the 19th Century many Quakers had left for America to live in Philadelphia. Emancipation came for the negro slaves in 1834, but the only work available was still on the plantations, where most of the ex-slaves remained. While many owners still provided clothing, medical care and living quarters, they were paid only a few pence a day but were able to grow their own food.

But trying to exist on the islands became more and more difficult and by the end of the 19th Century the population suffered as the plantations dwindled to a very few. Early in the 20th Century the British Government set up an Agricultural Experimental Station which first tried growing cotton and indigo for its blue dye. But a severe hurricane in 1916, followed by another eight years later in 1924, was a setback from which the crops never recovered, and Tortola's industry became livestock farming. In recent years the Agricultural Experimental Station has been grafting such trees as limes and mangoes as well as propagating vegetables to encourage market gardening in cooperation with the Laverty Stout College.

Today, with the huge growth of tourism the islands are now flourishing: as well as hotels, with water sports and diving facilities, there is a large marine industry with many marinas and charter boat companies, hiring out small yachts to visitors throughout the year. Part of the beauty of the Virgin Islands is its crystal clear waters, almost all of which in the B.V.I. are now a marine park reserve.

We found *Varuna* lying in a marina in Charlotte Amalie, the capital of St. Thomas. We settled on board and were happy to find friends there anchored in the harbour. The ex-skipper of *Varuna* spent the next two days showing us how everything worked on board. Life had been simple on *Golden Dragon* with a small gas refrigerator, paraffin cooking stove in the galley, and a 12 volt battery for starting the engine, lighting down below and the navigation lights. On *Varuna*, there was a large Perkins six cylinder engine, a small single cylinder diesel with a generator to charge an electric freezer, refrigerator, and the 32 volt lighting system. The compressor for the refrigeration had a salt water cooling pump. There was also the radar, autopilot, and the hot water heater; a fresh water pump to supply the wash basins and shower; and bilge pumps. The electrical and mechanical systems on board became a nightmare and most had to be replaced over the next few years. Later we were given an Australian wind generator which we rigged up forward at the bow when we were at anchor for long periods of time. It was the only piece of electrical equipment on board that never gave us trouble.

Varuna flew the American flag and when we came to register her at Lloyd's in London we found there was already a yacht called *Varuna* on the Register of Yachts so we could not keep the name. After much thought and discussion, we called her *Ramage* and she became our home for the next eighteen years. *Ramage* was a comfortable cruising boat, while *Golden Dragon* had been designed for heavy weather racing. The saloon was on deck level, with the galley and three self-contained double cabins below. William had the after cabin which he shared with equipment such as spare sails, ropes, shackles and tools. After William returned to Grenada his cabin gradually filled with everything else we could not stow elsewhere, including boxes of Dudley's books as he wrote more of them and National Geographic magazines we could not bear to throw away. The saloon in the deckhouse had a settee, dining table and two extra chairs. At the forward end there was the large chart table with stowage for charts beneath. Three steps down led to the galley to starboard and to port, the main stateroom. This was our cabin which became Dudley's office during the day. It was light and airy with a skylight overhead as well as portholes, so it was always cool. Forward was the third double cabin which became Jane's domain, where there was plenty of room for her to play when she was not up on deck or ashore on the beach with friends. There were two berths either side of this cabin, so Jane could have a friend to stay on board. A forehatch at the forward end gave her a separate way to get on deck.

We had a shakedown cruise to St. John and Tortola for a few days before our planned return to Grenada. In the meantime, the yacht broker based at Yacht Haven in St. Thomas, had found a buyer for *Golden Dragon*, who had visited Grenada to inspect her.

A purchase agreement was signed subject to survey. We sailed for Grenada during the second week of May with extra crew, who would bring *Golden Dragon* back to St. Thomas to the new owner. We had a fairly light breeze and a pleasant day's sail, but towards evening there were a few squalls of rain passing ahead along the horizon. Just after sunset the wind increased as a squall passed close to us and suddenly there were two loud cracks and the mainmast went over the side. It happened so quickly, at one moment the sails were drawing nicely, and the next the sixty-two foot mast was in three pieces, the jib, halyards and rigging and sails all tangled up together. The four men were able to gather it all and bring it back on board, where it made a surprisingly neat stow along the deck.

We then returned to Charlotte Amalie under power and just our mizzen set. Jane was below in her bunk and I was reading her a bedtime story. She had had her third birthday in February and was very aware of everything going on. The lowest part of the mast passed through the deckhouse to rest on the keel near the door of her cabin. We heard the two loud cracks and she immediately asked "What's that Mummy?" I was able to reassure her there was nothing to worry about and calmly finished reading the story, kissed her goodnight and much to my relief, she turned over and went to sleep. The first thing I saw when I came on deck, was Dudley holding on to William's feet on the bulwarks, while he, upside down over the side, passed pieces of rope round the broken mast, sails and riggings, to make it possible to haul it back on board. When Jane came on deck the next morning in Charlotte Amalie harbour, all she could say was "Oh, Papa!"

We could see in the wreckage that the port upper crosstree had parted and, sailing on the starboard tack, the rigging on the port side became slack and no longer held the mast. When Dudley cabled our insurance company in London to tell them about the loss, the reply was simply: "*How very unpontifical*". Dudley found a mast maker, Pigeon Hollow Mast Company in Boston, who could make us a new spruce mast and the next cable from the insurance company read simply: '*Pigeon is go bird*'. We also decided to replace our mizzen mast, which was made in St. Thomas.

Soon after, a new crew member joined *Ramage* and was given the name Jackson after the captain's coxswain in *Ramage* and all the later novels. He cost $15 and was a blue point Siamese kitten. In July *Alano* arrived from Grenada, bringing mail for us. Fred and Joan decided to stay in the Virgin Islands, chartering *Alano* for several more years. In little ways William was showing signs of homesickness; he went home to Grenada for a holiday early in August and we didn't expect him to return, but he did. But at the end of the year he did decide to leave us and return home, where he became a champion body builder. While in St. Thomas he had regularly gone to the gym with friends from St. Lucia, and we heard later he won championships in the United States.

Besides losing the mast, there were several other setbacks during our long stay in the marina. The first in July was a cable from the Pigeon Mast Company to say that a fire had destroyed their offices and needed copies of Dudley's letters and drawings. We had had mechanics on board *Ramage* on and off all summer, but Dudley became quite adept at changing the small water circulating pump himself for the refrigeration and adjusting sticking carbon brushes in the motor for the compressor. There were also problems with the large Onan generator, which charged the 32 volt system. In between working on the boat all summer and autumn and a busy social life, Dudley struggled to write some of the *Battle of Copenhagen*, but at the time he remarked to me that he was really only copying notes. The new mast arrived late in October and as soon as *Ramage* was ready to go sailing again, we left in company with *Alano* bound for St. John, a few miles to the east to anchor in Francis Bay, where we resumed our chess and Scrabble games with Fred and Joan. Some evenings when we sat in Alano's cockpit or on board *Ramage* in Francis Bay, we had a clear view to the west with St. Thomas in the distance on the horizon and we watched the sky change colour with the sunset.

While St. Thomas has many hotels and houses built almost all over the island, St. John is unspoiled with a large portion of the island a national park from land bought and donated by Laurence Rockefeller in 1956. The hillsides are covered with trees and bushes and the many beautiful beaches have long strands of sand. There are coral reefs and islets surrounded by clear water and it is possible to see the sand and corals as deep as eighty feet. When Fred and Joan had to return to St. Thomas to prepare for a charter, we sailed to Cruz Bay to go through the U.S. clearance formalities and then went on to Road Town, Tortola where, once the paperwork was completed with the B.V.I. Customs and Immigration, we sailed on to Marina Cay, which lies among a group of islands at the east end of Tortola. The anchorage is protected by the islands of Great Camanoe and Scrub on its north and west sides and Marina Cay and a large reef to the east and south. From here there is a beautiful view of the many small islands across the Sir Francis Drake Channel and the large island of Virgin Gorda to the east. We never tired of watching how the light changed on the sea and islands as the trade wind clouds drifted by casting their shadows. As in the Tobago Cays, the water is light aquamarine in the shallows, becoming turquoise as the water deepens, until nearer the horizon, a deep cobalt blue.

Marina Cay is a very small islet with a collection of cottages, forming a hotel with restaurant and bar at the highest point. The English owners had laid out mooring for yachts and welcomed everyone with their informal atmosphere. Lunch and dinner was always available and guests could serve themselves at the bar and write down the drinks they took in the bar book. We were encouraged to come and go as we pleased, use their little beach and pay our bar bill when we left. We found the Forsyth family on board their yacht *Iona* already in the anchorage in the lee of Marina Cay and other children lived on Great Camanoe Island close by, so that there were heavenly days for Jane playing with new friends on the beach.

For the first time for many months we were able to relax. We swam and snorkelled on the coral reefs there and looked for seashells. While at Marina Cay, we heard from the U.K. publishers that the page proofs of *Ramage and the Freebooters* had been posted to St. Thomas. Reluctantly we sailed after a few days to collect the proofs and on our way we found Alano anchored in St. John. Fred and Joan were on charter and we were delighted to find John Fearnley was their guest. By the time we anchored in Charlotte Amalie the proofs had already arrived and we began reading them immediately, with Dudley remarking to me that he really liked the book.

We were back at Marina Cay for the end of the year and Sandy Richardson joined us with two young ladies, his daughter and a school friend. We began 1969 cruising the Virgin Islands with Sandy and the girls for ten days, ending the holiday in St. Thomas where we stayed for the next three months. Again we were often alongside in the marina with mechanics coming on board to work on the generator. At this point Henry Chatfield came into our lives. He had just arrived from Antigua with his comfortable power yacht *Grampus* where he had been helping Eric Hiscock in his new yacht, *Wanderer IV*. Dudley had read Hiscock's articles in the magazine *Yachting World*, describing his many mechanical and electrical problems on board. Henry was not only an industrial engineer, but also a chemist and had worked for Du Pont for some years. Before he retired he designed and retooled factories, and his wife, Betts, told us his ideas were so advanced many manufacturers would not accept them. Now Henry was introduced to the disastrous state of our engine room and over the next year he solved our problems by instructing us how to do it. He also recommended two books, one on refrigeration and the other on mechanics, which we ordered. In time, we both became quite knowledgeable electricians and mechanics.

When the generator was working well again, we sailed to St. John to anchor in Francis Bay for a month before returning to Marina Cay. *Grampus* joined us at times as did Fred and Joan when *Alano* was on charter. Many other charter yachts from St. Thomas also brought our mail, which went to our address at the marina, when cruising with guests among the Virgin Islands. We were also able to arrange for letters from the publishers to come directly to Marina Cay and later to a small hotel in Virgin Gorda when we were more permanently anchored in the North Sound.

While we were still at Marina Cay, there was more trouble when our small diesel engine for the generator stopped working. Henry came over to help us and in the midst of the repairs, Putt Humphries arrived with his beautiful old and comfortable

173

power yacht, *Golden Scimitar.* We had met Putt in Porto Santo Stefano and had seen him briefly in Grenada. We were all invited to lunch, very happy to exchange *Ramage's* cramped engine room for the luxurious dining saloon on board *Golden Scimitar.*

With the beginning of the hurricane season in June, everything was running well again and we sailed for Culebra, a small island lying nearly 20 miles west of St. Thomas. With the island of Vieques a little further to the west, both were part of Puerto Rico, which had been a colony of Spain until the end of the Spanish-American War, when in 1898 Spain ceded the territory to the United States. At first we anchored inside a huge bay, called the Ensenada de Honda, on the south side of Culebra. The entrance was narrow with reefs on either side, but the bay beyond opens up into a long expanse of calm water with small inlets on each side. Later, in good weather we anchored outside in lee of the outer reef on the west side of the entrance, but as soon as there was a bad weather forecast, we sought shelter inside the first inlet called Ensenada Fulladosa. Here we hoped we would have good shelter if there was a hurricane. We were surrounded on three sides by mangroves and fields, and cows came down in the heat of the day to stand in the water in the shade of the mangroves.

From time to time the U.S. Navy used a large part of the eastern half of Culebra for a bombing range. Yachts wishing to visit some of the off-lying cays in that area, had to call up the Control on the radio telephone for permission to enter, and could do so if there were no manoeuvres or bombing practice in progress. But the island's fishermen were not able to lay down their fish pots in this area. The population was small and we quickly got to know everyone, including the mayor. The resentment against the U.S. Navy presence on the island was becoming more vociferous, and the following year they had the support of some senators in the U.S. Congress, with the result that within a few years the Navy withdrew.

There was no water available ashore in Culebra. Following a few years of very dry weather, the wells had become contaminated with salt water. Every house on the island had a cistern with a water catchment system using their roofs and gutters. We had some purple heart battens that we used for the awning on *Golden Dragon*, and with pieces of garden hose, Dudley made a rainwater catchment system on our deckhouse that fed rain water into the water tanks through the deck inlet fittings. With heavy rain we could catch over one hundred gallons very quickly.

At the end of June, *Grampus* joined us for a few weeks. She had a large generator on board for the air conditioning and TV. So it came about that we were able to watch the Apollo Eleven moon landing on 20 July. It was an exciting and awesome moment when Neil Armstrong and Buzz Aldrin stepped from the lunar module Eagle on to the dusty surface of the moon.

Before *Grampus* left to sail to Puerto Rico, Henry introduced us to the innovation of 'Voice Mail'. Instead of writing, he and Dudley both could dictate their letters to each other on a tape recorder with tape cassette, which we put in an envelope with the two words 'Voice Mail' written on the outside and mailed it at the Post Office. Later Henry sold *Grampus* and went to England to build a catamaran. But, even so far away, he still continued to be our technical consultant, answering Dudley's questions on tape cassettes, giving clear instructions and also enclosing drawings and electrical diagrams to help us. Dudley liked the tape idea and was soon sending them to Peter Janson Smith, his agent in London. They gave him free rein to express all his thoughts on a 30 or 45 minute cassette, instead of being confined to the pages of a letter.

At the end of July the first hurricane of the season had formed in the Atlantic; it was called *Anna* and was soon followed by *Blanche* and *Camille*. Tropical storm Debbie came next, but by then *Camille* was a hurricane and threatened Cuba with winds blowing at 115 mph. Two days later she came ashore at Mobile, Alabama, killing over 100 people in the area with winds up to 160 m.p.h.

Dudley had still not finished the first draft of *Copenhagen* and had been complaining to me for some months how tired he was. He began saying that he had lost all his creative urge, lost the will to fight and get things done. All the many problems we had had on board *Ramage*, as well as the amount of work involved with writing *Copenhagen*, had left him very tired and depressed. Before we left Culebra, at the end of the hurricane season, we received a royalty statement from Doubleday for *Drumbeat* and *The Triton Brig* which said the sales figures for both books had not yet reached the advance payments. This shocked and worried us because we had the mortgage repayments for the boat, and Dudley complained: "in spite of achieving a fine reputation as a naval historian and writer, the financial reward made him wonder what was the point of it all".

Shortly afterwards, Dudley's dejection and weariness lifted as he suddenly had an idea to set the next Ramage story in Culebra. Meanwhile, work on *Copenhagen* continued. When we had reached the battle sequence there were so many notes and reference books around him, he had little space on his table to write. Near the end of October he had described the details of the truce after the battle and was finally close to finishing the first draft. As well as mechanical problems so often interrupting Dudley's writing, there was other maintenance he sometimes had to cope with. Since William had returned to Grenada, I had taken over the painting and varnishing work on deck. But the book was advancing slowly, I was also able to keep up with him, typing the first draft mostly in the evenings. This made it easier for him to read the previous day's work before writing the next sequence.

But it was not always hard work, particularly when the weather was calm and it became too hot to work in the afternoons. Instead we went out with our masks and flippers to snorkel, looking for seashells to add to our collection, and sometimes Dudley went spear fishing to find a lobster. While anchored in the sheltered water of the Ensenada Fulladosa we also painted *Ramage's* topsides from our dinghy alongside before we had to return to Tortola in November, when our six month permit to stay in U.S. waters expired.

We settled down in Marina Cay and work continued on *Copenhagen*. At the beginning of December Dudley had written up to page 825 and a few days later he finished the first draft. It was far too long, coming to more than 250,000 words, and it involved an enormous amount of work to cut and rewrite. He immediately drew up a page by page synopsis and followed this with a chapter by chapter outline to discover the duplications and rearrange sections. By the time the book was published in 1972, *Copenhagen* was finally reduced to180,000 words, but there was a great deal more work ahead before the manuscript was ready for the printer.

But all this was interrupted by a visit from Sandy Richardson just before Christmas. Dudley had written to Ivan von Auw as well as Sandy to complain about the poor sales for *Drumbeat* and *The Triton Brig,* and pointed out that Lippincott had in fact, still done better with the first book, *Ramage.* Before Sandy arrived, Dudley wrote his demands on a memo to give to him, demanding Doubleday spend $10,000 on promotion and a guarantee for a print of 17,500 copies for future Ramage books. Sandy readily agreed and in their discussion he explained his position at Doubleday. One senior editor had already retired and another, Ken McCormick, was due to retire soon, Sandy felt sure he would get his job. He claimed it had taken him time to get to know how to work 'The Organisation', but now he had the strength and power to do what he wanted. Sandy's explanation was not entirely convincing and I wondered what would happen if he did not get Ken McCormick's job? It seemed to me Sandy had lured Dudley away from Lippincott's with promises which we did not realise he could not keep.

The following February Dudley came to a decision about Sandy, and wrote to Ivan von Auw to say that Doubleday would not be getting the Copenhagen manuscript. In fact, by a strange, coincidence, his letter crossed in the mail with one from Ivan, saying Sandy had met him for lunch and suggested Dudley would be happier with another publisher. It seems that Sandy was unable to keep his promises that he had made just before Christmas and those he had made in Grenada to persuade Dudley to follow him to Doubleday. I know Sandy admired Dudley's books and I am sure he would have liked to continue publishing them, but in a large publishing company like Doubleday, part of a conglomerate, the bottom line on the balance sheet probably showed the returns were not profitable enough. With Dudley insisting on more advertising and a guarantee of higher sales figures, it must have put Sandy in a difficult position. He had no choice but to suggest Dudley would be happier elsewhere.

A second letter arrived from Ivan later in the month to say that Norton, Scribners and Simon & Schuster were all making offers to publish Dudley's books. He should have chosen one of the smaller publishers, but instead Dudley decided to go to Simon & Schuster. This was a hasty and wrong decision that he later came to regret, as Simon & Schuster were as large as Doubleday. Years afterwards, Dudley acknowledged it probably would have been better if he had stayed with Lippincott's while some years later, Sandy Richardson made the comment to Barley Alison, who became Dudley's British publisher, that Doubleday did not do too badly with the Ramage series, but Simon & Schuster let it die. It took Dudley two years to write *Copenhagen* and another year passed before it was published. By the time the next Ramage novel was published, the impetus of the earlier sales had been lost.

During the spring of 1970, while we were at Marina Cay, Dudley began cutting and rewriting *Copenhagen*. But we had social times too, with friends sailing into Marina Cay and interrupting the daily work routine. There was one memorable occasion when we had one of those beautiful Caribbean days, with bright sunshine and a light breeze, and we went swimming and snorkelling at one of the little islands nearby with friends from three other boats. Dudley shot a large fish and we had a barbecue on the beach, finding among the detritus along the high tide line, a grill; two large stones; and enough paper, kindling and wood to make a fire.

Early in March we sailed to St. Croix to have *Ramage* hauled out on the slipway in Christiansted. We had gone there the year before and had enjoyed the tranquillity of the island. St. Croix is the largest of the three U.S. Virgin Islands lying in the Caribbean Sea some sixty miles south of the others. There are two large towns, Christiansted on the north shore protected by a large reef and Frederiksted on the west coast, where the large cruise ships visit. There are many lovely old colonial buildings in Christiansted with an attractive waterfront which was made a National Historical Monument. The north-west coast has the highest land on the island which slopes gently southward to the south shore. The island is rural with gentle rolling hills, and at one time had ninety established plantations growing sugarcane, tobacco, cotton and indigo so that the colony was profitable. Christopher Columbus was the first European visitor and named the island Santa Cruz in 1493, anchoring by Salt River to take water on board. Sugarcane became the major crop, but with the discovery of sugar beet in Europe and the abolition of slavery in 1848, the crop became less and less profitable and today is no longer grown on the island. However, Crucian Rum is still distilled and bottled in St. Croix, with sugarcane imported from the Dominican Republic.

When we were launched back into the water, we sailed in company with friends to Tague Bay at the eastern end of the island and sheltered also by a long reef, where we stayed for a few more weeks. We were repairing various things on board, snorkelling in the afternoons on fine days and visiting each others' boats in the evenings. Dudley did not get much done beyond revising chapters one and two of *Copenhagen*, which he had already done at Marina Cay.

We returned to Tortola near the end of March and were soon back at our anchorage in Marina Cay. There we found mail and parcels waiting for us and among them were Jane's school books from the Parents' National Educational Union, which later became the Worldwide Education Service. This school system by correspondence was founded as a charity in 1887 by Charlotte Mason, who was a pioneer in her belief that education should be a partnership between parents, teachers and students. It was ideal for families living overseas, and many schools in the colonies became affiliated also. Today, as the W.E.S, it has become a large non-profit organisation, and as well as the correspondence school, it also gives curriculum advice to foreign governments. Jane was now five years old and very keen to begin school. We were amazed how quickly she learned to read. It was as though she had blotting paper in her head and soaked it all up immediately. We began a notebook for her nature studies and had fun going ashore to any one of the small islands around Marina Cay or wherever we were anchored, to find an insect, flower or plant, bird, fish or seashell for her to draw and describe. Several years later we met an entomologist from Yale University visiting a home on Great Camanoe who invited Jane along with friends on a nature walk. Jane returned triumphant, having received an accolade for finding a stick insect. As Dudley began work early in the morning, Jane and I did school together. The first year school time was fairly short, but it became longer as she grew older. Although we hoped to continue school at home on board for as long as possible, when Jane was twelve years old she went to school in the United States.

Dudley finally finished his revised manuscript in July and he then drew the battle diagram for the book, using Nelson's detailed instructions to his captains and the positions noted in the Captains' and Masters' logs. Meanwhile, we had received a letter from Commander Jorgen Teisen in the Historical Section of the Danish Admiralty enclosing photographs of drawings made by Robinson Kittoe, who was private secretary to Rear-admiral Graves on board the *Defiance* at the battle and which proved satisfactorily to Dudley that his positioning of the ships was correct. We were able to use one of the drawings on the dust jacket of the British edition of the book when it was published. Letters came from London and New York when the copies of the manuscript had been read. Tony Godwin, who was now Dudley's editor at Weidenfeld's began: *"Magnificent, truly magnificent . . ."*, but the next day the letter from Michael Korda at Simon & Schuster, enclosed a list of suggested cuts. In ten days, Dudley cut three thousand words from our spare copy of the manuscript, and he grumbled how it was *"hard, boring work."* Two weeks later, the manuscript was reduced by15,000 more, and by the end of October, having cut all he could, he was working on substitute pages to send to the publishers. Unfortunately, there was still more work to be done the following year when Tony Godwin in London asked for more cuts before sending it to the printer.

We had stayed in Culebra again during the hurricane season that year and, in November, with our U.S. immigration permit for six months almost expired, we returned to Tortola for a well-deserved holiday. Friends flew up from Grenada to cruise the Virgin Islands with us for twelve days. Most of the time we were snorkelling and looking for seashells, staying in one anchorage for one or two days, and then leisurely sailing to the next. We visited the North Sound of Virgin Gorda, a beautiful stretch of enclosed water about two miles long where we remained for several days to explore the many reefs and beaches there. We returned to Culebra immediately afterwards and planned to visit Puerto Rico in the coming year. In the meantime, Dudley was thinking about the next book he would write, feeling it was essential to consolidate the Ramage series. He had already noted down several ideas, setting a large part of the book in Culebra.

We left Culebra on 2 January 1971 bound for the east coast of Puerto Rico, where we stayed a month. We anchored in the lee of Isleta Marina, which has a boat yard and slipway. As the name suggests, the marina is on a small island which lies quite close to the coast at Fajardo, and with a second smaller islet close by forming sheltered anchorage as well. After we had *Ramage* hauled out on the slip and were back in the water again, we were ready to sail to La Parguera at the western end of Puerto Rico. The village had been recommended to us as a place which had very little rainfall and was perfect for maintenance work outside. Dudley had been replacing the black seam compound when our decks leaked, but they had reached the point where they needed a more radical solution to keep them water-tight. We had decided to cover and paint them to make them leak proof once and for all. La Parguera was the perfect place to do it.

CHAPTER TWELVE

La Parguera 1971–1972

The south-western end of Puerto Rico at La Parguera is lined with mangroves, cays and reefs, lying in an east to west direction for almost two miles offshore with the long, outer Margarita Reef extending from La Parguera to Cabo Rojo at the southern end of the island. Henry Chatfield had marked our chart of the area with courses we should steer to reach the village safely. There are many more cays just offshore, forming a canal, which narrows and widens, giving yachts a sheltered anchorage. The mangroves themselves are dense and have huge tortuous trunks close to sea level with thin roots growing down into the water.

Close to the village there are wooden houses called *casitas* nestling among the mangroves, both along the shore and also a few on the small cays, standing on stilts in the water and each having an open wooden deck. Rhesus monkeys were being bred by a research institute on one of the offshore cays to the west of the village and occasionally one escaped across the channel and leapt from mangrove to *casita* roof to mangrove until the keepers arrived to catch it.

Whereas Ponce and Guanica on the south coast and Mayaguez on the west coast are large towns, La Parguera is a small and quiet village where nothing much happens except pigs and scrawny dogs roamed freely near the shore and regularly knocked over the open oil drums which served as dustbins, and hens wandered in and out of the few shops there. It is a delightful place, an unspoiled backwater which has been discovered by only a few who are seeking to escape the pressures of modern life. We found the villagers friendly and helpful, many speaking only Spanish, whereas in San Juan and Fajardo, English was more frequently used. At that time, there was one hotel with a restaurant, the Villa Parguera, a café, a bar, one small guesthouse, and a small supermarket in the village. Lajas, the nearest town, is about four miles inland and the nearest hospital at San German a few miles farther away. The large town of Mayaguez has the western campus of the University of Puerto Rico and we soon discovered that the owners of the *casitas* in the mangroves were professional people; doctors, dentists, lawyers and lecturers at the University who came to La Parguera at the weekends, making the village more lively. During the week though, we shared the canal only with birdlife, the herons and bitterns in the mangroves, black buzzards, hawks and Tropic birds soaring high above us on the rising warm air.

Puerto Rico has a central mountainous ridge, La Cordillera, which begins inland of Fajardo at the eastern end of the island, and runs westwards to Mayaguez. The El Yunque rain forest is on this central ridge not far from Fajardo. To reach San Juan from almost anywhere on the island, the easiest and safest route was to use the coastal road. The exception is from Ponce on the south coast, which has a winding road across the mountains directly to San Juan, but this road and a few others in the Cordillera could sometimes be closed temporarily due to flooding, particularly in the hurricane season.

There is a second lower ridge of hills between the Cordillera and La Parguera, with the verdant Lajas Valley in between. Here and in Mayaguez it rains often late in the afternoon, sometimes accompanied with thunder and lightning, while in La Parguera it remained remarkably dry and was the perfect weather for us to do our decks.

Frank Casper soon joined us in La Parguera with his yacht *Elsie*. He needed to have an operation for a hernia and since we had already met a few of the surgeons and doctors at the weekends and learned there was also an excellent Seventh Day Adventist Hospital in Mayaguez, we were able to make the arrangements for him before his arrival. Frank had just been awarded the Blue

Water Medal for Cruising by the Cruising Club of America and there was an article about him in the then current edition of *Yachting* magazine which we had on board *Ramage*. The doctors were keen to meet him and the thoracic surgeon insisted on performing the operation. Frank stayed with us in La Parguera until early May and then sailed on his annual cruise to Bermuda, England, the Canary Islands and back to the West Indies. He so loved La Parguera that the village was added to his annual itinerary. Frank could have had his boat hauled out in Fajardo or other yards in the Caribbean, but he loved sailing back and forth across the Atlantic and spending a few months in Plymouth each summer.

Puerto Rico was invaded at Guanica by the United States during the Spanish-American War which began in 1898 and ended with the Treaty of Paris in 1901. The island was ceded to the United States and became a Protectorate. By 1917, the people had been given more rights, including U.S. citizenship and by 1947 could elect their own governor. In 1952 a new constitution for Puerto Rico was ratified by Congress and signed into law by President Truman, when the island government adopted the name "Estado Libre Associado", which translates into English officially as the "Commonwealth of Puerto Rico".

The island is not incorporated into the United States, but has full autonomy, allowing the people to run their own affairs. There have been several referenda to see if there was a wish for the islanders to change their status, but the majority like the current arrangement. The exception is a small vociferous minority who would like to be independent. In April, after our arrival, the members of the independence movement suddenly became more violent in their campaign. There were a few bomb explosions in San Juan, while in La Parguera it was feared that the *casitas* and boathouses would be set on fire. One day at this time we needed to visit San Juan to buy spare parts for our generator and while we were at the *Plaza de las Americas* we saw police checking the dustbins for bombs. The police began patrolling the canal also, but nothing happened immediately and the scare died down. A year later, however, there was more trouble and a fire engine from Lajas was temporarily stationed in La Parguera. There were scores of police in boats on patrol in the canal again, and in fifteen days eleven houses or *casitas* were burned.

At the end of April a letter came from Tony Godwin in London to say that he wanted to make more cuts to reduce *The Great Gamble* (as it was now named) to 180,000 words. This meant there would be no October publication and it was rescheduled for the following year. We did not receive the manuscript until early in June when Dudley was shocked to find how very badly the cuts had been done. He was furious and stormed around the boat *"all the blood had been removed from the story for the sake of 5.7%."* He wrote immediately to Weidenfeld's to say he wanted to leave, sending a copy to Peter Janson Smith. He felt there was *"no point in trying to work with such a man: sits on the manuscript for 6 months without telling anyone, cuts out the Introduction without telling me; and would have sent off the book to the printers without me seeing it unless I'd insisted . . ."*

It took five weeks to work on the manuscript and just as he was nearing the end, he received a letter of apology from Tony Godwin.

Dudley's choice of the title for the book, which came to him while reading Nelson's correspondence written at the time, exemplified the latter's understanding of the strategic situation, along with the enemy's advantages and disadvantages. But Nelson did not know the exact strength of the Danish fleet moored in the Sound to defend Copenhagen, and he gambled with his unorthodox tactics.

Just as Dudley finished and I was typing new pages for the manuscript, we received a very distressed letter from Henry in England: Betts, his wife, had died in her sleep and he wanted Dudley to come to Sandwich where he was building his new boat.

Dudley left three days later, taking the revised manuscript with him and leaving me with instructions to cable should a storm threaten Puerto Rico, since we were now in the middle of the hurricane season. In fact there was and I did send a telegram, but Dudley was unable to change his ticket to get on an earlier flight. By the time he was home the storm had passed south of La Parguera and was heading towards Cuba.

In Sandwich, Dudley met the owners of the pub where Henry and Betts stayed. They had become very fond of the Chatfields and described the slow decline of Betts's health. As a young woman Betts had contracted scarlet fever and she had suffered with attacks of heart fibrillations ever since. Sadly, her heart deteriorated rapidly during the last few months and nothing could be done for her. Dudley stayed with Henry for three days, during which time he was relieved to see Henry's mental state improve. During this time Henry offered to take over *Ramage's* mortgage from the Walkers, the previous owners. He knew that it was a struggle for Dudley to make the six monthly payments and had recently sent us a cheque for the May payment. But Simon & Schuster had sent an advance for *The Great Gamble,* and Dudley had returned the cheque to him. As well as seeing Peter Janson Smith, his agent and the publishers, Dudley also met Michael Korda, his editor at Simon & Schuster for the first time, who was in London for a working visit.

A whole series of mechanical problems prevented Dudley from settling down to resume writing until early September. We met Ernesto Martinez who was the head of the Engineering Department at the Mayaguez campus of the University of Puerto Rico, who kept his small sloop *Antares* in La Parguera. She had a shallow draft and when we sailed with Ernesto we could navigate easily around the series of reefs offshore without fear of going aground. But there were many Sunday evenings when Ernesto returned home with pieces of *Ramage's* equipment, which he took to various machine and electrical shops in Mayaguez. Many Sundays, Ernesto tied up alongside us for the day and sometimes he and Dudley mended equipment on board *Antares.* Ernesto was about the same age as us and a family man with two children. Plump and wearing spectacles he loved food and cooking. Sometimes he arrived with a chicken and cooked a *coq au vin* in my galley for lunch. These meals could last four hours and on one occasion Ernesto also made a special meal for my mother when she visited us. We met all his family and on our birthdays he brought a cake made by his mother-in-law. During these months Dudley was feeling desperate about the continual mechanical problems, but plans were being made to replace most of this old equipment. By the end of the next year we had installed a new diesel generator, with alternators that Henry recommended for keeping the batteries charged, and also fitted a new alternator on the Perkins main engine. We persevered with the refrigeration for another seven years, by which time Jane was away at boarding school. We then bought a small gas refrigerator and shut down the refrigeration for good, so there was no further need to charge the batteries so frequently.

Again and again we discussed if we should live ashore so that Dudley could write without the maintenance problems which were taking up so much of our time. We never did resolve this problem, but the truth was we both loved living on the boat. It would not be until 1987 before Dudley's ill health finally forced us to sell *Ramage*, when we were in St. Martin in the northern Leeward Islands. Back then, at weekends friends from San Juan, whom we had met in Culebra, would occasionally hail us from the shore and stay with us. Although we loved to be in remote places, Dudley did miss the stimulus of discussion with friends. He loved a good argument and there were always lighter moments when Dudley was entertaining with his tales about himself, all related with a little embellishment. He loved exchanging funny jokes back and forth between friends, one joke triggering the memory of the next.

As well as meeting many members of Ernesto's family, there were American families with young children living in or near La Parguera, which enabled Jane to have young friends. During our second year there, when she was seven years old, we gave her a little rowing dinghy which for so long she had wanted. At every opportunity, she had learned to row by borrowing friends' small dinghies. She was so excited with her own dinghy and it was a joy to see her set off after school to row herself down the canal to another boat to play with her friends, wearing her lifejacket and with a whistle in case she ran into difficulties. Jane loved watching the birds and looking for shells, and often returned with little treasures for me which she had found with her friends.

The University had a marine laboratory on Magueyes Island, which lay at the eastern end of the canal beyond the village and there was an old U.S. Coast Guard cutter tied up at a jetty which had been used as a marine research vessel. There was also a phosphorescent bay, very rich with plankton, just a short distance to the east of La Parguera, where manatees lived. At night they could be clearly seen moving under the water, and when swimming there we were surrounded with millions of tiny pinpoints of light. In fact I found La Parguera a perfect place for all of us. We had a social life with friends at the weekends, Jane had her own friends also and it was paradise for us to go snorkelling and find seashells on the series of reefs beginning just outside our anchorage.

Also, during one summer at La Parguera I was pleased to go out shelling with an experienced shell collector. Her name was Nadine and she was married to Bill Aheam, the lecturer on coastal geology at the University in Mayaguez. We went out once a week with Jane to wade on the shallow reefs covered with turtle grass looking for shells, turning over and looking under isolated clumps of coral which had become detached from the reef and which we always carefully replaced. One week we took our dinghy to explore the mangrove roots in the canal just offshore, where Jane and I had already discovered beautiful murex living amongst the oyster shells close to the water line. Nadine showed us how to pull off the green algae from the roots beneath the oysters, which were then put in a bucket. Nadine took the bucket home to rinse it in her kitchen sink until the shells dropped out. She returned the next week with a matchbox containing microscopic shells no more than three millimetres long. These were the unusual little green Berthelinia caribbea which only live on the mangrove roots.

Unfortunately before the summer was over, Nadine and her husband returned to the United States. We did miss her and our afternoon outings together. So often during my years in the Caribbean it has been hard to lose friends when they return home or sail away elsewhere. At the beginning of 1972 we covered our decks with dynel, a hardwearing cloth and several coats of epoxy glue, followed by two coats of epoxy paint. This took almost three months, but we were pleased with the result and there were no more leaks. There was one hiccough though when one morning, while we were waiting for the glue to dry, Jackson, who normally slept on Jane's berth most of the day, made an appearance. He panicked as soon as he felt the glue on his paws, raced back aft and down below, leaving a trail of paw prints in his wake. For months afterwards we were finding them in odd places and they took some time to remove. Jackson was up and about late in the afternoons when it was near his meal time and had the habit of roaming on deck at night. He was heavy on his feet when leaping down the three steps from the cockpit to the saloon and the next three between the saloon and galley, before coming into our cabin to jump on my bunk and curl up by my legs. The two sets of thuds very often woke Dudley, who was not sleeping well at this time.

I was worried about Dudley's health during in 1972: there were many days when he did not feel at all well, particularly when he was winding down from the extra work cutting *The Great Gamble*. He was not only depressed, but stressed and worried about our financial situation which was becoming critical because the book had taken so long to finish. *Ramage and the Freebooters* was published in 1969 and now, more than two years later, any royalty payments on books still in print were becoming smaller and the May mortgage repayment was soon due. He was also overwhelmed by the amount of work still to be done on board *Ramage*. He complained he had a sense of unease and physical weariness which later in the year developed into episodes where his heart was beating faster than normal, and one of the doctors at La Parguera arranged for him to have a series of tests at the hospital in San German. In fact he had tachycardia paroxysms, caused by stress and worry, which is relatively harmless, and with medicine the problem went away. Dudley had written to Peter to ask him if he could raise any more royalties from the publishers and on 10 February we received a cable:

WORKING HARD TO SOLVE YOUR PROBLEM WITH BARLEY'S
HELP STOP BARLEY FLYING TO NEW YORK MONDAY, HOPING
VISIT YOU EARLY MARCH STOP ON NO ACCOUNT DESPAIR
BUT CONCENTRATE ON GETTING WELL QUICKLY STOP WILL
WRITE FULLY WHEN CURRECT NEGOTIATIONS FURTHER
ADVANCED STOP MEANWHILE ALL BEST WISHES

A second cable came from Peter a month later in which he told Dudley to *ACCEPT BARLEY'S ADVICE STOP SHE KNOWS MY THOUGHTS*. Barley arrived from New York during the first week of March with the news that she wanted to publish Dudley's books: her publishing imprint, The Alison Press, was becoming very successful under the umbrella of Secker & Warburg. She was with us for three days of talks, although we had a break in the afternoons to go out to one of the reefs with Ernesto's Boston whaler to snorkel and look for seashells. Weidenfeld's, apparently, would be glad if Dudley left them, and he was amazed that there should be so much resentment over him in London. While in New York, talking with publishers over lunch, Barley reported she was told Dudley was difficult to work with, but even so she said both Lippincott's and Sandy Richardson would have Dudley back. It was hard to think those two American publishers would now be willing to publish his books again and, in Sandy's case, I rather suspect he was feeling mellow towards Dudley after a few lunchtime drinks.

As it was, Dudley was happy with Simon & Schuster at this point: the editing of *The Great Gamble* manuscript had gone well with Michael Korda and their relationship continued to be cordial. The problems had arisen in London at Weidenfeld's when Tony Godwin had held the manuscript for six months instead of returning it to Dudley sooner to make the cuts. It was a long book and it is possible Weidenfeld's were concerned about the printing costs and the resultant sale price in the bookshops which might not make it a commercial success. During their talks, Dudley told Barley he would like to write a biography of Sir Henry Morgan, the seventeenth century buccaneer. He had first thought of the idea the year before, when he had sent a short synopsis of Morgan's life to Peter. The early days of Caribbean settlement had begun to fascinate him and he wanted to discover more about the buccaneers. Having experienced seven years in the West Indies, its tropical climate with hurricanes and even a few small earthquakes, he felt he could add more to his subject than just the bare historical facts.

By the time Barley left she had offered Dudley contracts for three Ramage novels and one for the biography of Sir Henry Morgan, which Dudley accepted. He would leave Weidenfeld's and Barley would be his publisher: she had been his editor for the first two books in the series when she was still at Weidenfeld's, and he had liked working with her. As well as being good friends, they would have a long and fruitful publishing relationship together. When Barley returned to London she would prepare the contracts, while Dudley would draft a more detailed synopsis for a biography of Sir Henry Morgan. Peter would arrange Dudley's release from Weidenfeld's and as soon as the new contracts were agreed and signed, Barley would pay the advances on all four books.

Later in April, we received another telegram from Peter telling us the contracts with Weidenfeld's had been terminated amicably and he was drawing up the new contracts with Barley. Early in May, just as we were down to our last $6 in our bank account, Lippincott's sent us a cheque, paying royalties received from Pocket Books earned by *Ramage,* the first book in the series.

One Sunday, at this time, we went for a sail with Ernesto in *Antares,* sailing westward the whole length of the Margarita Reef to Cabo Rojo, the most western point of Puerto Rico. It was a warm, sunny day and the beauty of the reef, the sea and the land, made Dudley reject any wish to return to the Mediterranean. He did have a great deal of nostalgia for Italy at times, but he loved the Caribbean more. A few days later he told me that the fifth *Ramage* would be about the Post Office Packet Service, and then drafted the first idea for the story in his notebook. Three days later he was writing *Governor Ramage* and said he was really feeling better now he was writing again.

Dudley had now the plot of *Governor Ramage* completely thought out from beginning to the end in which Ramage is shipwrecked on to the reefs of Culebra, losing the convoy he was escorting except for one merchantman. Dudley was able to draw on the very heavy weather we experienced in the Eastern Atlantic when Hurricane *Carol* passed to the north of us and the loss of our main mast south of St. Croix in the Virgin Islands. Work progressed steadily throughout May and near the end of June the first draft was finished. He immediately began editing the manuscript, first by making page by page notations to spot any repetitions, and then carefully reading through, rewriting odd phrases here and there, but not making many alterations. Copies of the manuscript were posted off to London and New York and we received a letter from Barley when she had returned from her summer holiday. She liked *Governor Ramage* and suggested only a few small changes. She had seen Michael Korda while on a visit to London and they had discussed the manuscript together.

The Great Gamble was published early in June 1972 in Britain and in the United States in November. The first review to appear was by Vice Admiral Sir Peter Gretton in The *Observer* of 11 June. The Admiral describes the book, the political events that lead up to the battle and the battle itself. He pointed out that the book is:

> *"the first account written with the full access to the Danish papers as well as to a number of new British sources. As a result many mistakes by previous historians have been corrected, the positions of the ships, and shoals established with accuracy and the whole course of the battle described fully for the first time."*
> But the Admiral's final paragraph summed it up: *"This is a monumental work and it is not surprising that Mr. Pope has taken three years over it. The illustrations and charts are excellent and the book is good value for money."*

Other reviews appeared in magazines such as the *Economist* and *The Spectator,* and also provincial newspapers all over Britain. More reviews came from the United States and the Danish press, including one in the *Berlingske Tidende,* written by Admiral Saabye, who had made a lifetime study of the battle. Unfortunately, we did not meet the Admiral during our visit to Copenhagen to do the research for the book, but later a correspondence developed between them when Dudley was reviewing his notes and writing the book he found he had more questions relating to the Danish side of the battle. After writing to thank the Admiral for his generous review when it was translated for us, we received the following reply:

"29 August 1972.
"Dear Dudley Pope,
"Thank you for your letter of 21 August. I am glad that you now can look at your great work with satisfaction and I hope you can relaxe [sic] a little and also that the result of your effort shall amount to at least an admiral's pay.

"I have already noted the two errors you mention, but you cannot expect to write a book of that size without an error . . . The book has been very well received in Denmark and I do hope also in England and USA. I have had the opportunity to read Vice Adm. Sir Peter Gretton's review in some English paper, and it was very fine. I am now looking forward to see the Ramage enter the Sound through the "Kongedyket" one day so that we can have real staff conference!! I hope this may reach you some day! All good wishes, yours sincerely, E.J. Saabye."

With the hurricane season now showing signs of more activity, we moved *Ramage* back down the canal to our hurricane season anchorage among the mangroves. We had been anchored not far from the Caracoles Reef, the first in the series of reefs off La Parguera and quite close to the shore at this point. Dudley now wrote the first draft of his fifth *Ramage* novel, which continues the story after *Governor Ramage*, with Captain Ramage waiting in Jamaica for his next appointment. In *Ramage's Prize*, he is ordered to investigate the disappearance of Post Office packet ships at sea which were either not arriving in the West Indies with mail from England, or not returning to Falmouth with the West Indies dispatches and mail. Dudley finished this first draft at the end of August and then put it aside.

In the meantime, Peter had written to tell Dudley that Pan Books were offering an advance to publish The *Battle of the River*

Plate providing he cut the first nine chapters. Dudley started by doing a précis of these chapters and then wrote them in a condensed version for the paperback edition. For the rest of the year we were busy with maintenance work and preparing for the installation of the new generator. Everything was finished just before Christmas and we then prepared *Ramage* for sea.

We sailed from La Parguera and reached Roosevelt Roads at the south-eastern end of Puerto Rico on the last day of 1972. We anchored near the entrance to the U.S. Navy base and opened a bottle of champagne which friends had given us just before our departure. We sailed early the next day, bound for Isleta Marina just off the east coast at Fajardo and arrived there in the late afternoon. *Ramage* was hauled out nine days later, and we stayed up on the hard for two weeks, getting all the necessary work needing to be done.

The day *Ramage* was back in the water Frank Casper in *Elsie* arrived from La Parguera. He stayed six days with us and then slipped away again to visit Culebra first, and then on to Grenada.

Dudley now began revising his first draft of *Ramage's Prize* and continued until the middle of February when the proofs for *Governor Ramage* arrived. He was shocked to find there were so many "small and silly" alterations to the manuscript that it took much longer than usual to read and correct the proofs. The changes appeared to have been made after Dudley had last seen the manuscript with Barley's editing. He was angry and said he wanted to quit the whole business. Dudley was also perplexed by what or who could have caused the proofs to be in such a mess, but he painstakingly reinserted the missing words so the narrative made sense. There were even whole lines that had disappeared, perhaps dropped out by the printer, and more than a week later, when reading the proofs for a second time, he was still finding errors.

Although at the time Dudley was angry and really did feel he wanted to stop writing on this, and on another later occasion, I never believed him. Ideas kept coming into his head for the Ramage novels and the urge to write was too strong for him to resist. In arguments sometimes, it would annoy him even more that I did not appear to take him seriously, accusing me of regarding it all as 'melodrama'. Nevertheless, Dudley did return to *Ramage's Prize* soon after and six weeks later, the manuscript was finished and copies were posted off to Barley and Michael Korda. In May Barley wrote to say she did not like the new manuscript and a few days later he received a letter from Michael Korda which said that the book "would be better with more action and love interest . . ."

Dudley received a second letter from Michael Korda shortly after, in which he made a good suggestion to improve the story. Dudley liked the idea and rewrote the episode where the Post Office packet is attacked and captured by a privateer. He also included Gianna, the Marchesa di Volterra for the "love interest" near the end of the story. We sent off the typed pages with the changes to the manuscript and a few weeks later we received a cable from Barley, which said: "*Ramage's Prize* basically splendid".

In the meantime, Secker's had to print a second edition of *Governor Ramage* before publication because of a strong demand from bookshops. A few weeks after publication the first edition of 7,500 books and half the reprint of 2,500 were sold.

Dudley had already begun doing research for his biography on Sir Henry Morgan, visiting the Biblioteca Regional del Caribe Norte y Sur in San Juan where he was able to borrow books and bring them back with him to Fajardo. By August he had finished his research at the library and was going through all his notes. He then wrote a synopsis, dividing it into three parts: first, the period in general (1650–1680) at the time of Charles II; second, a description of the buccaneers and third, Morgan's life during that time. He did not begin writing this biography until we returned to the British Virgin Islands the following year. Moreover, three more Ramage novels appeared before it was finally published in 1977 with the title *Harry Morgan's Way*.

On the last day of August we sailed to Culebra: a tropical storm had formed in the Atlantic and we decided to seek shelter in our hurricane anchorage in Ensenada Fulladosa. Culebra was one of our favourite islands, it was so quiet and peaceful and where we had spent many happy hours snorkelling by the reefs. The village of Dewey was a twenty minute dinghy ride away from where we often lay at anchor, and we could buy all we needed at the shop and share the time of day with the people there.

CHAPTER THIRTEEN

Virgin Gorda 1974–1976

Dudley had now entered a period of great creativity, with many ideas for future adventures of Captain Ramage. At the same time we were still short of money as more financial problems overtook us. There were just two mortgage payments remaining on *Ramage*, but as Barley Alison commented, Dudley wrote best when under pressure and from 1974 onwards he was writing two books each year. Although *Governor Ramage* and *Ramage's Prize* were well reviewed in the United States, Pocket Books in New York decided they did not wish to continue with the series, although they had published the first three *Ramage* novels in paperback. Simon & Schuster were unable to find another paperback publisher and, not wishing to publish without their share of the paperback royalties, discontinued the series as well. Thus, Dudley's books were not published again in the United States until the nineteen eighties. Dudley began the first draft of the Morgan biography after *Ramage and the Guillotine*. *Ramage's Diamond* was written before Morgan was finished, and *Ramage's Mutiny* and *Ramage and the Rebels* followed quickly afterwards.

These four novels were written during our hardest times financially, yet perhaps they are among his best. *Ramage's Prize* was the first to have one continuous narrative rather than being episodic, but I believe *Diamond*, *Mutiny* and *Rebels* are favourites among many of Dudley's fans. His compulsion to work so hard was not only because of our financial circumstances, but as the ideas came into his mind and the plots took shape, he simply had to write them.

We returned to Marina Cay in October 1973 where we were reunited with friends. But we missed *Alano* because, while we were still in La Parguera, Fred and Joan had written to tell us that they had sold her. They were both feeling their age and had decided to retire from the charter business. The new owner wanted to sail across the Atlantic to the yard in Falmouth for a refit where *Alano* was originally built. They sailed with him and after the voyage Fred and Joan stayed a little while in England before returning to California.

Dudley began reading his notes for *Ramage and the Guillotine* in which Ramage is sent to France to discover how advanced Napoleon's plans were for the invasion of England, and began writing immediately. I liked the idea of Ramage being a spy because it reminded me of my teenage years when Dickens' *A Tale of Two Cities* and Baroness Orczy's *The Scarlet Pimpernel* were among my favourite books. He then did some research on the French correspondence system and experimented with sealing wax, to see if letters could be opened without damaging the seal. He found a way of doing it and used the trick where Ramage is seen intercepting the Admiral's dispatches at Amiens. Dudley resurrected the character of 'Slushy Dyson', cook's mate on board the *Triton* brig in *Ramage and the Freebooters*. He had been a smuggler in the area of Romney Marsh until he was caught and pressed into the Navy. It is arranged for him to take Ramage and three trusty members of his crew to Boulogne is his fishing boat, the *Marie* of Dover, more often used to take whisky, gin and woollen goods from England to France and returning with brandy, lace and other luxuries. The book progressed well and Dudley had finished the first draft by the middle of March. We both had memories of Romney Marsh. Dudley, while still a boy, had lived to the north of the marsh and had often gone on his bicycle to Hythe and Dymchurch, while I knew the west side at Rye, which was not that far from Bexhill.

Early in 1974 a three-masted steel schooner came into Marina Cay and we had watched her anchor, only to have to anchor again when her anchor did not hold. Unfortunately, she anchored some way ahead of us so that later in the evening when her anchor dragged again, her stern hit *Ramage's* bow. This caused some damage which we had to have repaired during the next few months, but the whole affair was dealt with in a friendly manner with the captain of the schooner paying for all the necessary repairs. When we had first visited Marina Cay in 1968 there was only one charter boat fleet in operation, but some four years later there were several companies all with thirty, or more, small yachts. Visitors who hired them for one or two weeks, usually sailed by themselves, but they could have a skipper to accompany them. The anchorage in Marina Cay was becoming too small for the large number of boats coming in each evening and seamanship sometimes left much to be desired. In anticipation of a large group of boats coming into Marina Cay shortly after we were hit by the steel schooner, we moved *Ramage* over to Trellis Bay on Beef Island, only a short distance away from Marina Cay and Great Camanoe.

The airport for the B.V.I. is nearby and the large Boston Whaler from the hotel on Marina Cay could cross the channel in ten minutes or less to pick up their guests. On fine days it was safe to make the crossing in our smaller dinghy. We found this new anchorage a pleasant backwater compared with Marina Cay and we also enjoyed snorkelling over all the reefs in the bay.

Within a day, or two, we were surprised to find we had two remoras attached to *Ramage* about four feet below the waterline under the curve of the hull. These long and slender fish have a flat, laminated disc, like a suction pad, on their heads and are able to stick themselves to large fish, including whales. We often saw the Right Whales during February and March every year which come from the North Atlantic to their breeding grounds close to the Virgin Islands. Our remoras probably came detached from a whale and found a comfortable berth with *Ramage:* they stayed a little while and then disappeared. Later, on some evenings when we were in Virgin Gorda during these two months, there was often a distinct oily smell of fish in the air, which I was sure came from the whales and was carried by the light trade winds from out beyond the reefs.

With *Ramage and the Guillotine* completed and in the post, we sailed to Virgin Gorda, and anchored in the North Sound near a little hotel called The Bitter End. We so loved this area that it became our permanent anchorage and we only sometimes visited Marina Cay when friends were on holiday at their homes on Great Camanoe. The Sound is a large area of calm water, enclosed by the north shore of Virgin Gorda on one side and by Mosquito and Prickly Pear Islands on the other. There are two passages for yachts to enter but narrow enough with reefs to prevent the Atlantic swells coming in. There is a narrow passage past Saba Rock at the eastern end which leads to Statia Sound and Statia Island in another area of calm water with many reefs and channels, all protected by a large barrier reef beyond. There is also another hotel near The Bitter End, in a small inlet called Biras Creek from which the hotel took its name. The charter boats tended to congregate at these two establishments, the people on board going ashore for an evening meal.

Later, we anchored *Ramage* close to Prickly Pear Island and discovered a paradise for snorkelling and looking for seashells around the many reefs, and bays. When there was bad weather in the hurricane season we moved to Biras Creek, which gave more shelter than the Sound itself. We came to The Bitter End also to see our friend Elizabeth Simonette, who was now the manageress. Elizabeth was Swiss and had lived in Africa, where her husband built highways. She had dived with Jacques Cousteau in the Red Sea in the early years of scuba diving, which was developed by him. Elizabeth had come to the Caribbean after her divorce and we met her first when she was at Marina Cay. Now, not too far from retirement, she was spending the last of her working years in Virgin Gorda. Don Neal, a Texan, ran the Reef Sampler, a small sports fishing boat and helped Elizabeth around The Bitter End. He went down to St. Thomas every week to buy the hotel's supplies and also made a regular visit to Anegada to buy fish and lobster from a family who laid fish traps in deep water some way off the north coast of Tortola and Jost van Dyke. We arranged for our mail to come to The Bitter End, but Don also brought any mail for us waiting at marina office in St. Thomas. He also posted letters for us, even the bulky parcels containing Dudley's manuscripts.

The only road to the area was at Gun Creek near the western

end of the Sound and it is here that the staff of The Bitter End live, crossing the Sound by boat each day. They brought the mail for the hotel addressed to a box number at the Post Office.

One evening during the summer, when it was Elizabeth's birthday, she invited us to dinner at the hotel. The nephew of one of the Rockefellers arrived with a party of friends and while we were there we heard the news that President Nixon had resigned. There were loud cheers that the Watergate scandal had at last been put to rest and we all celebrated with glasses of champagne that evening of 8 August 1974.

Dudley was by now writing his biography of Sir Henry Morgan. After revising his synopsis, he drew up a chronology, listing briefly all the dates and incidents of Morgan's life. He began the book with Morgan's funeral and the earthquake that destroyed Port Royal, but later put this at the end of the book. But work on Morgan was interrupted by some mechanical problems, first with the refrigeration, and then the generator's fuel injector. We had no choice but to send it to a friend in San Juan, who took it to Bosch for repair. To do this, we took *Ramage* down to the Virgin Gorda Yacht Harbour, a marina on the west coast which is near the airport, to put the injector on a flight to San Juan. Unfortunately, Bosch had to order the replacement parts from New York, so the injector eventually came back a month later. Living as we did, far from civilisation, there were times when it was difficult to get things repaired.

Even before *Ramage and the Guillotine* was finished, Dudley was noting down ideas for the next Ramage novel. He was about one third of way through the biography, having just completed Morgan's first raid on Villahermosa and Granada, when he had the whole plot worked out in his mind and he could not resist the urge to begin the next in the series. The story flowed well and, putting Morgan to one side, he finished the first draft within two months. The title quickly became *Ramage's Diamond*, in which Ramage is promoted to post captain and given command of the frigate *Juno* with orders to sail to Barbados with dispatches. A large part of the book describes how Ramage captured and fortified Diamond Rock to attack French shipping and in a postscript at the end of the book, Dudley explains that Diamond Rock was indeed captured in 1804 by Commodore Samuel Hood, who was blockading the French in Martinique. Hood "put his 74- gun *Centaur* alongside the Rock and swayed up 24-pounder guns to the top" a feat of "seamanship of epic proportions." The manuscript was finished and posted off to London early the following year.

Early in October we had quite a bad earthquake which was measured as seven on the Richter scale. It lasted about ten seconds and sounded like a roll of distant thunder. The epicentre was near Montserrat and both steeples of the cathedral in St. John's, Antigua, were damaged. St. Kitts also had some damage; all three islands are visible from each other on fine days and form a triangle in the northern Leeward Islands. At times, we also felt earthquakes under the water that made a ringing sound on our iron keel. All the islands, from Grenada to Cuba, sit on the edge of the Caribbean plate and tremors occur from time to time.

The same week we received a letter from Dudley's agent in London with three pieces of bad news. Peter was trying to sell *Ramage and the Guillotine* in the United States, and McGraw Hill were the latest to be approached, but they also turned it down. Worse still, there was a claim from the Inland Revenue for one year's tax, from April 1972 to April 1973, because the double taxation agreement between Britain and Tortola had expired and had not yet been renewed. Dudley had visited the accountants in Road Town a few months earlier and learned that the negotiations for a new tax treaty had broken down between the two governments. Worse was to follow when Peter was not permitted to send out any more royalties to us until the tax bill was paid. As a result there were no payments from October 1974 until May 1975, when the tax bill was paid off, which was a period of seven months. Those seven months passed agonisingly slowly.

In fact we were helped by our friends who had a home in Great Camanoe, who sent us a cheque which saw us through those dreadful months. But even more upsetting, Peter had sold his literary agency to Campbell Thomson & McLaughlin and would leave at the end of the year to join the Oxford University Press. However, a long and friendly relationship began with John McLaughlin, who would be Dudley's agent for the rest of his life.

Later, in November, we heard from Barley who sent us encouraging sales figures for *Governor* and *Prize,* predicting that there would be a steady sale of 10,000 copies for each book. *Ramage's Prize* at this time was still on the best seller list. With the paperback sales as well, there was a good income in the pipeline, but not yet available to us. Corgi sold over 50,000 paperback copies of *Ramage and the Freebooters* and 35,000 of *Ramage and the Drumbeat.* The paperback of *The Battle of the River Plate* was due to be published soon, and Pan were also planning to publish *73 North.* Besides all this, *Ramage and the Guillotine* would be published within six months. Peter's next letter had better news: he had a tax lawyer working on our behalf and Weidenfeld's, having already reprinted *Ramage,* were now going to reprint *Ramage and the Drumbeat* and *Ramage and the Freebooters.*

With the first draft of *Ramage's Diamond* finished Dudley then turned to long overdue maintenance work. As well as the diesel engine for the generator developing an oil leak, we had decided the main mast needed painting. The Sound was the perfect place to do this while we were anchored in calm water and Dudley had hoisted me up in the bosun's chair, which was not just a simple short plank with two ropes passing through each end to hoist it. Because Dudley did not like heights and suffered some vertigo, he had a chair made in St. Thomas with stiff, thick storm canvas, which wrapped round three sides of the body and had a narrower piece across the front. Accordingly, after stepping in and sitting down, my legs passed out under the front piece. I felt completely safe in this chair and could move around easily holding onto the rigging. There was always a fine view sixty feet up as I sanded with one hand and held the mast with the other to keep me in place.

While I was busy sanding the mast, I found some rot in one of the upper crosstrees. Elizabeth allowed us to go alongside the large boat dock at The Bitter End, where we could use electricity from the hotel's generator. We unshipped the upper crosstree and brought it down on deck to repair it while we were alongside the dock.

Near the end of the year, Dudley received a letter from Peter Shepherd at Harold Ober Associates in which he said Simon & Schuster had been in touch with him concerning the paperback rights for *Governor Ramage* and *Ramage's Prize*. Although Pocket Books had decided not to publish the two titles, under the terms of the contract Simon & Schuster were legally obliged to pay Dudley royalties within two years for the paperback edition of *Governor Ramage*. They wanted to know if Dudley would agree to them trying to sell the rights to another paperback publisher.

Late in November 1973 Dudley had written to Peter Shepherd to say he was making arrangements for his London agent to handle his books on a worldwide basis. But a year later he was having second thoughts and thinking it might be better after all to have an American agent again in New York. He therefore wrote in reply to Peter Shepherd on 31 December 1974 that in *"conversation with various American authors I have learned a good deal about American publishing that I did not know before, and it became clear to me that I owe you an unqualified apology, and would like to make the same unqualified apology to Ivan von Auw. Over the last year or so it has become increasingly obvious to both Peter Janson Smith and myself that it was impossible for him to handle the U.S. end from London."*

Moreover, as Peter Janson Smith had now left the agency after many years he felt it would be better to be represented in New York by an American agency. There was a lot going on at the time; *Ramage and the Guillotine* was due out in the U.K. the following July and was available for a U.S. hardback publisher; the manuscript of *Ramage's Diamond* would be ready in March, with the biography of Henry Morgan, also commissioned by Alison Press/Secker & Warburg, available in July.

Additionally, the eighth Ramage manuscript would be ready within a year. In a postscript to his letter, Dudley added *"I read recently in the Miami Herald that Pinnacle Books are reprinting all the Hornblower series again in paperback at the rate of one a month [sic]. Is there any chance that they would be interested in the first six*

Ramages?"

In reply, Peter Shepherd wrote on 21 January 1975 with an anecdote. *"Thanks so much for your letter of December 31. I emerged from a rather short and harmless trip to the hospital to find it in my office, having been set up for it by my anaesthesiologist who is a passionate admirer of yours. He happened to notice that I was reading a book entirely unrelated to your work except for the fact that the word 'commodore' appeared in its title. That was enough. He reads all eighteenth century sea adventure stories, but particularly admires your work, has copies of everything you've written, and wants more. Well, of course, we'd be glad to resume representing you, in any event. It's plain from your letter that a major campaign is called for . . ."*

With the manuscript of *Ramage's Diamond* in London, we were preparing *Ramage* to sail to Antigua soon, to have her hauled out on the slipway at the boat yard in English Harbour. At the end of March we left the Sound to cross the Anegada Passage. There was a full moon that night, but little wind and an uncomfortable swell. We sailed under power with the staysail and mizzen set and reached Oranje Baai in St. Eustatius (always called Statia) twenty-four hours later.

We stayed in Statia for two days to rest and explore the town a little. The anchorage on the west side of the island is an open roadstead, which meant landing with our dinghy on the beach. On our first foray ashore to clear Immigration and Customs we were met by a fishermen, who helped us pull our dinghy out of the swell waves and up the beach He then drove us in his truck to the town which is perched on the cliffs above. Here, also, Fort Oranje overlooks the anchorage and is maintained in good condition, housing some of the government administrative offices. We also visited the ruins of the Jewish synagogue, once used by the large Jewish community which had dispersed after Admiral Rodney sacked the town and left it in ruins in 1781.

Holland had been persuaded to recognise the Government of the United States after the Declaration of Independence in 1776 and Statia had become a free port with a huge depot of munitions and war materials of all kinds, supplying the rebel army against Britain. The warehouses on the waterfront below the cliffs were destroyed and, when we were there in 1975, there were a few walls visible at low tide. Hurricane *Luis* swept most of these away in 1995, but the beach and the sea in this area is now a national park and when swimming with a mask and snorkel, the submerged foundations of the sea walls, warehouses and piers, cannons and anchors can still be seen in the sea close to the shore.

A few days later, we left Statia and sailed past St. Kitts, where we could see the large fortress on Brimstone Hill and fields of sugarcane in the low lying areas stretching from the coast until the land begins to rise up to Mount Limuiga at nearly four thousand feet. We had to visit Nevis, which is separated from the southern lower end of St. Kitts by a channel just two miles wide. The two islands of the Federation of St. Kitts and Nevis are among the earliest to be colonised in the Caribbean and although sugar became the primary export from the1640s, tobacco was also grown in the early years.

We anchored in Charlestown, the capital, and stayed several days. We found the town very attractive with quite a few of the old colonial style houses. The island is small, not much more than nine miles long and seven miles wide, while Nevis Peak dominates the centre of the island and rises to just over three thousand feet. Many places along the shore have a grove of coconut palms growing, with road going round the island, further inland. Some of the old plantations houses have been converted to hotels for tourists who come in the winter months to enjoy the atmosphere as it was in colonial times. We visited Morningstar Plantation, which was privately owned by Robert Abrahams, a retired American lawyer from Philadelphia, who had a lifelong interest in Nelson. He restored the sugar mill on his property and turned it into the Nelson Museum, where he put all the memorabilia he had purchased on his many visits to antique shops in Britain. His collection is impressive with many framed prints of Nelson around the walls and he even had Dudley's books, *England Expects* and *The Great Gamble,* on display. The fact that Nelson had come to Nevis, met and married Mrs. Nisbet in the church near Morning Star, had brought the Abrahams to Nevis and they bought the plantation as soon as they discovered it was for sale.

We were invited to stay to lunch and in the afternoon the Abrahams took us to see the church where Nelson and Mrs. Nisbet were married and also to Fort Charles on the shore just south of Charlestown.

Nevis was so peaceful that we would have liked to stay longer, but unfortunately the anchorage is an open roadstead like that in Oranje Bay in Statia, and it is uncomfortable lying at anchor with the boat rolling in the swell. We sailed for Antigua next day and again the wind was east and our course for Antigua was also east: it was an uncomfortable trip, heading *Ramage* directly into the wind, we motored all the way with mizzen and staysail set, passing the little island of Redonda in the moonlight.

We found many yachts anchored in English Harbour, some cruising the islands having crossed the Atlantic the previous November. Others were charter yachts, carrying their guests up and down the island chain on weekly or fortnightly holidays. We could see life could be decidedly social. *Ramage* was hauled out early next morning and we stayed up on the slip for three days. The men worked well and we had the topsides painted and other work done while lying alongside a jetty at the boat yard. By the middle of April we were anchored out in the harbour, and after making a few notes, Dudley found himself writing the first few pages of *Ramage's Mutiny*.

Shortly after arriving in English Harbour we met Ian Spencer, an old friend who had been living there for many years. As a young man he had not only been in the Merchant Navy, but had been on board a ship in the same convoy as Dudley when his ship was torpedoed in the Atlantic, south of Madeira. Ian's ship survived the submarine attacks and had reached England safely. After the War, he had an eventful life on the sea as a yacht skipper in the Caribbean. Dudley also met Edward Dodd, chairman of the U.S. publishers Dodd Mead who was on holiday in Antigua, and as a result of the meeting Dodd Mead later published Dudley's biography of Sir Henry Morgan.

Antigua Race Week had begun during our last few days in Antigua, and yachts from all over the Caribbean had come to English Harbour for the races and the anchorage became very crowded. As soon as we were ready, we sailed for Virgin Gorda at the end of April in bright sunshine, passed St. Martin in the moonlight and sighted the peak of Virgin Gorda early the next morning. We went into the Yacht Harbour to clear Customs and stayed the night there. Although we were tired, it had been a fine trip with the wind on our quarter and we returned to the North Sound the following morning.

Ramage and the Guillotine was published in May and we received some good reviews from the London papers. Among them there was also an article in *The Sunday Express* written by Graham Lord, which had the headline: "*When Home is a Luxury Yacht in Paradise . . .*" It was a very nice article about Dudley, his work and our lives in the B.V.I., with a book review of *Guillotine*. It was true we were living in paradise, leading simple lives close to nature, still short of money and always hard at work to keep ourselves afloat. But the North Sound was not paradise for everyone – I met a visitor on the beach at *The Bitter End* who told me she could not live there because there was no hairdresser! I reassured her that I cut Dudley's hair and he cut mine.

John McLaughlin also wrote to report that Barley was offering a new contract for four more *Ramage* books. It was several weeks before Dudley began writing but when he did, it was to pick up the Morgan manuscript which he had abandoned to write *Ramage's Diamond*. At times, he felt overwhelmed by the mass of material he had to work with. He first read through the chapters he had already written, making page by page notes, so he could rationalise the sequences. At the end of May, with this task finished, he began rewriting the first chapters. By the end of July, feeling more confident about the way the story was developing, he reached the end of his original manuscript. He then began working on the chronology for the rest of the book before continuing. This first draft of the manuscript was finished just before Christmas and like so many of his non-fiction books, it was far too long and would have to be cut. But early in the New Year we sent this first draft to Barley to have her comments and suggestions.

With the hurricane season over in November, we moved from Biras Creek, where we had sheltered from Tropical Storm *Eloise*, and anchored *Ramage* out in the Sound off Prickly Pear Island again. During the Christmas holiday we, and nearly everyone at *The Bitter End*, went off in the Reef Sampler to a party held in a home two miles away at the western end of the Sound. On the way we changed course to pull a boat off the reef at Mosquito Island.

In the first weeks of January 1976, Dudley tried to relax and have a few weeks rest. Frank Casper sailed in with *Elsie*, in company with *Halben* which was owned by friends from La Parguera, who were having a holiday in the Virgin Islands. At the end of the month we returned to Marina Cay to visit friends who had returned to their homes on Great Camanoe for their winter holidays. While we were there we suddenly lost our cat Jackson. He died very quickly and we buried him in our friends' garden, planting a seedling of a flamboyant tree on his grave. Dudley had collected the seeds in Fajardo, Puerto Rico, and we were growing a few in a pot on board. For a long time afterwards we missed him: he always came on deck to greet us whenever we arrived alongside from a visit on shore or a shelling expedition.

At Christmas we had given Jane a sailing dinghy which we had found was for sale at The Bitter End. Soon she would be eleven years old, was growing up fast and had become a very able sailor, often sailing in the laser races organised by the hotel for their guests. Most afternoons Jane sailed ashore to The Bitter End to see her friends there and brought letters for us, if any had arrived, when she returned on board. School on board was still going well and she continued with her nature notebook. Among the subjects she described and drew was the century plant or Agave cactus, which with a climate often dry and irregular rainfall, grows all over the Leeward Islands. When the cactus begins to bloom early in the year, it first produces a long stem, growing to a height of thirty feet and is visible on all the islands' hills, often standing out on the skyline. The stem looks like a giant spear of asparagus before the clusters of yellow flowers appear, which are much loved by the humming birds. By December, the flowers and stalk have dried enough to be cut and used as a Christmas tree. The cactus flowers just once in its lifetime and when the flowers and stem have withered and dried at the end of the year, the plant itself also begins to die. But there are already many shoots around the base, growing into new Agave plants.

Jane also described the resident population of large iguanas which basked in the sun on the large boulders that rise up the hill a little way behind The Bitter End. These creatures, like huge lizards, are greyish in colour, some with bodies as long as three or four feet and even longer tails ringed with dark stripes and spines running down their backs.

While Dudley was waiting for Barley to return the *Morgan* manuscript with her comments and suggestions in January he began retyping the first twenty-seven pages of the eighth *Ramage* he had begun while we were in English Harbour in April the year before. This was published with the title *Ramage's Mutiny,* which Dudley based partly on the true story of the mutiny of the *Hermione,* which he described in his book, *The Black Ship.* The first draft was finished in March and within six weeks, after a few revisions, the manuscript was sent off with two sketches Dudley drew of the port on the Spanish Main, where the mutineers had taken the frigate and which had helped him plan the attack. One sketch was of the port itself, and the other was an offshore view with Ramage's new command, the *Calypso,* in the foreground.

As he always was after finishing a book, Dudley felt listless and at odds with himself. But we were snorkelling every afternoon, and found beautiful murex and cone shells. One afternoon, Dudley returned triumphantly to our dinghy holding a trumpet triton nearly fourteen inches long and the largest we had ever found.

John McLaughlin had written earlier to tell Dudley that there were very complex negotiations going on between Barley and two paperback publishers, Fontana and Futura Books. Futura had offered a higher advance payment for one book in the series, while Fontana was bidding on all the Ramage books, but their advance payments were less. When Barley wrote early in May to explain the details of the offers, she gave Dudley the choice. Without any hesitation he chose Fontana.

With the manuscript of *Morgan* back from London, Dudley next began sorting out the early chapters. Although depressed at how much had to be cut, he hoped it was not going to be too difficult. It was at this point that he decided to start the book with his resumé of the early history of the Caribbean and the Spanish quest for gold, while he put Morgan's funeral and the destruction of Port Royal during the earthquake at the end. However, cutting the manuscript was much more difficult than he thought. He said to me at the time that the story was so long and so complex "the more I cut the longer it gets." In June he finished the first cut and calculated the manuscript came to 165,000 words, having cut fifteen thousand. He then went through it again and managed to cut another five thousand more and then wrote the Notes, Bibliography and Index. As soon as they were finished and typed, we posted the manuscript back to Barley a few weeks later.

In the meantime, a friend had lent Dudley some papers on the loss of H.M.S. *Astrea*, which had foundered on Anegada Reef. Dudley decided to write a book about the *Astrea*'s working life ending with her shipwreck. He drafted a synopsis and sent it to Peter Janson Smith, who liked the idea and commissioned Dudley to write the book for the Oxford University Press. But later, when he was writing the book, Dudley began to think and refer to it as 'Man of War' as his working title and not the *Astrea*, so that it changed from the working life of the frigate H.M.S. *Astrea* and her loss on Anegada Reef, to a book which eventually became *Life in Nelson's Navy*.

During the next few months Dudley read and made notes from his background research material he still had in his files on the *Victory* for his book *England Expects*, and all the notes for the mutiny of the *Hermione* which he used for *The Black Ship*. We still had the set of small line drawings illustrating pieces of equipment found on board, which Harold Wyllie had drawn when they discussed collaborating on a book about the construction and working of the great ships. These were used as illustrations, appearing at the end of each chapter. Then he wrote a new outline and decided there would be twenty-seven chapters, all of which were noted down on his index cards. By late October the first chapter was written. Meanwhile, in London, Steve Cox in Barley's office was busy editing the *Morgan* manuscript. He sent Dudley his list of queries, which were helpful, while Barley wrote that she was very enthusiastic about *Morgan*, but there was a long delay before we received the edited manuscript, because after photocopying the first fifty pages, the office Xerox machine caught fire. However, when the manuscript did arrive at the end of October, Dudley spent a few days reading through it and made his last alterations.

Early in November we stowed and prepared to sail to Antigua. *Ramage* needed to be hauled out again and have the bottom scrubbed and painted again, and also the topsides. We were thinking we would perhaps stay there for a while and not return to Virgin Gorda. We had left the busy and crowded anchorages in Marina Cay and Trellis Bay to find tranquillity in the large expanse of water in the North Sound near The Bitter End and Biras Creek. But now, as more charter boat companies were starting up in the Virgin Islands, even the Sound was becoming crowded. Every evening we were finding more and more of the little charter boats anchoring around us, some so close that if the wind changed direction, they would be alongside. The boats began coming in about 4 p.m., so we often took our afternoon cup of tea out on deck with the boat hook ready to fend off any anchored too near. Whenever Dudley pointed out they were too close and suggested they re-anchor further away, the answer was always: "It's all right!" Often it was not, and Dudley had to resort to stronger language. On one occasion, we hauled in *Ramage*'s anchor and moved closer to Saba Rock, to get out of the way.

We left the Sound in the morning at the beginning of November and headed out into the Anegada Passage. It was going to be another uncomfortable trip sailing to windward with mizzen and staysail set. We saw the sunrise over St. Barts and soon we were anchored in Gustavia Harbour. We rested there for a few days before continuing to Antigua.

CHAPTER FOURTEEN

Antigua 1977–79

The island of Antigua has low rolling hills of grassland and just one high area at the south-west corner, where there is some tropical rain forest. The two most outstanding features of the island are the many beautiful beaches and the large number of ruined sugar mills. Today, the economy depends on tourism but, from the time Europeans first arrived and settled on the island, sugar became the major industry and cotton was grown also. In 1705, there were thirty-four sugar mills, but this quickly grew to 175 by 1748 and many of the ruins of the towers can still be seen. Most of the fortifications at English Harbour and Falmouth were built early in the eighteenth century, but when Nelson was sent out to the Leeward Island Station in the frigate H.M.S. *Boreas* in 1784 the dockyard was not quite finished. Nelson was in English Harbour during two hurricane seasons and today it is also called Nelson's Dockyard. While cruising the surrounding islands under the orders of Admiral Sir Richard Hughes, he visited Nevis where he met the widow Mrs. Frances Nisbet, whom he married in March 1787. Late in 1786, Prince William Henry, Duke of Clarence, later King William IV, arrived in English Harbour from Nova Scotia in command of H.M.S. *Pegasus*. He and Nelson were friends, having been shipmates in a previous posting and the Prince insisted on giving away Mrs. Nisbet at the wedding.

The remains of the forts and army barracks on the hills surrounding English Harbour can still be visited on Shirley Heights, while Fort Berkeley is low down and guards the entrance of English Harbour. Most of the original buildings of the dockyard are on the west side of the harbour and have been beautifully restored. The large copper and lumber store has been turned into apartments. The small apartments of the officers' quarters were rented to individuals, but more recently hold small shops. The superintendent's house is now the museum, the pay office in 1975 had a grocery and offices upstairs, with the yacht chandlery below. The capstan house used to be between the pay office and the quayside, but the capstan still stands there, while the galley is close by and is still serving food and drinks to residents and visitors to the dockyard. On the east side of English Harbour, Clarence House stands on a hill between two small mangrove inlets and Prince William Henry was the first to stay in the house when it was finished. The Antigua slipway lies just to the south of Clarence House near the eastern entrance to the harbour.

In early 1950, Commander Nicholson sailed into English Harbour with his wife and two young sons, Rodney and Desmond, in the schooner *Mollyhawk*. The family pioneered the development of the charter yacht industry in English Harbour and the Society of Friends of English Harbour was formed with the aim of raising funds for the restoration of the dock yard, which was successful and it is now an interesting place for tourists to visit. As well as a busy and important yachting centre, it is still very much a working dockyard. *Ramage* was hauled out at the slipway for a few days and then stayed tied up alongside for more work to be done on board.

Christmas came and we were drawn into the social life, including Commander and Mrs. Nicholson's Sunday cocktail parties at their home, converted from the powder magazine. We met Desmond and Lisa Nicholson again, and Jane soon became friends with their two youngest girls. Desmond Nicholson became closely involved with the restoration of English Harbour and was also a charter member of Antigua's Historical Society, raising the funding for Antigua's two museums. He was also very knowledgeable about the Arawak Indians who lived on fish and shellfish found in the shallow water around the islands and whose small villages were built near the sea on some of the

Leeward Islands, from 700 to 1500 AD. Teams of archaeologists and students from Yale University excavated four sites in Antigua, beginning in the late 1950s. The last visit was at Indian Creek, where the Arawaks built their village on a plateau half a mile up the narrow inlet just to the east of English Harbour. We went one Thursday afternoon to see the site with Desmond when he took a group of visitors on his weekly field trip to Indian Creek. After Desmond finished his talk, we were allowed to poke around in the diggings. Anyone fortunate enough to find a good arrowhead and showing it to Desmond would have it taken for the museum collection.

Early in the New Year of 1977, we took *Ramage* round to Falmouth Harbour, the next bay to the west, which we shared with only one other yacht. It was quiet and pastoral, surrounded by hills and the imposing Monk's Hill, which rises steeply beyond the village of Falmouth, with Fort George on the summit commanding the whole bay. Blake Island, in fact a fortified islet, lies near the west side of Falmouth Harbour, and has the remains of Fort Charles built in 1672, making it one of the oldest in Antigua. The low walls and four large cannons occupy the whole area of the small island. We spent many afternoons there, exploring the coral fringing the island and a shallow sandy area covered with sea grass, finding many seashells in piles outside the octopus holes. It was only a short walk to English Harbour from Falmouth across a narrow neck of land. From where we were anchored we could see the island of Montserrat on the horizon with its high, jagged, volcanic mountain peaks, and had a beautiful view of many glorious sunsets.

We liked the bay so much we did decide to stay and not return to the Virgin Islands. We were anchored close to the Falmouth Beach Apartments managed by Amy West, who took us under her wing. When Amy mentioned that Martha Gellhorn was one of her guests and wanted to meet Dudley, we introduced ourselves and invited her to *Ramage* for a drink one evening. Martha was the well-known journalist and war correspondent besides having been the third wife of Ernest Hemingway. She published many books about her travels and collections of her articles. She reported from Germany the rise of Adolf Hitler and was in Czechoslovakia in 1938 when Germany invaded and occupied the country. She covered the Spanish Civil War for *Collier's Weekly* and the Second World War, sending reports from England, Finland and in the Far East. When she could not obtain credentials to be on the beaches at the D-Day landings in 1944 she dressed herself and went as a stretcher bearer to obtain her news reports. She continued as a war correspondent after the end of World War II and wrote reports from Vietnam, the Israeli Six Day War against Egypt and civil wars in Central America.

Dudley had many questions to ask about her experiences as a war correspondent and Martha was interested to learn about Dudley's books and how we lived on board *Ramage*. Tact prevented us mentioning Ernest and Martha volunteered nothing. She certainly enjoyed her visit to *Ramage* and, since she seemed reluctant to leave, we invited her to share our supper, which Dudley noted in his diary was 'stew'.

Desmond and Lisa Nicholson's house at the top of the hill above the Falmouth Beach Apartments, overlooks the whole bay. When we were invited to lunch one Sunday in January we met Luis Marden who was a regular contributor to the *National Geographic* magazine. He wrote three articles on H.M.S. *Bounty*, Captain Bligh's command, and when her sunken remains were found at Pitcairn Island, he visited the Pacific island during her discovery. Luis was in English Harbour with his own yacht, which he called the *Bounty*, and we very much enjoyed his company over the next two months. Desmond wanted a record of all the guns on the island and when he discovered Dudley had published a book on guns, he asked for help with a survey. On two Sundays we went round the island together, visiting forts to inspect their armament. Afterwards Dudley drew up an inventory for the island's historical records. At Fort James, which is at the entrance to St. Johns Harbour and another of the oldest forts on the island, we found there were ten very fine 24-pounder guns still there with the insignia of King George III embossed on top of the barrels. There were great guns from the men-of-war that once visited English Harbour, standing with their barrels partly buried and used as posts in the dockyard, including a few near the copper and lumber store and the officers' quarters; just as they can be found in London still, often marking the entrance to old alleyways for pedestrians only. Dudley spotted a carronade that was in good condition at the entrance to the dockyard and when H.M.S. *Danae* made a courtesy visit to Antigua on their Caribbean tour, groups of sailors came ashore each day to work on anything that needed repairing or painting. While they were in the dockyard they were asked to dig up the carronade so it could be displayed elsewhere. We found the oldest gun at the old fort on Blake Island, a 24-pounder on the north side, made before 1714 and with the Rose and Crown embossed on the barrel. Later when we were snorkelling below the walls of the island we found two more large guns in the sea.

Early in December, we had received an offer from Pocket Books which came through Doubleday, to reprint *Drumbeat* and *The Triton Brig*. Dudley accepted the offer in the hope they would change their minds from an earlier refusal and publish more of the other available *Ramage* titles. But they showed no further interest, which was hard to understand, since they had now reprinted the first three in the series.

Once we were settled down in Falmouth, Dudley continued his first draft of the book which would become *Life in Nelson's Navy*. He finished it very quickly and found the manuscript needed very little editing. We were living in an appropriate place for Dudley to write this book, with the atmosphere of the dockyard nearby and all the forts on the surrounding hills. A letter came from Peter Janson Smith when he had received and read the manuscript. Dudley was shocked to learn that he did not like the book at all, and could not publish it. Peter's objection was that it was not the book described in the synopsis which Dudley had written when we were still in Virgin Gorda. When Dudley found it among his papers and read it again, he realised he had quite unwittingly written a 'serious standard work' for the Oxford University Press about the Navy in those days. There was no denying the manuscript was nothing like the synopsis: instead of writing about the life of one ship, H.M.S. *Astrea*, he had written about the organisation of the Navy, the ships and the way the men lived on board them. Nevertheless, Dudley was surprised Peter did not like the book, because he felt it was very much more the kind of book that the Oxford University Press would publish. However, John McLaughlin did like the book and set out to find another publisher. Eventually, it was accepted by Allen & Unwin who published it in 1981 with the title *Life in Nelson's Navy*.

When *Ramage's Mutiny* was published in the spring, Barley wrote to say it was at number five on *The Sunday Times* best seller list. Also, Fontana were ready for the publication of their paperback edition of their first two Ramages. They had chosen to begin the series with two titles, *Ramage and the Drumbeat* and *Ramage's Diamond*. Dudley's association with Fontana lasted until the end of his writing life: they published the whole series of the Ramage books with *Ramage and the Dido*, the last he wrote, coming out in 1990. They commissioned the artist Paul Wright to paint the jacket illustrations, which pleased us enormously and Barley liked them, also using them for the dust jackets of her hardback editions. Paul Wright's paintings of those old wooden warships were accurate and full of detail, catching the atmosphere of the ships and the sea.

When the weather was fine and there was not too much wind and swell running, we went round to English Harbour in our Zodiac dinghy, powered by the outboard motor. In this way we could visit our friends anchored out in the harbour. Antigua at this time was suffering with a severe drought so we were unable to catch rain to fill our water tanks. Amy West told us because of a lack of grass to graze, goats and cattle were dying and that some years it did not rain in Antigua until August. But when carnivale began at the beginning of the month, the rain would come. In the meantime she let us fill a few jerry cans with water. The alternative was to take *Ramage* round to English Harbour to take on water at the slipway's fuel dock.

Jane had plenty of opportunities to go sailing while we were in Antigua. Now she was twelve she would be off to school in the United States within a year. She had become a very good sailor, very quick to anticipate before things happened, such as ropes getting caught up or jamming in blocks. She became a permanent member of one of the racing boats for the Thursday afternoon races. It was a short course, leaving English Harbour at five p.m. and returning just before sunset in time for the cocktail hour at the flagpole in the dockyard. She also crewed occasionally on one of the yachts that went out on charter for the day, and we loved to see her go, happy to miss a day's school. About this time, she had one glorious week on board the brigantine *Romance*, owned by friends based in the Virgin Islands. They collected her when they arrived in Antigua, cruised through a few islands and, when they reached St. Kitts, put her on an aeroplane to return to Antigua. The latter part of the week had been very wet and when we met her at Antigua airport, Jane came through the arrivals door looking like a little wet mouse in a huge yellow oilskin jacket.

Suddenly, in May, the whole plot for *Ramage and the Rebels* came to Dudley and he began writing the ninth in the series. A major part of the book is set in Curaçao and is adapted from a true incident when in 1800 the governor surrenders the island to a passing British frigate. The first draft was finished at the beginning of September and he spent the rest of the month editing the manuscript. *Ramage and the Rebels* was published in May 1978 and soon after it reached number seven on *The Sunday Times* best seller list.

Barley and the sales people at Secker & Warburg were anxious to have Dudley in London for the publication of *Harry Morgan's Way* to generate some publicity and promotion for the book and she invited Dudley to stay with her. As soon as he arrived in London he was busy with radio and newspaper interviews, as well as visits to bookshops. He went to Chatham, still a naval town, for an interview with the Chatham News and was also on Radio Medway. On a visit to Yorkshire for the weekend with Barley, he was interviewed by the Yorkshire Post and Radio Leeds. He went to Bush House and was interviewed for two B.B.C. World Service programmes, the Caribbean Magazine and the Book Writers' programme. Barley also arranged many dinner parties for him to meet and get to know everyone at Seeker's, including Tim Manderson, the Director for Sales. A few days earlier he also met John McLaughlin, his agent, for the first time at a quiet dinner at Harley Gardens and had lunch with Simon King, his editor at Fontana, where he learned the sales so far for *Diamond* were 37,500 and *Drumbeat* 34,100 copies.

Simon King, who was always enthusiastic about the Ramage books, wrote late in November to say Dudley's visit to London was 'a triumph'; while Barley sent a cable to tell us *Harry Morgan's Way* had won the Brighton Marina award, which was a gold medal for the best Book of the Sea in 1977. Barley received the prize on Dudley's behalf at the London Boat Show early in January of 1978 and, in a letter to us, she described receiving the medal and since it is heavy and encapsulated in plastic, called it *'absolutely the most upmarket paperweight'* anyone could have. The biography was published in the United States five months later by Dodd Mead with the title *The Buccaneer King*.

While in London, Dudley also saw a neurologist and an ear, nose and throat specialist. Even when walking the short distance to the dockyard from Falmouth Harbour he arrived feeling quite distressed with dizziness and nausea. He first noticed and complained of his vertigo when we were at Marina Cay in the British Virgin Islands, but the condition was becoming worse and he was now using a walking stick. After tests and a head and ear X-ray, the diagnosis was that the balance mechanism in his left ear was permanently damaged. When Dudley was on his ship the *Silver Willow,* during World War II, he had been in charge of a Bofors gun, standing on its right side, giving instructions to the gunners and close enough to the firing without ear protection, which caused the injury to his left ear. For many years his right ear had been compensating for the left, and we recollected instances in the past when he had had bad falls and it also explained why he never enjoyed dancing during the days of our courtship. A year later on a visit to New York, Dudley had a scan by Computerized Axial Tomography (CAT) of his brain which also showed an old trauma, most likely caused when his ship was torpedoed and he was thrown from the bridge.

Dudley began writing his Second World War novel early in 1978. His hero, Ned Yorke, has to discover why certain convoys of merchant ships are attacked in the Atlantic by German U-boats which appear to get inside the convoy without being detected by the Royal Navy escorts. The idea first came to him when we were in Virgin Gorda where he made a rough sketch of the plot. All the background for this modern novel came from his own wartime experiences, when he was at sea in the Merchant Navy in convoys, his months in hospital at Ashford, and life during the bombing in wartime London. He certainly evoked the atmosphere of London at the time and the last three or four chapters are quite dramatic. When *Convoy* was published in May 1979 it became the Book Club selection.

During the summer, Dudley began thinking over ideas for the next book, writing them down when they occurred to him. He considered setting a Ramage at the Battle of Copenhagen or during the Treaty of Amiens, when there was peace between Britain and France from March 1802 to May 1803. But another completely different idea came to him, setting the next book back in the Mediterranean. He decided he would like Ramage to capture two bomb ketches, and after searching through his files all day for an illustration of a bomb ketch to help him write a description, he found one finally in his own large illustrated book *Guns*. He wrote the book quickly and after editing and polishing, the manuscript was posted to Barley at the end of the year.

We heard Antigua's veterinary surgeon had two Siamese kittens for sale, so taking one of English Harbour's taxis, I went over and brought back a little male kitten, carrying him fast asleep in a canvas holdall bag wrapped in a towel. We called him Jackson also, and he soon proved to be a very active kitten. He settled down on board, investigated everywhere, ate voraciously and drank a great deal of milk. He used his sandbox within an hour of being on board, and played all evening and night too, bringing down a pile of paperback books from the bookshelf over my bunk in the early hours of the morning. After shutting our cabin door, Jackson stayed in the saloon the rest of the night.

Early one morning when he was older, we had a call by radio telephone from neighbours anchored nearby, to tell us we had a rat climbing up our anchor cable. It was a very wet cat trying to climb up and get over the fairlead at the bow, and it was possible he had fallen back into the water a few times. Dudley prepared a short piece of thick rope and put three knots in it to hang over the side amidships for Jackson to climb up and get back on board if he ever fell over the side again. But he never did, which was surprising as I often saw him walking along the bulwarks. He had a 'mad' hour early each evening, rushing round the deck, up along the booms, through one window of the deckhouse and out another on the opposite side of the saloon, alarming any visitors sitting there. When I was in the galley and rattled a saucepan, Jackson would fly through the saloon from the cockpit, taking the two sets of steps almost in one great leap, hoping his dinner was ready for him.

There were plans for Dudley to visit London again in May to go on a book tour for Fontana, visiting nine cities as well as London itself in two weeks. He had a quiet weekend with Barley before a hectic week began, first going to Glasgow and Edinburgh, followed by visits to Newcastle, Manchester, Birmingham, Norwich, Plymouth, Leeds, Bristol. In all of these cities he had interviews with the press, radio and TV, visited bookshops and attended receptions in the evenings for sales representatives and booksellers. Dudley enjoyed meeting them all and hearing how his books were selling. Everywhere he went he recorded the day's events on tape, so I could hear how the tour went, and we played them back when he returned to Antigua.

Although it was most unusual for the time of year, it rained for most of May when Dudley was away, with a low pressure system that remained stationary over Antigua. Being unable to work outside on deck, I was busy down below and painted the saloon, our cabin and galley as well as laying new carpets. It was a perfect opportunity to do this whilst Dudley was away.

We had experienced a little difficulty in renewing our residence permits for six months at the beginning of the year. Many more yachts were coming to Antigua, besides the regular working yachts with their charters. English Harbour was overflowing and more were coming to anchor in Falmouth Harbour. Friends had already sailed to St. Martin and they had recommended Simpson Lagoon as an excellent anchorage. Accordingly, we were thinking of leaving.

Two days after Dudley's return, however, an event occurred that really unsettled us and made up our minds to leave the island as soon as possible: at lunchtime a launch came alongside *Ramage* with armed police and a Customs officer who ordered us to go to English Harbour. When we asked why, we were told it was for security reasons. It would appear something was worrying the authorities.

We were able to have *Ramage* hauled out at the slipway immediately and stayed at the yard three weeks to have the bottom and topsides painted. Amidst all this work, a cable arrived from Barley to say the proofs of *The Ramage Touch* had come in early and had been sent to St. Martin. As soon as we were ready we sailed at the end of June, just after some bad weather had passed through the area. We made good time with a fair wind and reached St. Martin just twenty hours later and anchored in Marigot.

CHAPTER FIFTEEN

St. Martin 1979–1982

The village of Marigot nestles on the water's edge under a hill capped by Fort Louis. From *Ramage's* deck we could see more hills behind the fort rising until they reach Peak Paradis, the highest point on the island at almost 1,400 feet. Although Christopher Columbus was the first to claim the island for Spain during one of his voyages of discovery at the end of the fifteenth century, ownership of St. Martin was also disputed between France, Holland and Britain until 1648. In this year France and Holland signed the Treaty of Concordia in which it was agreed to divide the island of thirty-seven square miles between them and have shared it ever since.

Thus the name of the island has two spellings: St. Maarten for the Dutch side and St. Martin for the French. The early Dutch colonists settled in the southern part of the island, and built their main town, Philipsburg, on Great Bay. The French, in the northern part, have the town and port of Marigot, and also a small fishing village called Grand Case a few miles further up the coast on the north-western shore. The border between the two sides of the island is open and marked only with a monument on the road near Oyster Pond and another at Bellevue on the main road between Philipsburg and Marigot.

The most striking feature of the island is the number of salt ponds and lagoons, large and small. Those behind Philipsburg were used commercially to harvest salt: there was a system of canals and sluice gates to allow sea water to enter the ponds and evaporate under the hot sun, leaving the salt residue to be collected. This industry continued until 1949 and was for many years one of the most successful on the island. In the early days with slavery, cash crops such as sugar cane, cotton, indigo and even tobacco were grown, as well as the subsistent crops of cassava, sweet potatoes, yams, tomatoes and pimentos. But the crops failed at times with the uncertain and irregular rainfall, which plagues the northern Leeward Islands from Antigua to the Virgin Islands.

Simpson Lagoon is the largest and stretches along the southern shore from a few miles west of Philipsburg, almost to the western end of the island. It is nearly five miles long and perhaps half a mile wide in some places, bordered by hills on the landward side. There are a few lower hills at the south-western end, which curve in a semicircle, suggesting it may have been the remains of an old volcanic crater. The lagoon stretches northward for three miles along the western shore on the French side and in 1979 was lined with mangroves as far as Sandy Ground and Marigot. Unfortunately, these disappeared by 1990 with the rapid expansion of the whole island, when many hotels were built in an attempt to develop a viable tourist trade. This lagoon is a good hurricane shelter for fishing boats and yachts and where we anchored *Ramage* each hurricane season during the next eight years. There are two ways into the lagoon, one with a short canal on the south shore at Simpson Bay and the other in Marigot Bay at Sandy Ground, both with a lifting bridge which open daily at regular times for vessels to enter and leave the lagoon.

We settled down in St. Martin, first anchoring in Marigot on the French side, but within a few weeks we moved into Simpson Lagoon for the hurricane season. There we had a safe anchorage at the western end between the mangrove shoreline and two islets so that we were well inside the boundary on the French side of the lagoon. *Ramage*'s bow always headed into the trade winds, eastwards towards the beautiful view of Marigot and the hills of the island rising to Peak Paradis.

In July, Dudley accepted an offer from the U.S. Naval Institute Press to publish *Life in Nelson's Navy*. While Allen & Unwin in London were preparing the manuscript for the printer, there were a few copy editor's queries to be answered and they agreed to use Colin Mudie's cutaway drawing of the *Victory* that was published in *England Expects,* as well as Harold Wyllie's little drawings of equipment on board a man of war, which were put at the end of each chapter.

Dudley began writing *Ramage's Signal* soon afterwards, although the plot was not completely fixed in his mind. The book progressed slowly at first and the passage of two hurricanes interrupted his work in September. Because he was feeling unhappy about the way the story was developing, he decided to go through the manuscript from the beginning only to find it was not as dull as he feared. Reading the manuscript helped clear his mind and soon he was writing ten pages a day. The story features semaphore towers along the French Mediterranean coast and how messages were relayed to and received from ships cruising offshore.

The hurricane season became very active in September with two hurricanes forming out in the Atlantic. The first was *David,* and as it came near, old friends from Antigua and the Virgin Islands cruising close to St. Martin sought shelter in Simpson Lagoon. The bridge opened frequently to allow yachts and dozens of island trading vessels and small merchant ships to come into the lagoon. *David* proved to be one of the worst of the century and fortunately passed south of St. Martin, although there were some strong gusts of wind during the night. However, Dominica and Martinique had a great deal of damage as the hurricane passed through the passage between those two islands. We heard later that *David* crossed Santo Domingo and Haiti where 600 people died. In Dominica it was reported 60,000 could be homeless, with every building in Roseau without a roof. A British frigate, stationed in the Caribbean every hurricane season to help any of the British islands, went to Roseau to help restore the infrastructure. They would have run an electricity cable from the frigate's generators to the hospital and command centre during the emergency, as well as sailors going ashore to clear the roads and airport runway. Our turn came six days later on 3 September with Hurricane *Frederick,* the centre crossing the island in the afternoon. We had strong squalls for hours which heeled *Ramage* to the bulwark capping, and torrential rain reduced visibility to a few yards. We listened to St. Thomas radio and heard the commentator talking to a French meteorologist in the neighbouring island of St. Barths, where gusts of 119 miles per hour were recorded. The trimaran *Zelina* was anchored near us with the Clark family living on board. Early in the morning before the wind became strong, Raymond, the elder of two small boys, swam over to *Ramage* to stay with us. He slept in Jane's bunk all afternoon and woke to find that *Zelina* had lost her mast. The rain continued for several more days after the centre of the hurricane passed over the island. The Great Salt Pond behind Philipsburg filled and overflowed, flooding much of the town and two supermarkets.

St. Martin is one of a group of five islands: the British island of Anguilla lies five miles to the north-west at the closest point between the two islands, while St. Bartholomew (always known as St. Barths) is twelve miles to the south-east from Oyster Pond, on the east side of St. Martin. It takes one and a half hours by ferry to St. Barths, but longer for a for a yacht sailing to windward. The Dutch islands of Saba and Statia are further to south, but can be seen on fine days from the south shore of St. Martin. Like the French side of St. Martin, St. Barths fell under the Department of Guadeloupe until 2007, when the two islands voted to have direct ties with France. The two are known collectively as the 'Isles du Nord' (Northern Islands).

Jane began going to boarding school in the United States this year. Her homecomings for school holidays were always eagerly awaited and yet each time I faced the devastation of her departure. We were able to meet and return her to the airport by *Ramage*'s dinghy, and because Dudley also found the 'goodbyes' stressful, I took her across the lagoon to a landing not far from the airport terminal. After seeing her to the door at immigration, I so often returned to the dinghy with tears in my eyes. In the cabin one day soon after she began going away I found her diving wet suit, which completely rocked me and I found myself standing there crying. She came home from school a week before Christmas and we sailed to St. Barths for the holiday.

We always found the little town and port of Gustavia delightful with a typical tropical style of architecture used in the French Caribbean islands and, at that time, completely untouched by tourism. Between the years of 1785 and 1878 St. Barths had belonged to Sweden and then, under the Treaty of Sale, to France. The Swedes had insisted St. Barths should remain free of all taxes and duties in perpetuity. In 1979, there was a large warehouse on the quay, stocked to the rafters with all kinds of liquor and wine. The quay was always busy with small trading vessels coming in to load up with duty free liquor to take to islands, and was also smuggled to Venezuela. The houses around the rectangular harbour are set back on a wide quay. All have red roofs and white painted walls, and there is a clock tower, with its sides covered with wooden shingles halfway up the hill and a church beyond. We stayed six days in Gustavia, making new friends among the yachting community. On Christmas Day there was a turkey barbecue on the quay and all were invited.

We were back at anchor in Marigot for New Year's Eve and 1980 was ushered in with fireworks and long barrages of fire crackers set off along the shore. This past year had seen the Germans and Japanese beginning to translate and publish the Ramage series, *Convoy* and *The Ramage Touch* had been published, and Dudley had done a successful book tour in eight cities for Fontana in Britain.

To make a change from writing the Ramage books, Dudley decided to write one or two novels set in the Caribbean during the time of the buccaneers. He had compiled a large amount of material for his biography of Sir Henry Morgan and decided to call his hero Ned Yorke, a forebear of his Royal Navy hero in Convoy. In fact, Dudley wrote four of these books set in Jamaica in the 1650s when Oliver Cromwell was in power and many Cavaliers fled to France with King Charles II, while others went to the Caribbean. They converted their sailing vessels into privateers, joining Henry Morgan and the Brethren of the Coast. Some of the episodes in these novels were adapted from Morgan's raids on the Spanish Main. Although Ned Yorke's second in command, Sir Thomas

Whetstone, was indeed a buccaneer with Morgan, Dudley never considered including Morgan himself. I found these Yorke novels more romantic than the Ramages, possibly because of the period. When the first manuscript arrived in London John McLaughlin wrote that it had been enthusiastically received.

We were still going out to snorkel and look for seashells some afternoons and one of our favourite places in St. Martin became La Belle Creole, where we were finding many species in a lagoon enclosed from the sea by a natural rocky barrier. We bought an 18-foot Boston Whaler with a powerful outboard motor so that on calm days we could go quickly up the coast to the reef at Crole Rock on the edge of Grand Case Bay. Other days when the weather was calm, we went further to Pinel or Tintamarre Island. Dudley had made me a strong net with a stout handle which I used to sieve sand. I brought the samples of the dredgings back to the boat and, after a few days when it was dry, I went through the tiny grains and pieces of coral with a magnifying glass and tweezers. I had begun doing this in the Virgin Islands and in St. Martin I found many more shells I did not have, and a few I could not identify. Some years later I was able to go to Holland and visit the Museum of Comparative Zoology at the University of Amsterdam and meet the staff there. Later, one marine biologist identified most of my shells, but one was new to science, which he very kindly named after me.

Early in July we received a very sad letter from a friend in Bermuda to tell us Frank Casper had died and was buried in Bermuda on 6 June. It would appear that Frank was taken ill during his voyage, confined to his bunk and *Elsie* sailed him to Bermuda with the self-steering gear and wind vane, coming close to shore on the reef at the Castle Harbour Hotel. Later, divers on the reef found Frank's Blue Water Medal for Cruising awarded to him by the Cruising Club of America for his circumnavigation round the world and his many other voyages. Frank had written to us a few weeks before he sailed, giving us his views on the political situation in Antigua at the time; sympathising with Dudley's difficulty in walking distances, which Frank himself had experienced, and also describing his 'hurricane experiences':

"About 100 yachts in English Harbour for hurricanes David and Frederick; no damage. A few boats anchored out, but most boats went into the mangroves, which I believe is necessary because of lack of swinging room. David *had the stronger winds, and I had two anchors out and dragged about 50 feet while anchored in the Cove. When* Freddy *came along, I chickened and ran bow into soft mud in the mangroves (about 5 ft of water under the bow) with two anchors out astern. About 10 feet spacing between adjacent boats. The eye passed directly overhead, a 20-minute calm (during which one anchor was reset), then a wind reversal. The wind reversal caused a heavy current surge, broadside to the boats, but no damage."*

He also gave us news of his sailing plans for the spring, hoping to sail up to Bermuda, possibly returning to the Caribbean via the Azores (possibly even the U.K.), the Canaries, Barbados etc. and maybe end up in St. Martin. Alas, it wasn't to be.

Between July and December Dudley wrote *Ramage and the Renegades,* the twelfth book in the series. The story is set during the Treaty of Amiens, that short period of peace between France and Britain. Ramage is ordered to sail to South America where he is ordered to make a survey of the island of Trinidade, several hundred miles off the coast of Brazil. He obtained details about Trinidade Island from the ships' logs published in the book called *Private Sea Journals 1778-1782,* kept by Admiral Sir Thomas Pasley, edited by a descendant and published in 1931. He had bought this volume in a second-hand bookshop in England many years before and kept it among his books and papers in his small research library on board *Ramage.* Ships often called at Trinidade to rendezvous and fill up with fresh water. Captain Pasley put an expedition ashore to survey and colonise Trinidade in October 1781, establishing a small settlement. It was abandoned just a year later, when twenty-eight men and one woman were taken off by the captain of H.M.S. *Bristol* while passing with a convoy in December 1782. Before Dudley finished the book he suddenly had an idea for Paolo to deliver a letter from his aunt to Ramage at an appropriate moment during the voyage. This was in fact Dudley's solution to writing *Gianna, the Marchesa di Volterra,* out of future *Ramage* books. In the letter she says her duty lies with her kingdom in Italy and is returning there, while Ramage's duty will always remain with the Navy. Making it clear she will not see Ramage again, Gianna hopes he will eventually marry and find happiness.

When the printers' proofs for *Life in Nelson's Navy* arrived in July 1980, there were so many errors that Dudley asked Allen & Unwin to send him the revised proofs once they had been reset. These came a few weeks later and while reading through them for one last check, more printers' errors had crept in. The most extraordinary was 'telescope' which had been changed to 'telephone' and Dudley was afraid what else could be changed before the book came out. In fact, there were more problems before the book reached the bookshops. Both the American and British editions were printed in the United States. Peter Leek, Dudley's editor at Allen & Unwin, wrote a year later:

". . . The saga of the book seems to be unending; the Naval Institute Press delivered our copies to the shippers early in April, but apparently the shippers failed to dispatch the books to us until well into May, allegedly because of industrial action by New York dockers protesting against Mrs. Thatcher's treatment of the IRA hunger-strikers. In fact, we suspect that the shippers were waiting to fill up a container. Eventually, after several cables and phone calls they established that the books had been shipped and landed at Felixstowe, where they were held up by a British dock dispute. The latest news is that they are now in Northampton and are likely to be in our warehouse at Hemel Hempstead by the time you receive this letter. The moment they arrive I will air mail you some copies . . . In rash anticipation of the book's arrival we have now rescheduled publication for July 23rd. If you offer us another book, which I very much hope you will do, I have a feeling we shall use different typesetters and print it in Britain!"*

We received another letter from him eight days later to say

the books had finally arrived. But there was a postscript to the saga: the container was impounded by H.M. Customs at Felixstowe because some other books in it did not have the right documentation. Fortunately Allen & Unwin persuaded the Customs to release their boxes of *Life in Nelson's Navy*.

Dudley finished the first draft of *Ramage and the Renegades* just before Christmas. Jane returned home, followed by Barley, who was coming to stay for a winter holiday at the little Pirate Hotel on the beach close to where *Ramage* lay at anchor. The New Year of 1981 was ushered in at midnight with fireworks from the fort above Marigot and many firecrackers. Dudley was in a more buoyant mood at this time, feeling the past year had been a good one.

When Barley arrived she persuaded him to allow her to read the *Renegades* manuscript and was busy editing it for him. Even so, we did go out together some afternoons to La Belle Creole to look for shells. Jane returned to school early in January, while Barley left a few days afterwards. Dudley then read through the manuscript himself and made a few more changes, before the final version was sent off to Barley at the end of January. In the meantime, Barley was negotiating with John McLaughlin, having offered new contracts for two more *Ramage* and two *Yorke* novels. Soon Dudley began jotting down ideas for the next book, *Admiral*, which would continue the story of the buccaneer Ned Yorke. By early April, he had written about 30,000 words and the story was at last going well. Late one afternoon while we were having our usual cup of tea, an army mutiny idea came to him, as he said to me, *"right out of the blue"* in exactly the same way an idea had come for an episode while he was writing *Buccaneer*.

Then suddenly towards the end of April, Dudley began having tachycardia paroxysms, which he had had when we were in Puerto Rico in 1972. Caused by stress and overwork, his heart began beating rapidly for short periods of time. After finishing *Ramage and the Renegades* just before Christmas, he was finding it hard to relax and it was not long afterwards that he had begun noting down ideas for *Admiral*. After resting and reading for a few days, taking medicine to calm his heartbeat, Dudley began to feel better. But during June he went through a period of feeling tired and not very interested in writing. As he said to me at the time, he just did not want "to respond to the challenge". Yet he had completed Yorke's raid on La Providencia and was writing about the buccaneers attack on Portobello. Because he was not happy with the way it was developing, he decided to leave this last episode in the book for a while and began editing the manuscript instead.

Later Dudley rewrote the buccaneers' entry into Portobello and the attack that follows. Then he was finally satisfied with the way the book ended.

Collins in Canada had invited Dudley to do a book tour for their Fontana paperbacks of the *Ramage* series. He flew to Toronto on 17 October and had thirteen gruelling days visiting six Canadian cities, crossing the country from Nova Scotia in the east to British Colombia in the west. Just before he left, Barley sent a telegram to say she loved *Admiral* and it was being edited; Fontana had bought *Ramage and the Renegades* and she wished Dudley 'bon voyage'. His first day in Toronto was a Sunday and friends, who lived in Chicago, drove up to spend the day with him; they lunched together and then took Dudley on a tour of Toronto and the surrounding countryside, where he saw the leaves of the maple trees turning gold and red.

A very intensive schedule then followed with radio, TV and newspaper interviews. On the first day, a radio interview was followed by another with the magazine *Canadian Yachting* and then a newspaper interview with the *Globe & Mail*. He then flew to Ottawa, where he was met by Collins' Eastern Division manager. Here, the next day, he had two TV and three radio interviews as well as one with the newspaper, the Ottawa *Citizen*. They had lunch at the Town Mess of the Royal Canadian Navy and then Dudley visited the War Museum.

Later in the day, the tour continued with a drive to Montreal, where he had three radio interviews the following day. Halifax was the next destination and the pace became even more intensive with five radio, or TV, interviews and with one newspaper and the day after six more radio interviews and one with *The Daily News*. After dinner at the officers' mess in the wardroom of the Royal Canadian Navy's Fleet School, Dudley was given ten minutes' warning to give an hour's talk. Unfortunately I was not there, but I am sure he carried it off without any difficulty and the evening was apparently a great success.

For the second week of the tour he flew from the Atlantic Ocean to the Pacific: a flight that took nine and a half hours from Halifax, Nova Scotia, to Vancouver in British Columbia, including a call at Montreal airport, where there was a one hour delay followed by another at Calgary caused by snow. He finally arrived at his destination on a Saturday evening and the following day was able to visit friends in Vancouver with whom we had spent many Sundays in Virgin Gorda, going on picnics and shelling. The week continued with interviews on radio and TV, and with newspapers, both in Vancouver and then Victoria on Vancouver Island. Another friend we knew in the Virgin Islands telephoned the radio station while Dudley was being interviewed on the air. A visit to Winnipeg followed with more interviews and then Dudley had one more working day in Toronto. The last day ended with a reception at H.M.C.S. *Yorke* and Dudley was asked to give another one hour talk, which was also a great success. Barley had sent a shipment of *Ramage and the Renegades* by sea which was very delayed. So at the last minute she sent more copies by air freight so they should be available with all the publicity of the book tour. In his letter to Barley giving her a report, Dudley wrote:

". . . the figures were formidable – 12,000 miles of flying, 6 TV appearances of more than twenty minutes screen time, 21 radio interviews of more than fifteen minutes, 10 major newspaper interviews (i.e. counting only big cities), two 1-hour talks to 100 R.C.N officers of commander and upwards . . ." ". . . BUT RAMAGE AND THE RENEGADES was delivered late in Canada, and despite the 400 air freighted extra copies, was not on sale in any of the cities at the time I was on radio or TV until I reached Victoria and Winnipeg, the last two of the tour.

KAY POPE

SIGNAL was thick on the ground – six feet of shelf space in some shops. But most of the rest are out of print. So Collins, Canada, did a truly fine promotion job of the tour – quite up to Fontana, London, standards, but questions need asking in London . . ."

Early in November, in spite of the fact that after the Canadian book tour he was so mentally exhausted he could not read more than a few paragraphs of a book or magazine, Dudley drafted a vague idea for the next Ramage to follow *Renegades*. In fact we were busy doing maintenance work on board *Ramage* most of the next two months to make *Ramage* ready to sail to Antigua, as we had an appointment to haul out at the slipway in January.

So 1981 ended; during which Dudley had finished *Ramage and the Renegades* and written *Admiral,* as well as visiting Canada for the promotion of the Ramage paperbacks for Fontana. As a result of this tour, which Collins considered a great success, Dudley received a letter from Nick Harris, president of Collins Canada, written on 12 March 1982. He reported that in 1980 the sales for *Ramage's Signal* were 6,983, while for *Ramage and the Renegades* up to the date of his letter, the sales were 14,660 – more than 100 per cent increase.

When we returned to Marigot after our visit to Antigua, Dudley was soon working on *Ramage's Devil*. The story begins while Britain and France are still at peace in 1803 and Ramage with his wife Sarah are in Brittany on their honeymoon. When hostilities begin again between Britain and France, Ramage and Sarah escape from Brest and find the Channel Fleet and Ramage regains his command of the Calypso. He is then ordered to sail across the Atlantic to Devil's Island at Cayenne. When the manuscript arrived in London it was sent off to the printers without any cuts or alterations.

This left Dudley feeling more than just the usual let down after finishing a book. He wrote in his diary at the time that he was feeling *"absolutely exhausted: absolutely drained. I simply have no feelings for anything and this is what I cannot get Kay to understand: that I want a complete rest. She has got so used to me producing books and solutions to problems that she thinks any complaints are melodrama."* This was said to me many times during these years when he was writing two books a year and was feeling so tired. Whatever I said in reply never mollified him. With my more optimistic outlook on life, he felt I did not worry as much as I should and it irked him that I appeared not take him seriously enough.

But apart from the usual exhaustion and feeling low after finishing a book, he was always anxious about providing enough income for us to exist. Although the payments for the mortgage on *Ramage* were paid off by 1975 and we had also repaid the money we owed our friends, he had the financial worry of being sure we had enough income for Jane's school fees now that she was going to boarding school in the United States. Fortunately, he did take a long break from writing and did not begin another book until three months had passed. He tried to relax, but was deeply worried about his lack of ideas for a buccaneer Yorke he had planned to write next. After doing nothing for a while, he kept himself busy doing maintenance on board *Ramage*, while trying to work out a Morgan period story. Finally, Dudley wrote to Barley to tell her that two books a year was too much and received a very understanding letter in reply. She was also worried about the strain caused by the number of books that he had written during the last few years. However, he did have an idea to write another World War II Yorke in which his hero captures a U-boat to get an Enigma machine. He wrote a synopsis and sent it to Barley on 17 August, saying this was the book he would like to write next:

". . . Quite apart from the fact that I am very keen on the new WW II story, the fact is I have not yet dreamed up a 1660s story that is sufficiently different from 'Buccaneer' and 'Admiral' to fire me into starting it. However, so we don't get too behind I am anxious to start the next Yorke book and have at least a first draft ready for you to read at Christmas, if not the final MS. Although I hate you knowing what the story is until you read the complete MS, because it takes away from some of the surprise, I'm in fact enclosing a fairly stark synopsis because I'm sure you will want to talk over the proposal with Tim. The final story might well

vary in detail as new ideas usually tumble round me once I start writing . . ."

Barley was coming to St. Martin to stay at Le Pirate again for Christmas and already Dudley was putting pressure on himself to have the rough draft of this book written in time for her to read when she arrived. Barley sent a cable on 31 August which said: *OF COURSE WRITE A SECOND WORLD WAR YORKE STOP LETTER FOLLOWING. LOVE BARLEY.* We received the letter ten days later:

"My Dear Dudley,
"Of course you need not write another seventeenth century YORKE next if you don't want to. For that matter, nor need you do anything you don't want to. You write of yourself rather as though you were one of those Robot drink dispensers one finds on motorways: you put in your 30p and press the required button to get a plastic beaker of luke-warm chocolate, tea, tomato soup or black or white coffee. You will be dumbfounded to hear that the picture of you in the minds of those at Poland Street is nearer to the last *lot of photographs Jane took of you* [on board Ramage] *than to the aforementioned machine. We actually think of you as a live human being who eats, sleeps, breathes, gets bored, has ideas that fire the imagination, feels enthusiasms, etc . . . Dare you believe it? Moreover, those of us who have read the WW II YORKE synopsis actually share your enthusiasm and think it sounds like a marvellous story. I can hardly wait for Christmas. I have never fully understood what anyone did at Bletchley, let alone the Enigma machine, but the build-up, then the life boat and finally the captured U-boat sound not-put-downable . . . I must now sound a slight note of caution. Tim Manderson, as you know, thinks that it is your name that sells the books, but you will recall that he thought too long a seventeenth or nineteenth century interval would make fans nervous lest you had killed off one or other of their heroes . . . There are also those in London who say that World War II is no longer as popular or fashionable as it was eighteen months or two years ago. It is also rumoured that there are several novels with Enigma backgrounds on the stocks. This does not worry me at all since, though vital, it is*

quite a small part of your plot. All of which is another way of saying that we will publish the book with enormous pride and enthusiasm but would not like to say, at this stage, that we will sell quite as many copies as we do of the RAMAGES. But rest assured that we shall do our damnedest to do so."

Barley then wrote about lengthy high-level discussions going on to decide which paperback publisher in the U.K. and Canada should be offered the book: Corgi, Hamlyn or General-Publishing. She then continued her letter with the comment: *". . . We could do with a few more authors whose books raise problems of a 'which' rather than a 'whether' kind in Canadian and paperback circles! . . . So full steam ahead please and if I can bring a typescript back with me in January we will publish W.W.11 Yorke IV in July or August 1983 . . ."*

Dudley began writing *Decoy* at the end of August and by the middle of November he had reached the most difficult passage in the book where a German U-boat surfaces alongside Yorke's lifeboat. But he did not have any books on board giving descriptions of German submarines, so Dudley wrote to our friend in Chicago, where at the Museum of Science and Industry the World War II German submarine U-505 is on display. Soon we received a packet of photographs and literature which gave him everything he needed to describe the U-boat that his hero had to capture with his boarding party, disguised as seamen in a lifeboat who had abandoned ship.

In December, *Ramage* was anchored in her usual place off Le Pirate Hotel in Marigot and Dudley was close to finishing the first draft of *Decoy*. Jane was home from school for Christmas and when Barley arrived the manuscript was ready for her to read each morning. She then came over to *Ramage* for lunch and, weather permitting, we went snorkelling in the afternoons. On Dudley's fifty-seventh birthday at the end of the year, he said to me he felt his body was a bit like *"a boat, developing defects here and there."* However, he was cheerful because Barley told him that she expected sales for *Ramage's Devil* to be fourteen thousand,

while Iris Murdoch's sales were often not more than eight to ten
thousand hardback copies sold.

CHAPTER SIXTEEN

St. Martin 1983-1986

During the early months of 1983 we experienced a very social time with several friends who, having sailed across the Atlantic to Grenada late the year before and cruised leisurely up the island chain, came to Marigot to visit us. We were planning to take Ramage to the slipway in Antigua after everyone had departed to return to England in May. In the meantime, we were catching up with the maintenance work on board.

Dudley had edited *Decoy* quickly as it seemed Barley only had a few minor queries and we posted it to London early in February. Two months passed and there had been no word from her that the manuscript had gone to the printers. Dudley was at first worried and then began to be irritated. So when a letter did arrive from Barley in the middle of April, asking for cuts to speed up the narrative, delete some duplications and several other pages that Seckers' lawyer said were libellous, Dudley became exasperated. He finally answered her on 1 May asking her not to publish the book and release him from the contract.

Five days later a telex came from Barley, saying she had sent *Decoy* to the printers. This astonished us, because of what Barley had said in her letter. Dudley assumed she sent it to the printer to avoid returning it while he was insisting to be freed of the contract. He had pet hates and one of them was the British Foreign Office, their policies, and the embassies overseas. He had very little time for politicians and always had strong opinions about British foreign policy. But he regarded Mrs. Thatcher an exceptional woman and supported the invasion of the Falkland

Islands that had taken place just the year before. He deplored the lack of intelligence that should have been reported from Argentina and had said at the time: *"What the devil were our intelligence people doing and the embassy.in Buenos Aires while the Argentines are assembling ships and 'planes to invade the Falklands?"*

In *Ramage and the Freebooters*, Dudley had portrayed the governor of Grenada as inadequate and in his buccaneer series his hero Yorke is contemptuous of the governor of Jamaica. More to the point, in *Decoy* he had made strong criticisms of the Foreign Office, the Ministry of Transport for the design of their lifeboats and lifejackets for seamen, politicians and civil servants, and until we received the *Decoy* proofs, he did not know what cuts Barley had made. Just as Dudley was always critical of the Foreign Office, this establishment was Barley's great love, having worked in the British Embassy in Paris and then in London. Dudley had offended her loyalties and it was inevitable she would object to some of the passages in *Decoy*. As the years passed Dudley's opinions were becoming more conservative and in conversation with Barley he was finding himself more often disagreeing with her.

In fact, Barley confided to me a few years later when I was helping her in the kitchen, that she regarded Dudley as her "right wing anarchist!"

But Barley was one of the few people Dudley knew who could talk more than himself. It was hard to stop her when she was in full flow, and once in frustration Dudley said: "Barley, you even interrupt me interrupting you!" Barley smiled and admitted Saul Bellow, who was also one of her authors, makes the same complaint. Having written to ask Barley to cancel the contract, Dudley had then very wisely allowed John McLaughlin to discuss and resolve the problem of *Decoy* with her.

We went to Antigua shortly afterwards to haul out *Ramage* at the slipway. Our visit took much longer than usual because our mainmast had some rotten wood that had to be replaced and it was lifted out by a crane for repairs. At the time, there was a Test Match taking place between India and the West Indies, and there were days when the carpenter just did not come to work. The general consensus was he had gone to watch the cricket.

When we returned to Marigot in July we found the *Decoy* proofs were waiting for us at the Post Office. Dudley saw that most of Barley's cuts were indeed political and became angry again. He wrote to John McLaughlin on 26 July 1983:

". . . Decoy galleys had been waiting here five days for us and I've done them and sent them back to Barley. As I expected, going through her 'suggestions' made me realise I don't really want her to publish any more of my books. The reason is simple: she wants to censor a manuscript for politics and all her pet subjects. It was not clear from her covering letter – a copy of which she sent you – but she sent me about twenty pages from the manuscript with anything from a page to a paragraph crossed out with "?delete to speed narrative". One, and one only deletion was suggested by the libel lawyer because 'Bomber' Harris is still alive, and was justified. But the others included description/ criticism of British lifejackets and lifeboat design, criticisms of Foreign Office, Ministry of War Transport, comments on civil servants in general, mention (of not widely known fact) that many M.P.s get subsidies (in fact bribes) from unions and business, comment on Aneurin Bevin (mild) and so on. The whole thing was staggering because 'speeding the narrative' meant cutting out politics and reference to the F.O. and Civil Service, Barley's two pet subjects. I had the same caper over the Convoy MS. I would not change anything and I thought Barley had learned her lesson, but no; her Decoy effort is worse . . . So either she has got to agree I write without her censorship, or I must move. I welcome (as you know well) anything that improves a manuscript, and have always accepted any editorial suggestions from her, but I will not accept this . . . She even argued about Bevan's speeches, quoting Roy Jenkins' memories of what Roy's father said – but I listened to scores of debates where Bevan was attacking Churchill. Oh, yes, she even poked her finger into the lifeboat scene – something I have had first-hand experience of. Even from an editorial point of view, 'speeding the narrative' made nonsense: a novel can't be a high speed race all the time: without the slow parts, the

climaxes merge into a blur, and I think Decoy is well paced . . ."

A month later Dudley received a letter from John, dated 9 August in which he described his talk with Barley:

Now, Barley, and Decoy: I had a talk with her on the telephone just before she went off to Australia, and I think that you have made your point of view very clear to her; in fact, you threw the fear of God into her. I do not think that you will have the same sort of trouble again, and of course it is only likely to arise with second world war books, when the subject matter engages her own political susceptibilities. Thank God she does not have strong views about politics in the 17th and 19th centuries! . . . Clearly there are other publishers who would be eager to take you on, but the sales people at Heinemann do such an excellent job with your books that it might be quite tricky to replace them with a force that did as well   . . . But we have plenty of time to decide; as you say, there is a Yorke contracted after the next Ramage . . ."

Dudley replied to John the next day: *". . . your comments are wise and you are right, particularly over the Heinemann sales force (thanks to Tim Manderson). Likewise 'better the devil you know'. But the political censorship angered me. I know (she told me when she was here) that I am the financial mainstay and I am glad I put 'the fear of God into her' . . ."*

But since he did not write another modern day novel any quibbles from Barley about his opinions did not arise again. Our friendship survived and we were soon receiving letters from her beginning with "Dearest Dudley and Kay".

The problems with *Decoy* now resolved, Dudley began writing *Ramage's Trial*, in which Ramage is ordered to escort a convoy to England and during the voyage an incident occurs with another frigate with the result he faces a court martial when he reaches Plymouth. Work progressed well and the manuscript was finished in four months.

More maintenance work kept us busy on board *Ramage* during the first months of 1984 while Dudley turned his thoughts to writing a buccaneer *Yorke* story. He began reading *Buccaneer* in the evenings to regain the atmosphere of the seventeenth century Caribbean and made notes for the background in Jamaica to ensure the continuity of the next story. While reading *Buccaneer* he was surprised how much of the book he had forgotten and commented in his diary that he was interested to see *"how much Aurelia resembles Kay. I don't think I was conscious of this when writing it, but Clare in Convoy and Decoy . . . was intended to . . ."* But he thought Aurelia was more successful. He continued: *"And Ned in Buccaneer seems more like me than anyone else I have written about. I am now looking forward to reading Admiral to see if the likenesses continue. "*

A month later it seemed working on *Ramage's* mizzen rigging was advancing better than the buccaneer *Yorke*. At the same time, John McLaughlin was renegotiating with Barley the agreement for the advance royalties to be paid for this book. The sales figures for this series were still only half those of the *Ramage* books, and Barley could only offer a small increase. Dudley had written to John on 28 March to complain it *"would cost more per week to have your bathroom painted than I would earn writing a Buccaneer, and secretaries earn a lot more . . ."* and felt he could either accept Barley's offer, or write a new *Ramage,* or retire from writing altogether. John had replied on 12 April, thanking Dudley for his letter :

". . . containing the gloomy news of your disenchantment with the business of writing books. I obviously have a vested interest in your continuing to do so . . . What I am saying is that the advance *you would get for the new 'Buccaneer' is not the total final sum of your expectation from the book. Barley's sales are building, Hamlyn's sales are building, and as they build we shall hope to add more translation sales for Yorke. I am under no illusions that it is not hard work writing books; it is only the authors who are as talented and hardworking as yourself who*

*stand any chance of getting anywhere in today's extremely tough
market. But over a period when everyone else's sales (with few
exceptions) have been falling, yours stand out like a lighthouse.
A lot of novelists have been put out of business altogether by the
latest recession; your situation, although I appreciate all you say
about it, is not anything like as bad as theirs . . . At any rate I
shall hope to hear the results of your deliberations in due course;
I know what I hope to hear, and I expect you know what this is
as well . . ."*

Barley did not even blink; in her reply, she agreed that the
advances paid on the Yorke novels bring in less than you would
earn as a house painter and pointed out that she was passionately
addicted to author's royalty statements containing good news . . .
If Dudley needed a large amount of money she was always ready
to offer contracts for several books at once and she explained she
had a little black book in her office in which details of authors'
contracts are listed and advances paid.

*"The Pope pages are especially tatty since we tend to turn to them
for comfort after looking up some other author to see whether
he is in credit . . . it was more the realisation that we had no
undelivered Ramages in the pipeline than any lack of enthusiasm
for the Yorkes. John is, of course, right in saying that the Yorkes
are not yet as saleable as the Ramages – but it is in the nature
of series to build. I would expect the next seventeenth century
novel to do much better . . . But please, Dear Dudley, take a
well earned rest for a month or so and then go back to Yorke 5
. . . Your suggestion that 58 is a good time to retire from your
profession is not one I can be expected to go along with in my
65th year. I am even now thinking vaguely of working only three
and not five days a week at my trade in my 75th . . . There
are also excellent precedents for authors going from strength to
strength in the prime of life."*

In the meantime, Dudley did decide to abandon the *Buccaneer
Yorke.* He still did not have enough enthusiasm for it, although
he had written three chapters and had most of the plot worked

out. Instead, he decided to write another Ramage first. He wrote to Barley on 9 June:

> *"Dear Barley, Now to answer your delightful and very flattering 4 May and tell you that, on condition you stop smoking, Ramage is Back, to be followed by Ned is Back. I've written to this effect to John, who'll be getting in touch with you. I was a retired gent for about six weeks, and it was wonderful; no withdrawal symptoms and plenty to do . . . I've explained to John that YORKE 5, on which I was working when I decided to quit writing, has gone cold on me so I have put it (three chapters) and complete synopsis to one side for the moment, to be resumed later. So it is a 'Ramage' and then a 'Yorke'. This switching has nothing to do with the disparity of advances: simply that leaving YORKE 5 let it get cold, but it is a good story and will warm up . . ."*

In *Ramage's Challenge* Ramage is sent to the Mediterranean to rescue British subjects held as hostages, among them his wife Sarah, in central Italy since the war against France had begun again. Work on the book began slowly, but Dudley finished editing the manuscript near the end of year.

In the Caribbean the hurricane season is normally over at the end of October, but a low developed in the central Caribbean south of Santo Domingo on 6 November and rapidly became Hurricane *Klaus*. Instead of taking the usual track of west-north-west, it moved eastwards over Puerto Rico and then St. Thomas in the U.S. Virgin Islands, where the cruise ship *Nordic Prince* hit yachts in Charlotte Amalie harbour and one hundred other yachts were swept ashore. The hurricane passed just to the north of St. Martin, but heavy swells in Great Bay at Philipsburg drove thirty-five yachts on to the beach.

During 1985, Dudley complained more about his health; how it was exhausting for him when walking ashore: as well as the dizziness and lack of balance, he felt shaky and short of energy. With the manuscript of *Ramage's Challenge* in London we decided to visit England for two weeks at the end of January. So we made appointments for Dudley to see the specialists again. We found some people to look after *Ramage* while we were away, so that for the first time for many years we were able to travel together. Barley, knowing how hard it was becoming for Dudley to get around with his walking stick, insisted on holding dinner parties to invite our friends to her home. We had the most enjoyable evenings together, our friends loved Barley and she adored meeting them all. There were also lunches and dinner parties with publishing people: Simon King at Fontana told Dudley no other author could sustain fifteen novels in print at the same time, and Peter Lavery at Arrow Books was delighted to be publishing *Decoy,* which would be the Hamlyn and Arrow Group's number one title for January.

When Dudley visited one specialist he was told his problem was disseminated sclerosis. But two days later he saw the neurologist, Dr. Reynolds, who reassured him that this diagnosis was mentioned only as a possibility. It was necessary for Dudley to have two weeks of tests and a scan of his brain with the new Magnetic Resonance Imaging machine (M.R.I.) before a diagnosis could be made. Because there was a long wait for appointments we would have to return at a later date.

Once back home on board *Ramage,* Dudley picked up where he left the third Caribbean Yorke novel, the first forty pages of which he had already written before breaking off to write *Ramage's Challenge.* The novel ends with an attack on a Spanish galleon laden with gold and silver plate which had gone aground off the small town of Marigot in St. Martin, giving the book an exciting ending. By the time this first draft was finished, Dudley had decided the title would be *Galleon.* The manuscript was sent off to London in July and an enthusiastic letter came from Barley, who loved the book. She had only a few queries, which Dudley dealt with immediately, posting the small number of changes at the end of the month.

In the meantime, he had learned that Alexander Kent, who also wrote sea books under the name of Douglas Reeman, had left Hutchinson and joined Heinemann, part of the publishing group with Secker & Warburg and Barley's Alison Press. While Dudley was convinced that Reeman had been headhunted by

Brian Perman at Heinemann, who was at one time also Reeman's editor at Hutchinson, he felt there would be a conflict of interest to have two writers publishing similar sea books in the same group, and feared his share of the budget for promotion and publicity for the Ramages would be less. In August a merger was announced between the Hamlyn and Heinemann groups and again Dudley feared Secker & Warburg and Barley would suffer, to the point of shutting them down to save costs and absorb all the authors into Heinemann. In fact, there never was any danger of this, but at the time Dudley became so concerned he asked John McLaughlin to consider approaching another publisher for his books. In his letter to Dudley dated 2 September 1985 John wrote:

". . . I had a session with Barley, as promised, and discussed the implications of the Heinemann purchase of Reeman/Kent. You might be entertained to know that Reeman, when he realised that Secker and Heinemann belong to the same group was equally alarmed, and was within an ace of calling the whole thing off . . . But they feel very strongly that there will be no conflict; and that neither you nor Reeman will suffer in sales from being handled by the same sales force . . ."

In his reply of 16 September, Dudley wrote to John :

"If Barley comes up with decent promotion guarantees and improved advances, I will stay and you can hint this to her if and when she 'phones you . . . I am very very serious about the effect on my reputation of this 'massive promotion' of Reeman/Kent.

"However, one must plan that no guarantees and improved advances will be forthcoming, so we must look for another publisher . . ."

John replied on 25 September, stating that others were interested in publishing Dudley, including Antony and Rosemary Cheetham of Arrow and that he already had an enthusiastic paperback publisher in the firm in Peter Lavery: *"and that combined with the fact that Antony's published intention is to build Arrow up from being in the second division of paperback publishers to the first division would make the prospect of doing the Ramage and Buccaneer series extremely appealing . . . If I take one step back and look at this situation, it seems to me that however matters work out you should finish up being the gainer. Either we will get a strongly reinforced commitment from The Alison Press [Barley] or a new improved commitment from elsewhere . . ."*

The negotiations continued throughout October and into November, before on 22 November John cabled:

"BARLEY AGREES PROMOTION AMOUNT AND OTHER CONDITIONS. TWO LETTERS IN POST."

It had been agreed there would be increased advances for *Galleon* and the new *Ramage* and to advertise more widely, including in *Publishing News* and the *Yachting Press*.

Three days later Dudley wrote to John:

"With Barley we seem to have got the range and number of salvoes just right . . . I'd sooner she spent more money on ads in the yachting press – their circulation has grown enormously in the last ten years and every aspiring yachtie is an actual or potential fan: the books have the right mix of expertise and snobbery to appeal . . . Anyway, please go ahead and get a letter from Barley to you confirming the details – £7,500 promotion for 'Galleon' and the next Ramage. I'm sorry she's far from well. But for some thirty years Kay and I have been trying to get her to knock off the smoking, and for the last twenty years to ease up on the booze . . . I am pleased we are still with Barley because I like her and get good service . . . but I was sufficiently angry over Heinemann and Reeman/Kent to move . . ."

Later Barley proposed to put seven advertisements in the specialist yachting magazines and early in December Tim Manderson, who was strongly of the opinion that rather than spending the money on a *Bookseller* cover (which, according to him, no one looks at), proposed a colour insert for the Bookseller, which could also be printed separately and used by reps and bookshops.

In the meantime, Dudley had written the first thirteen pages of his next *Ramage* novel by early October. At first he was unsure whether at this point in the series to write a Romney Marsh story or go on to the Battle of Trafalgar. In fact, he did decide to have Ramage taking part in Nelson's last great victory and using fact and fiction wove an exciting story around the frigate *Calypso*'s role. He finished the first draft early in 1986 and the title became *Ramage at Trafalgar*. Unfortunately, Dudley's fear that there would be a conflict of interest with Alexander Kent joining the Heinemann group came true, much to the detriment of Kent. Early in March the next year Barley reported to Dudley:

> "My dear Dudley, The Bookseller and Publishing News insert has caused a fairly major hurricane at Heinemanns. This was their first intimation that we were publishing RAMAGE AT TRAFALGAR in October and reached them a couple of days after Mr. Alexander Kent had let them know that his previously untitled novel was to be called BOLITHO AT TRAFALGAR and unlikely to be ready until the end of '87. I lunched with Kent's agent yesterday who was distraught and told John, with whom I had lunch on Monday, the news on the telephone. He roared with laughter and agrees with me that this is Game, Set and Match to the incomparable Ramage. Love to you both, from Barley."

1986 was going to be our last year living on board Ramage. With much reluctance Dudley admitted not only was it becoming too difficult for him to take care of the maintenance work on board the boat, but climbing in and out of the dinghy from *Ramage* and up on to the quay ashore was also becoming hard for him. We would sell *Ramage* and the question of where we would live had been solved finally. *The Pirate Hotel* on the beach, where Barley loved to stay, had been sold to a development company, who planned to demolish the little hotel and construct a large building on the site. It would keep the name and be called Le Pirate. When we heard this news we made an unspoken decision immediately to buy one of the apartments overlooking Marigot Bay where Ramage was so often at anchor since we came to St. Martin. I too, was ready to move ashore: it had been hard work for eighteen years trying to keep Ramage looking smart with the bright work varnished and painted. I felt relieved that we would sell the boat to people who would take good care of her. We had had many happy years living on board Ramage, we had made many friends and met interesting people in the islands, but now we were both ready to retire from the sea.

Barley wrote on 26 February when she received and read the manuscript of *Ramage at Trafalgar*:

"My dear Dudley, I spent the weekend reading Ramage at Trafalgar and have invented a new publishers' cliché – it is not merely unputable down but was so exciting at times that I actually had to put it down and go and calm myself with a mug of coffee and fiddling with the dead flowers before I could bear to go back to the possibility that the Calypso might be about to go down with all hands. Apart from the plus factor of having Ramage actively engaged in the one naval battle everyone between the age of seven and 107 actually knows a bit about, it seemed to me genuinely the best yet . . . Steve Cox is picking it up later this week but I doubt very much whether he will come up with more than a couple of queries of a copy-editorial kind. Incidentally, TV's Mastermind, who announce their subjects at the eleventh hour, had a female school mistress answering questions about the Ramage novels for the second time in the programme's history. Steve Cox who happened to have bought the Evening Standard watched it with his family. To his intense shame, since he has read all the Ramages published by me three times, i.e. once to make a note about all the things like north and south and place names which crop up more than once, once to put on his magic little marks for the printer and again at proof stage, was only able to answer three of the questions. The poor woman scored only nine whereas the other two did rather better. We are trying to get you a list of the questions and answers, information about what the other subjects were on at the same time (Steve is not a

*Mastermind addict and only watched the Ramage) and thirdly
the name and address of the school mistress. Unless you violently
object we thought we would ask her what her top favourite
Ramage was and then airmail a copy out to you so you could sign
it for her as a consolation prize for having failed. Much love to
you both, from Barley."*

Dudley had decided his next book would be the non-fiction
story of the mutiny of the *Danae* and after he catalogued all his
material and wrote a timetable of events, he began writing the first
draft in March. We had found all the material Dudley needed at
the Public Record Office in London and also the French records
at the Citadel in Brest when we were living in Italy. The book was
published a year later with the title *The Devil Himself.*

There was trouble in Marigot in June when the police were
looking for illegal immigrants. Unfortunately they arrested
some local St. Martiners and there was a riot. Cars were burned
in the streets near the Town Hall and the police used tear gas. The
people in St. Martin are usually happy and friendly, but when
provoked they are quick to rise in anger.

A letter came from Barley on 23 May to tell us that *Galleon* had
sold 6,200 copies and was selling about 100 copies a week. She
had plans to reprint four of Dudley's non-fiction books that had
been published by Weidenfeld's years ago: *73 North* and *The
Black Ship* first and then *At 12 Mr. Byng Was Shot* and *The Battle
of the River Plate.*

Dudley intended to write a buccaneer Yorke next, but until
he felt ready to begin, he read a few books and listened to a
cricket match on the B.B.C. radio. We sometimes could not
avoid hearing the cricket commentaries on small portable
radios if the West Indies team were playing when *Ramage* had
been hauled out at the slipway in Antigua. One year, the men
were listening to a match between England and the West Indies
while painting *Ramage's* topsides. We became absolutely hooked
by the commentaries of Henry Blofeld and Brian Johnson on
the B.B.C. World Service. As they reported the state of play, they

253

included occasional comments about a red double decker bus driving along the road outside the Oval, or the cake which some kind person had baked for them for tea, all of which revived pleasant memories. We had by now lived abroad longer than we had lived in England.

It was not until the middle of September that Dudley began writing *Corsair*, but within a month he was writing nine pages a day and the first draft was finished in six weeks. The manuscript was posted to Barley before Christmas, where it would wait for her return from a visit to Key West.

Earlier in the year Barley had given us news about an apartment she was buying in Florida, which was in an old building being converted from a hospital. It was due to be ready for her in December, but she reported in May that it was still *'bulldozers and wires'*. Our building was finished and opened as a hotel just before Christmas. Almost all the investors who bought apartments lived in France. They chose to sign a contract for three, six or nine years with a management company which would run Le Pirate. As their contracts expired, the owners then rented their apartments privately through real estate agents in Marigot. We were able to buy our apartment and use it privately. But it was not quite ready for us because the carpenter had not finished the cupboards.

However, near the end of December we were there one morning to have some furniture delivered and Dudley found he was already enjoying the view of Marigot Bay from our balcony and all the yachts at anchor.

CHAPTER SEVENTEEN

Le Pirate 1987–1997

Barley went to Key West in December, hoping to be comfortably settled in her new apartment, but she experienced more problems than we did. She wrote to us on 15 January 1987 after her return to London to say she was just back from rainy Key West to find the corrections for *Devil* and the information that River Plate wouldn't be with her until the end of the month. She had experienced similar, if not more severe problems with her apartment which had not been ready and had even had to go to the lengths of having a drink at the nearest bar, or coffee bar, if she wanted to go to the toilet. She also looked forward to reading *Corsair*, which she had just received.

Dudley had been worried the narrative of *Corsair* was too episodic and was afraid Barley would not like it. But, to the contrary, she loved the book and in her next letter written on 21 January she wrote: *"Goodness, how much I loved CORSAIR. Not only is it a splendid unputdownable or unputabledown read but you have managed in a microcosm to explain everything that the Brethren of the Coast got up to, what the point of them was and what difficulties they faced. It really is a stunning performance."*

Although we were not quite 'happily settled' in our new home, we were packing all our books on board *Ramage*, including Dudley's small reference library, and our shell collection. Late in January, we began moving our boxes into our apartment with the help of friends who came with a van. Dudley went on to the apartment with the first load, while I returned to *Ramage* for

255

the second. We repeated this five days later and had most of our possessions stowed in the apartment by the end of January, but it was not until the middle of February that we spent our first night there. Thus ended more than thirty years of living afloat that included eighteen on board *Ramage;* and a new one began at Le Pirate.

Jane, after graduating from school, had studied photography and she returned home shortly after we moved into Le Pirate. She quickly found herself a job working for a photographer on the Dutch side of the island and also found a small apartment to rent in Marigot. Dudley was soon beginning to feel he should be preparing to start the next book, but he was worried because he had no ideas for the plot. Having written two books during our last year on board *Ramage,* he complained he was mentally exhausted with a burnt out feeling as well as "an awful lethargy which is physical rather than mental."

His lack of balance was difficult for him and made walking an effort. His deterioration was gradual and for several more years he was still able to manage with his walking stick. But it was so hard to see a man who had been active all his life, slowing down so much. We went to London in June and stayed a month with Barley – Dudley to see the neurologist again and an appointment was made for an M.R.I. brain scan.

There was one overnight stay at the Cromwell Hospital for Dudley to have a spinal tap. By the end of all the medical tests, Parkinson's disease, disseminated sclerosis and multiple sclerosis were ruled out. Instead, Dr. Reynolds diagnosed a cerebro-spinal degeneration: what was clear on the scan was that the brain tissue in his cerebellum had become smaller and was surrounded by more fluid. It is this part of the brain which is associated with the function of balance and coordination of muscle movement and was the cause of Dudley's vertigo. Friends who were in the medical profession took me aside to warn me that I would have to make the decision to move Dudley back to England at some point and not to leave it too long. This disturbed and frightened me: I had been so dependent on Dudley for so many years and some day soon he would be very dependent on me. Yet I knew there was no way that he would agree to return to live in England.

He loved his tropical home in the Caribbean, where from his chair in the apartment he could look out over Marigot Bay with all the activity of boats coming and going on a sparkling blue sea beneath a sky filled with trade wind clouds drifting by. How depressed he would be somewhere in England watching the rain falling in the garden.

Later in the year, Dudley woke one morning with severe dizziness and weakness, so that he could hardly stand up. By the evening he was better and fortunately this severe episode of vertigo did not occur again in this way, but his condition did gradually become worse.

We returned to Le Pirate early in July and Dudley was ready to start drafting the synopsis for the next Ramage novel which he decided to set in the Mediterranean. Work progressed slowly and the first draft was not finished until the end of November. After a break for a few days, Dudley began editing the manuscript which he finished just before Christmas. The book was published in the autumn the following year with the title *Ramage and the Saracens*.

On Dudley's birthday at the end of the year, during which *Corsair* and *The Devil Himself* were published, as well as Barley's reprints of *The Battle of the River Plate* and *At Twelve Mr. Byng Was Shot*, he described in his diary how hard he was finding it to write: *"Pirate 29 December. Aged 62 today and not liking it at all. The years have slipped by and I don't know where they've gone. Now, with my illness, life is a drag with every day an effort and writing increasingly hard. My concentration is going – whether it is old age or illness, I don't know."*

Early in February, 1988 we had our first earthquake since living on shore in our apartment. It was 5.5 on the Richter scale and shook us up: the doors rattled, our bookcases and the floor swayed. An aftershock followed the next afternoon of about the same intensity, but shorter in duration. It became very noticeable within a few days that the Pirate's swimming pool was leaking and soon there were men drilling holes around it to find the leak.

We finally sold *Ramage* early this year so that we no longer had the worry of her lying out an anchor in Simpson Lagoon with no one on board. I had been going out to check her regularly and pump the bilges when necessary. She had been our home for eighteen years and we had had a wonderful life living on board, although it had been hard work at times. We met many people and made friends in the islands, particularly among the yachting community.

Early the same year Jane had decided she would like to try living in England to see if she could advance her photographic career. There were few opportunities for her in St. Martin, although she had sold some photographs for the calendar printed each year for the island tourist trade. We still had many friends in England and we were delighted that she wished to spend some time in her country of birth. Barley had heard about Jane's plans and invited her to stay at her house while she looked for a job and somewhere to live. Some months later, when Jane was planning to move to her own apartment after she had found a job working at Crabtree & Evelyn, we received a letter from Barley which began: *"She has been a joy to have in the house"*, but Barley had been unable to find friends for her or help her photographic career. She had, however, been impressed by the many hours work Jane spent compiling her portfolio and slides and researching Latin and common names for her Caribbean flowers at the local library. Barley was sure the degree of dedication, determination and sheer hard work would pay off eventually, though it would take time, encouragement and probably financial help . . .

In April, Dudley began the eighteenth Ramage novel in which his hero is in command of a 74-gun ship. It was slow work at first, because he needed to establish the atmosphere. *Ramage and the Dido* was to be the last book Dudley would write and he dedicated it *'To Jane Clare Victoria with much love.'*

Most of September Dudley was busy editing the final typescript and at the end of the month the manuscript was sent off to Barley. Only a few minor queries came from Barley before it went off to the printers.

1988 came to a close and Dudley was worrying that he still had no idea for the next book to follow. Again he complained to me he was feeling utterly burned out and hoped it was not permanent. *Ramage and the Saracens* was published this year and also Barley's reprints of *The Black Ship* and *73 North*.

Jane continued to call on Barley who regularly sent us news about her. It should be explained that our daughter had been using her third given name, Victoria, since she was in America. We were very happy with this decision, but it took a little time to adapt. Dudley was much better than I was, while Barley had no trouble at all. In the last letter we received from Barley she told us: '. . . I *went to a delightful dinner party given by Victoria . . .'* Barley went on to tell us that she would be in Key West in August, having bought the house next door and would be arranging for an architect to draw up plans to combine the two. Alas this was not to be; on 31 May Victoria telephoned to tell us that Barley had died the previous weekend. It was so hard to believe: she had been our friend and Dudley's publisher for so long and although we knew her health was weakened by a heart attack and a recurrence of further trouble later, forcing her to work shorter hours at her office, it still came as a shock. Barley was indeed a marvellous person and had so many interests and zest for life.

On 2 June Dudley expressed his thoughts about her and his anxiety about the future of his books now that she had gone, in a letter to John McLaughlin:

". . . The news about Barley was indeed a dreadful blow to both of us: the end of thirty years' very close friendship. Ironically, we had spent much of that time trying to persuade her to eat more and drink and smoke less . . . As a publisher she was incomparable and, as you probably know, I simply wrote about whatever I pleased and she published it. It will be very hard to work with anyone else – over the years everyone I knew at Seckers has gone. I've no idea what plans for The Alison Press future are, although my contracts are of course with Seckers. One of the people most upset by Barley's death was my daughter,

whom Barley had known since she was a baby and treated like a favourite niece. Indeed, Barley's last letter to me began with the news that 'Darling Victoria' had Barley to dinner, arranging for a car to collect her and take her home . . . I'm asking my daughter Victoria to represent us at the memorial service for Barley whenever it is held . . . "

It took a little while before the decision was made about the future of Barley's Alison Press, but in August it was confirmed that it was to be fully incorporated into the group and Dudley's titles would henceforth be published as *'Secker & Warburg'* books.

On 17 September, the Caribbean was struck by a very powerful hurricane called *Hugo*, which hit Guadeloupe and destroyed the control tower at the airport. First reports said there were eight dead, eighty-four injured, and 10,000 homeless. The wind became strong here about nine o'clock in the morning and by the early afternoon was blowing more than sixty miles an hour. A ship dragged across bay and grounded south of La Belle Creole. The view from the front door was spectacular, with the wind scooping up spray and bending trees, as well as a few corrugated iron roofs flying. The only damage to us was the loosening of ceiling slats over the passageway outside our front door. Fortunately, the centre of *Hugo* passed about eighty miles to the south of us so that we did not have the extremely strong hurricane force winds. Victoria telephoned us and said the news of the hurricane was reported on the B.B.C.

In the following days news came in slowly from the islands to the south of us. The centre of *Hugo* went across Guadeloupe and Montserrat with winds of 140 m.p.h. *Hugo* crossed Montserrat leaving 12,000 homeless and Nevis lost eighty per cent of their buildings. Later we heard on our local radio station Chief Minister Osborn of Montserrat talking via ham radio to Dominica Radio, saying all buildings were flattened and people had nowhere to live. H.M.S. *Alacrity*, on station in the Caribbean for the hurricane season, arrived immediately afterwards, cleared the airport runway, and helped restore the infrastructure. Further to the west, Culebra, our favourite island and hurricane shelter while we were in the Virgin Islands, was also totally wrecked. Most of the yachts anchored in the great Ensenada de Honda sank and many lives were lost.

While editing the typescript of *Ramage and the Dido,* Dudley had found it difficult holding his pen, he explained to me that it felt as though he was holding a broomstick in his hand. Barley had once said to me that she believed that her life and Dudley's writing life would probably end together and this came to be. The degeneration to his central nervous system did become worse and on 20 November he wrote a letter to John McLaughlin to explain he would not be writing another Ramage novel.

"Dear John, I would like your advice. As you know, I was knocked around a bit in the War, and as a result have two problems, balance and walking. The balance business is a result of gun blast destroying the mechanism in my left ear, and the walking because of damage to the spine when I was blown off the bridge when my ship was torpedoed. Neither thing affected me immediately (i.e. during the war), but about 15 years ago I began to feel the effects. As you know, I often came to London to see specialists, staying with Barley. The balance thing was easily diagnosed: the left ear mechanism was not functioning at all, the right was doing its part for both. The result was poor balance, and over the years as I have got older, the right mechanism functions less, so now I can stand up only using a walking stick . . . The spine thing was diagnosed as cerebro-spinal degeneration and the effect is I can walk only about 40 yards, and barely get up stairs. I shall probably end up soon in a wheelchair because of that. Now for the 'cerebro' part of the spine problem: this naturally affects my brain, and in recent years has affected my memory. In the last year it has caused something like writer's block. I have not been able to write for the last year – no energy or inspiration. It means, I fear, that my writing career is over, as the 'degeneration' can only mean things get worse . . . I am sad at the thought that DIDO will be my last book, since the series has much more scope. Incidentally, all this has affected my handwriting, too, so poor Kay has a job deciphering all this. Yours sincerely, Dudley.

John replied that he would inform *Seckers* who, of course knew nothing of Dudley's difficulties and medical history, Barley being the only person with whom the story had been shared.

Dudley was overly pessimistic about his memory loss: it was no more than was normal for a person of his age. But the following year he did need to have a wheelchair and later I ordered a hospital bed so that it was easier for him to get up and sit in his recliner chair each day. It was so distressing to see his gradual loss of speech as the muscles in his tongue became less coordinated. For a man who enjoyed telling rattling a good yarn and funny jokes, he could only utter single words to indicate his needs. Yet his mind remained acute and he had a lively interest in watching daily events unfold on the television, as well as enjoying documentary programs and films.

Victoria returned home in the early nineties when friends telephoned to warn her that her father was becoming frail. She joined the English language newspaper *The Weekly Herald*, which soon after became *The Caribbean Herald*, published daily on the Dutch side of the island and Dudley watched her progress and development as a photo-journalist with much pride, reading with pleasure her stories under the by-line 'Victoria Pope'.

In a further exchange of correspondence with John at the end of January 1994, in which Dudley had been informed that the Japanese agent had written about the large number of *'Captain Ramage'* enthusiasts in his country, Dudley very sadly stated in his reply that he had almost completely lost the use of his hands, but apart from his spine problem was fit, albeit resenting being "anchored to a wheelchair."

We continued to live quietly at Le Pirate and Dudley had the satisfaction of seeing some of his books still being reprinted. Friends continued to sail into Marigot and came to visit us. *Ramage* was sold again and the new owners visited us often. They wanted to restore *Ramage* to her original state and had many questions to ask us. The previous owner had made changes to the accommodation below and they looked through all our photographs.

Early in September 1995, it was St. Martin's 'turn' for a devastating hurricane, as bad as *Gilbert* and *Hugo*. Hurricane *Luis* had winds of 140 miles per hour and it moved so slowly the hurricane took three days to cross the island.

Three days later, Hurricane *Marilyn* passed just to the south and homes were flooded again with torrential rain, drenching the interior of so many that had lost their roofs and just beginning to be covered with bright blue tarpaulins. The water desalination plants were out of commission for several weeks and many people on the island were without electricity for three months. The French Navy arrived with two ships, transport aircraft arrived each day with 40,000 litres of bottled water and we were rationed to two litres a day. Before Hurricane *Luis* approached 1,500 yachts and various vessels had anchored in Simpson Lagoon for shelter.

Afterwards only about 200 were left at anchor, while the rest were scattered around the shore on all sides of the lagoon, or sunk at anchor with their masts sticking up out of the water. Quite a number were jammed under the lifting bridge at Simpson Bay. *Ramage*, with her wide and heavy keel, was blown towards the shore with the weight of other yachts caught up in her anchor cables. But as she went aground, her keel caught firmly in the muddy sand, which held her off the rocks as more yachts piled up on her deck. Her deckhouses and hull above the waterline were damaged, but underwater she was relatively unscathed.

Le Pirate lost parts of the roof and apartments on the ground floor were flooded with sea water that left eight feet of sand inside. The nine year contracts for the hotel rooms were due to expire in 1996 and Le Pirate never reopened as a hotel again. But the insurance payments covered all the repairs and it became entirely an apartment building.

Ramage, our other real home for so many years, was sold following Hurricane *Luis* to a young couple with children. They took her to Venezuela where she was restored to her original condition.

By early 1997, Dudley's illness had slowly progressed to the point where he was very frail. On the morning of 25 April, while he was sitting in his chair after breakfast, he suddenly could not breathe. As I was trying to help him, I saw the light go out of his eyes and I knew I had lost my constant companion and friend after so many years together.

A few weeks later, Victoria and I filled two large baskets with red bougainvillea and golden allemanda blossoms early in the morning of 16 May and, late in the afternoon, we went on board *Ramage* with a group of friends. We left Marigot Bay to go a little way out into the Anguilla Channel with Father Charles, Marigot's much loved priest, who came to give a blessing. As we sang a hymn we scattered Dudley's ashes with the flowers and together they drifted astern on the calm sea in the reflection of the sun already low in the sky as it drew near the horizon.

In a letter of 23 May John McLaughlin sent me copies of Dudley's obituaries that appeared in the London newspapers, including the one he wrote for *The Guardian*:

> *"Dear Kay, Thank you for your two letters of 14 May, and for the paperwork which I shall file appropriately. I was very pleased to hear that you scattered Dudley's ashes from 'Ramage' – that would have pleased him. I remember a very moving occasion when the navy took Nicholas Monsarrat's ashes out from Portsmouth on a frigate, and scattered them in the Solent (with three retired Admirals of the Fleet on board!) I wish I could have been there. Here is a Times obituary – I don't know where they got some of the information – some of it they admittedly got from a digest of Dudley's life which I sent them, and some from the Independent obituary by Colin Mudie. We learn that the Telegraph did a piece earlier this week, and we have ordered a copy which we will send you when it arrives. That means that the four heavyweight dailies in London have now written about Dudley. Yours, John."*

The last time I saw her, *Ramage* was at anchor in English Harbour, Antigua.